I hope you enjoy the story about our family's journey of faith, Julius (Gyuszi)

Surviving
Through
FAITH

Remember, always have FAITH!

Zoltan Zocha

Surviving
Through
FAITH

A true story
of a refugee family's hope, faith, love,
devotion and determination.

Written by
Zoltan Zsohar

As told by
Elizabeth Zsohar

For information, please contact Brown Books
16200 North Dallas Parkway, Suite 225, Dallas, Texas 75248
972-381-0009
www.brownbooks.com

First Printing, 2001
ISBN 0-9714922-0-4
Library of Congress Control Number: 2001118919

Artwork on the dust jacket front: pen & ink drawing of Central Presbyterian
Church, Waxahachie, Texas, 1984, rendered by Dr. Julius Zsohar

Artwork on back of dust jacket: pen & ink drawing of the Zsohar home
in Waxahachie, Texas, 1985, by Dr. Julius Zsohar

Dedicated in loving memory

of Zoltan's grandfather
and my father

Dr. Antal Padanyi Frank

and

of Zoltan's father
and my husband

Dr. Julius Zsohar

BROWN BOOKS • Dallas, Texas

CONTENTS

PREFACE

Growing up in Waxahachie, Texas, even as a young child, I knew that a story existed about our coming to the United States. I knew that we were Hungarian immigrants, that my parents spoke with an accent, and that our family was a bit different from other families in this small town. Because my parents were very proud of their Hungarian heritage, we practiced some customs and traditions in our house that my friends and their families did not practice. For example, when I addressed my parents, I called my mother "Edesanya," which is Hungarian for "dear mother"; likewise, I called my father "Edesapa." This felt natural for me, but it was certainly considerably different from anything I heard my friends call their parents.

I always wanted to know, but I was always somewhat afraid to ask, how we came to be in this somewhat unique situation. Nobody in the family ever talked in any detail about what happened that brought us to this country. Somehow, I got the distinct feeling that this was a subject my parents simply did not want to talk about. Sitting around our dinner table, we never discussed anything related to World War II, living in Austria or coming to America. The only part of the story that I ever heard was an occasional reference to an illness my sister Helen had one time in Austria, and because of this experience Helen always asked for something related to nursing for every Christmas and birthday.

Various things occurred when I was a child that I did not and could not understand. For example, Edesapa was very strict, and he was particularly strict about wasting any food. We were to place on our plates only the amount of food we could eat. I never understood why he became so very angry when someone left a half-eaten piece of chicken on a plate after dinner. We raised chickens. We had many chickens, and it just did not make sense that this should matter so much to him! I noticed through the years that other things related to minor incidents of waste seemed to be blown totally out of proportion. I just assumed that this was one of Edesapa's eccentricities.

After I became an adult and started a family of my own, my wife and I moved to Kalamazoo, Michigan. Shirley was expecting our second child in June 1975, and I asked Edesanya to come to Kalamazoo to help me take care of Lara while Shirley was in the hospital giving birth to Amy. Edesanya came to Michigan a few days early. One day before the baby was born, I took her for a long drive through the countryside of western Michigan.

Sometime during this tour, Edesanya began telling me the detailed story about how we came to be in the United States. I was so moved and overwhelmed by the story, I could hardly drive. I knew at that moment that I needed to capture this story for my children and for their children.

Finally, in 1981, after several job relocations through the years, my company transferred Shirley and me back to Dallas. Soon after we were settled, I asked Edesapa if he would be willing to tell me the story of how he and Edesanya brought our family to America and let me record it on audiotapes. I was not at all sure how he would react because I still had not heard him tell the story or even talk in detail about those years. To my pleasant surprise, he agreed. Over the next three years, he recorded a number of audiotapes for me. After he began telling me the story, suddenly it became a popular subject at the dinner table when the family gathered. I held onto the tapes, planning to transcribe them to hard copy as soon as I had spare time. Being very busy with my career, I never could find the time to begin work with the tapes until the fall of 1999, when my career activities slowed down. That is when I began to transcribe the tapes.

Edesapa passed away on December 6, 1999, soon after I had started transcribing the tapes. As I listened to and transcribed the tapes, gaps and unanswered questions surfaced in the story. Fortunately, Edesanya, who is now eighty-two years old, has a very good recollection of the story and has provided me with the additional information I need to complete the story. After Edesapa died, I began recording tapes of Edesanya's responses to my questions about the story. I took both sets of transcribed notes and integrated them to get the complete story; however, after completing two drafts, I realized that the transcribed notes did not create a readable manuscript.

I started over. I rewrote the entire story, as I understood it from the notes, from Edesanya's point of view. I had talked to Edesanya so much about every detail in the story that I felt it would be much better if I wrote the story from her perspective, even though Edesapa had told me part of the story. After all, it was Edesanya who told me the story in the first place. After completing each chapter, I would take the manuscript to Edesanya to receive both her blessings and her comments. As I continued to write, I had more questions. Many questions seemed to trigger recollections of incidents and events Edesanya had not thought about or remembered for years. As a result, I have added to and modified the manuscript repeatedly. I also have done some historical research to support the story my parents related.

In 1985 my family and I visited Austria and Hungary, along with my parents. This was soon after I recorded the original audiotapes with my dad. I had visited Obertraun one time before in 1979 with my wife and two daughters. We had met Dr. Ballick and his family in Hallstatt on that trip, and they had taken us to Obertraun to meet the Perstls. Dr. Ballick spoke fairly good English, so we were able to visit with him, and he could interpret for our visit with the Perstls. I was very glad we had made the 1979 trip because Dr. Ballick died between that trip and our trip in 1985. During the 1985 trip, we had a very nice visit with the Perstls; but more important, Edesapa showed me around the area. How wonderful to see things with him and through his eyes!

After we left Austria, we went to Budapest. This was my first trip into Hungary and Budapest. Meeting my Hungarian family was a dream come true for me. It was wonderful to meet my aunts and uncles and especially my cousins. The cousins all spoke English, so we could easily communicate with them. From the very beginning, we formed a connection. I felt so close to them. The communist influence was apparent in the Red Star that appeared in many places and the soldiers who were at many intersections in the city. In western Hungary many people in the small villages did not have cars and still used oxen or horses pulling wagons to travel from place to place. It was wonderful to see the family house in which my parents had lived and in which my uncle, Marci, presently lives. It was also great to see the Teachers College that I had heard so much about when we recorded the audiotapes. I left Hungary wanting to return as soon as I could.

After I began putting the story together in 1999 and 2000, I wanted very much to visit Austria and Hungary again to take a closer look at the route traveled by my parents and a closer look at where we had lived in Obertraun. I approached Edesanya about making the trip. She immediately agreed to go, especially since it meant another opportunity to go to Hungary to visit with her brother.

Edesanya, my oldest sister, Liz, Shirley and I spent the entire month of June 2000 in Germany, Austria and Hungary. I took a tape recorder along to gather as much information as possible. The trip proved to be an emotionally difficult one for Edesanya. Not only was it the first trip she had made without Edesapa, but also it was the first time she had actually retraced the route they had taken when leaving their homeland. For this reason, it was sometimes difficult to persuade her to talk about some of the details and events that had occurred fifty-five years earlier. Observing her emotions, I certainly received a better appreciation for the difficulties the family experienced at that time. On two separate occasions during this trip, we met and visited with Austrians who had seen a group of Hungarians traveling in the same area Edesapa had said they traveled. In Budapest we again had a wonderful visit with my Hungarian relatives. I noticed that the city was dramatically improving with the absence of communism. Marci knew I was documenting my parents' leaving Hungary, so he brought out a box of photos for us to go through. I was able to gather many photos of family members taken during the years before the family left Budapest. I returned to the United States with several audiotapes of information, a folder full of photos and a new appreciation for the adversity my parents had to overcome to reach this country.

These trips helped bring to life the incredible journey my parents made to get to this country. Seeing the settings in person and meeting most of the people who were a part of the events aided me in visualizing the story. As I thought about these trips, I renewed my enthusiasm for producing and completing the story.

As I put this story together, I gained an understanding of my parents that I never had before. I especially understood the strict nature of Edesapa. I gained enormous strength from knowing what my parents went through so that their children would have the opportunity to live in this country. When I first began putting the story together, I had my daughters in mind. I wanted them to understand and appreciate what their grandparents had gone through in order for all of us to have what we now have. As the story developed and as the power of the story became evident to me, I soon realized I needed to make the story available to anyone who needed hope in his life.

This is a true story of hope, faith, love, devotion and determination.

One of the fringe benefits from writing this story has been the time I have spent with Edesanya. Shortly after Edesapa passed away, I began showing up on her doorstep in Waxahachie on a very regular basis with a tape recorder in tow. Losing her husband of fifty-nine years had been a very emotional experience for her. To compound that, I was asking her questions about another very emotional time in her life. A number of times during our taping sessions we paused to let her reactions to the memories settle a bit. We soon began to cherish these opportunities to talk about the past. I think in some ways recalling their life together helped her to deal with her grief. This project has provided a wonderful opportunity for me to be able to share remarkable, special moments with Edesanya.

To aid the reader, I have included a glossary at the end of the book to help with the pronunciation of the Hungarian names and words used frequently in the text.

Only my wife, Shirley, has any idea of the number of hours I have spent putting this manuscript together. She has been most patient with me, and I thank her for her love and her support. I also thank my children and friends for their encouragement during this long process. I implore anyone and everyone to gather their family history and to document it for future generations. If you do not, the story will be lost forever.

I also want to thank Sue Passmore whose editorial suggestions have enhanced the readability of the book.

Zoltan Zsohar

CHAPTER 1
THE LORD IS MY SHEPHERD

It was late in the evening on May 3, 1943. My husband, Gyula, and I had finished dinner and had just tucked the children into bed. Gyula was telling me about his day at the elementary school and how happy he was that he had completed his eleventh year of teaching. As he was describing the activities of the end-of-school celebration party, we heard the air raid sirens for the first time! Gyula exclaimed, "Erzsebet, we need to move to the basement quickly!" Immediately grabbing the children, some blankets and a case that contained our important documents, we hurried toward the basement. Frightened and shaking, I had great difficulty carrying eight-month-old Gyuszi and a blanket down the narrow, steep stairs into the musty, damp basement. Gyula followed closely behind me with two-year-old Erzsike, a blanket and the documents. Once we were safely in the basement, we closed the door and turned on a small light. Never had I been more terrified in my entire life. Gyula and I held our son and daughter tightly, waited and prayed.

Until now our prayer had been that this day would never come. Now we prayed for our very lives. We always believed Budapest to be a safe city that would never be bombed. In no way had we expected that anyone would want to destroy such a beautiful, peaceful city. Now, huddled with our children, we waited to hear the planes and the explosions. We heard nothing. The silence was deafening. In a matter of minutes, but what seemed forever, we heard the all-clear sirens; slowly and cautiously, we ascended the narrow stairs. Maybe this was only a drill; maybe no air raid had occurred; maybe this was just a bad dream!

But we soon learned that this was not a bad dream; it was not a drill! The radio confirmed that the Allied planes had dropped bombs, intending to destroy a defense factory on the Pest side of Budapest. Because we lived on the Buda side of Budapest, we had not heard the planes or the bombs exploding. The news reported that the planes had missed their target. Instead of destroying the defense factory, the bombs demolished some apartment buildings nearby, killing eighty-one people. With the exception of one policeman, the dead were the factory workers, their wives and their children. Everyone became outraged at this senseless loss of life. The resentment intensified when we learned that American planes had dropped the bombs. They were among the Allies we had hoped Hungary would be able to join! Now they were attacking our city!

Although we had hoped that this day never would arrive, we always feared that it would. Ever since the Germans had invaded Hungary and had installed what they considered to be a "loyal" government, the fear had gnawed deep in our very beings. We had hoped that Hungary would be able to join with the western Allies and avoid the wrath of the German war effort, but somehow we knew that Hungary was too strategically important to the Germans for them to allow that to happen. Hungary did not want to be drawn into the war by the Germans, but they had no choice. The German war machine simply marched in, took over the government, the army, and anything else its leaders felt useful. Small, weak Hungary had been unable to resist the German troops. After taking control of the government, the German leadership had sent the Hungarian troops to fight with the Germans against the Russians on the eastern front. Thousands of Hungarians perished against the far superior Russian troops. We were certain that this act of war against the Russians would attract retaliation, although, at the time, we had no way of knowing what the ultimate response would be. Would Russia and the Allies strike back by bombing Hungary, or would they invade the country? Now, with this attack on Budapest, it appeared we had the answer to our question; our worst fears were confirmed.

Stories had circulated for weeks of attempts by British and Russian planes to attack Budapest, but the German antiaircraft guns were either destroying the planes or forcing them to turn around before they reached the city. The American planes, on the other hand, were more powerful and thus flew higher and faster, often out of the reach of the antiaircraft guns. As a result, the American planes had penetrated the defenses and had attacked our city. The planes were frighteningly swift as they dived toward their target, dropped their bombs, and then quickly climbed out of sight.

Now, for the first time, the war actually had come into our own backyard. Never had I thought this would happen or had most Hungarians. I recalled listening to the radio on a Sunday evening a year and a half earlier in early December 1941: Pearl Harbor had been bombed. America was joining the war. I remembered thinking how this might affect the entire war effort and our lives. I had discussed the events at the time with my parents and with other older adults. We had talked about the expanding war and what effect it might have on Eastern Europe and specifically Hungary. All had agreed that we were safe in Budapest. "No one would ever attack us," they said. I remembered how comforting and reassuring their comments had been.

Even after the Germans had occupied Hungary, the impact on our day-to-day lives had not been significant, but some things did change. As soon as they had dominated Hungary, the Germans required all Hungarians to document their religious heritage. Because the religion of each parent is stated on the birth certificate, we were forced to acquire official copies for ourselves and for the previous two generations on each side of our family. After obtaining the documents, we were required to register them with the local government. This whole exercise was merely an inconvenience for us and did not affect our status at all. Gyula's parents were both Protestants belonging to the Presbyterian Church; my father was Catholic, but my mother was Protestant, and I had been raised in the Presbyterian Church. Of course, the purpose of the documentation was to aid the Germans in locating all of the Jewish people in Hungary. As the Hungarian Jews were identified, they were obliged to wear a yellow star at all times. They were always watched carefully, but to our knowledge, at the time, they were not gathered up and sent to death camps or concentration camps. Drafted into the military, rather than bearing arms, they served in labor battalions. On a day-to-day basis, we did begin to see increased discrimination against the Jews in Budapest, as the German stronghold on the Hungarian government increased.

We soon began to notice other changes after the German occupation. Shortages occurred in the marketplace. The Germans had begun siphoning the country's resources for the war effort. In spite of a rationing program instituted by the Germans, we still had all of the goods we needed to meet our basic needs. Initially, the rationing was more of an inconvenience than a serious problem.

To further support the war effort, the Germans forced the Hungarians to convert many of their industrial plants to defense plants. Since most of the plants in Budapest were on the Pest side of the Danube River, the Allied bombings appeared to be targeting those plants. But now that the much-feared bombings had started, everything was changing for the worst, and our future seemed very uncertain.

Because of the vehement protest brought about due to the civilian deaths from that first bombing on May 3, 1943, the Allied forces waited several weeks before they again bombed Budapest. Initially, only the American planes bombed, and they always attacked at night. As the bombings continued to occur every few days on a fairly regular basis, we had to adjust our lives considerably. Life was no longer carefree and relaxed. What had been a life of comfort, peace and hope, filled with dreams and plans for our young family, now changed severely. We lived in constant fear for our safety; in fact, we lived in fear for our very lives.

Obviously, my children were destined to experience a very different childhood than mine. My childhood had been wonderful, carefree and joyful. I had grown up in a beautiful three-bedroom house in a very nice neighborhood. My father, an instructor at the Teachers College near our home, became president of the college in December 1931, when I was twelve years old. It was after he became president and after we had moved into the apartment at the college that he first began to prepare me for the possibility that life might not always be as simple and as comfortable as it had been for me up to that time.

My father, who I always affectionately called "Edesapa," which in English means "dear father," always loved to take a leisurely stroll each evening after dinner. After a long day working in the office, he enjoyed this opportunity to relax and to reflect on the day. Normally, my mother, who I likewise affectionately called "Edesanya," which means "dear mother," would accompany him on these walks, but sometimes she was tired and just simply did not feel up to getting out of the house. It was on these occasions that Edesapa invited me to go with him. I loved Edesapa very much, but I did not particularly enjoy these walks. A young teenage girl at the time, I would have much preferred to stay at home, play, or read books. But I had been taught to honor Edesapa and Edesanya, and refusing to accompany Edesapa under these circumstances was not an option.

One evening during our walk, Edesapa began to talk to me about dealing with life situations. A very religious man, occasionally he would talk about his religious beliefs. On one of these walks, he asked, "Erzsebet, do you know what phrase in the Lord's Prayer is very easy to say but is very difficult to actually believe to be true and to accept in our day-to-day lives?"

Thinking like a child, and having just finished dinner and understanding the importance of food, very assuredly I answered, "Give us this day our daily bread."

Edesapa answered, "No; the most important thing to remember in the Lord's Prayer is 'Thy will be done.'" He went on to explain: "No one knows what will happen in this world, but it is very important to remember that whatever the Lord's will has for you, that is what will be done. This requires tremendous faith. I wish that you will always have a wonderful life, but sometimes things do not work out the way you would want them to. You are not guaranteed a life without difficult challenges and trials. It is possible that you may even lose everything you have, and you need to be prepared for whatever life presents you. Remember, the Lord's will be done. You must always have faith in this. Trust in the Lord. In life you can lose everything, but I emphasize to you, never lose your faith! Remember, never lose your faith! Often it is only through faith that people survive. The Lord will take care of you; he will be your shepherd."

I wondered at the time, "Why is Edesapa telling me these things? What is he talking about?" We had a very comfortable life. I had everything I could want. We lived in a very nice apartment at the Teachers College. Edesapa had a good, highly respected, well-paying job. We were all healthy and happy. Edesapa also owned the home we lived in before he became president of the Teachers College, as well as another home at Balaton Lake. Life could not be any better for me. We lived in a nice, secure, safe city. Life was wonderful!

Now, in the early spring of 1943, I recognized that life's circumstances can change quickly. The war, the Germans and the bombings were changing everything. I began to recall Edesapa's instruction. I began to think about what the Lord had planned for our lives. Maybe surviving these bombings was going to test my faith. I was now beginning to see how important Edesapa's words were going to be in my life. In my daily prayers, I gained strength merely by thinking about the need to have a strong faith and to trust in the guidance of the Lord.

Throughout the summer, the bombings continued. Although our routine certainly was not what it had previously been, we attempted to keep life as normal as possible. Since traveling was still feasible without too many problems, Gyula and I decided to take a short vacation to his father's home in Kisrakos, a farming village some 240 kilometers away. The war had not yet affected Hungary's extensive and reliable railroad system.

Even though the bombings had only recently begun, it was nice to get away from the anxiety of living under the threat of attack. The people in Kisrakos received very little news about the bombings and were so far removed from the big city that they were very relaxed about the whole affair. They never thought for a minute that the war would ever reach them. I remembered thinking the same thing only months earlier.

After a nice visit with Gyula's family, we spent a couple of days with my parents at their summer home on Balaton Lake. The peacefulness of the village and the serenity of the lake gave us some much-needed rest and somewhat relieved the stress of previous months.

We returned to Budapest in time for the schools to reopen for the fall, again attempting to resume as normal a life as possible. Gyula again was teaching elementary school during the morning and early afternoon. However, after coming home and having lunch, he would then report to the university to   teach a couple of classes and to work with the head of the natural sciences department in the evenings. He had completed his doctorate in botany, zoology and anthropology, but the head of the department liked him so much that he had offered Gyula a position as an assistant working for him. The department head could not put Gyula on the payroll because the government already employed him as a schoolteacher; the law did not allow anyone to be paid by the taxpayers for two jobs. In spite of this, the department head was able to work around the law by paying Gyula from a fund provided to him by the university for needs that he judged to be important and necessary for the work of the department. His assignments included creating illustrations, drawings and pictorial teaching aids for books and publications. Gyula loved art as well as the sciences, and he could combine them working for the university. Because he loved the job and because he could earn additional pay, he worked every weekday evening. Gyula always was eager to do whatever he could to provide a better life for our family. So, after a full day's work at the elementary school and after completing his duties at the university, about nine each evening he would leave to catch the streetcar home.

Soon after we had returned to Budapest, the bombings began to occur more frequently. Many evenings Gyula did not make it home from work before the bombings began. As soon as the air raid sirens sounded, the streetcars would stop and all of the lights in the city would be turned off. If this happened before Gyula arrived home, he would either have to wait until the all-clear siren sounded or he would have to get off the streetcar and walk home. On nights when multiple air raids occurred, he would sometimes walk as far as six kilometers.

During the early part of 1944, the bombings began to occur during the daytime. The Americans continued to bomb at night, and the British and Russians bombed during the day. With this increased frequency, we became much more concerned about our safety. Most of the bombings were still on the Pest side of the Danube River where the large defense factories and large apartment buildings were located. On our side of the river, the Buda side, fewer defense factories existed, and the homes were mostly single-family dwellings. But with the increase in the number of bombings, we were hearing more explosions. On some occasions, the explosions were so close we could feel the ground shake. We began to become more worried about the location of our home in relation to potential Allied targets.

We were renting our house from my parents. Our home, the house in which I'd been raised, was only three blocks from the Teachers College, where Edesapa was now president. Located across the street from the Teachers College was a factory building that had been converted into what we were told might be a munitions plant or some other defense-related facility. In the other direction from our house, less than a kilometer away, the military recently had installed antiaircraft guns on a high hill. We feared that eventually the planes would try to strike either the antiaircraft guns on top of the hill or the defense plant across from the college. Located on a direct line between the two and less than a kilometer from each, our house sat in a precarious position. The bombs had missed their intended targets before.

Gyula and I both spoke German, so we began to listen to a Vienna radio station that broadcast in German the estimated time that the planes would be expected to begin bombing Budapest. Because the planes flew over Austria on their way to

Budapest, the Austrians could estimate the arrival time of the bombers in Budapest. Erzsike soon learned enough German to understand that *zweiundzwanzig* meant twenty-two hundred or ten o'clock in the evening, which was when the bombing would begin. Much too young to understand the danger, she could tell by our reaction that something exciting was happening. Anytime she heard *zweiundzwanzig,* she knew that she would not be going to bed soon because she knew we were going to hurry to the basement. She always seemed more excited about the event than afraid.

About twenty minutes after the Vienna radio station announced that the bombers were on their way, the air raid sirens in Budapest usually sounded. Because we had heard the broadcast, we had enough time to make a couple of trips to the basement with coats, blankets and pillows before the planes were expected in Budapest. This was much easier than having to haul everything into the basement all at once in a near panic, as we had done the first time we heard the sirens in Budapest that night in May.

In February 1944, I learned that I was pregnant with our third child. Erzsike, our daughter and first child, had been born on May 19, 1941; her brother, Gyuszi, had been born on September 13, 1942. Being pregnant made the routine of regularly going down the narrow, steep stairs to the basement even more difficult. Very often we would hear the all-clear siren, move back upstairs and be almost settled in, only to hear another air raid siren, even before the radio was warmed up. This routine sometimes occurred several times during the day and evening. Now that I was pregnant, I would become even more tired taking the children downstairs, waiting for the all-clear sound, and then up again and later down again. Each time we carried blankets, coats, pillows and, of course, the documents with us to the basement. Because of the damp basement and the potential for mildew, we could not leave the items in the basement for any length of time. Thus, we hauled the children and supplies up and down each time. Especially tiring were the nights when the alarm sounded several times; the children, who were half-asleep, became heavier and heavier each time we began our trip to safety. Even then, we had a much easier time than most people, because we lived in a one-story house. Most people lived in multistoried apartments. They had to take several flights of stairs each time an air raid occurred.

By April 1944, the bombings were occurring with such frequency that the government announced a plan to evacuate women with young children from Budapest. They felt that the women and children would be much safer in the rural villages and farms, where bombings were not occurring. They announced that schools would close soon and that a systematic evacuation would begin, one that could take weeks to complete. The men would not be allowed to leave Budapest. Only the women and children would receive the necessary documents to relocate. The government could assign women and children to a particular home or shelter out in the Hungarian countryside, and that rural family or shelter had no choice but to accept the Budapest family for as long as was necessary.

Even though the schools would be closing, Gyula could not evacuate Budapest with us. As an employee of the government, he needed to remain to be assigned another government job to meet our living expenses.

Recognizing that the danger was ever increasing with the frequency of the bombings, and now that the government was initiating an evacuation, Gyula decided to secure government permission to immediately relocate the children and me to his family's farm in Kisrakos in western Hungary.

Gyula, the oldest of the six children, five boys and one girl, had been raised on the family farm in Kisrakos. He attended elementary school (grades one through four) in Kisrakos, but because Kisrakos did not have a middle school (grades five through eight), Gyula lived with his uncle in Kormend for four years. While in middle school, Gyula decided he did not want to become a farmer like his father; instead, he developed a passion to become a teacher. When he announced to his father that he wanted to go to college to become certified as a teacher, his father was a bit less than enthusiastic. He had counted on his boys to work with him and eventually to take over the family farm. He did not see the need for a fourteen-year-old boy to receive any more education; besides, he did not have any money to send his son for more education. Gyula's father strongly resisted his request until Gyula's paternal grandmother, who was also living on the farm, came to the rescue. She convinced Gyula's father that if the boy wanted to further his education, he should be allowed to do so. Gyula's father finally agreed to allow him to go to college, but only on the condition that he secure a scholarship to cover all of his expenses. Gyula's family barely had enough money to meet their needs. An advanced education was hardly viewed as a need. Some of Gyula's teachers at the middle school wrote glowing letters of recommendation, soliciting scholarship money from various schools. As a result of the letters, the Teachers College in Budapest offered him a full scholarship to attend the school to become certified as an elementary teacher.

Now with the intensified bombings, the safety of rural Kisrakos and the family farm was most appealing. Gyula contacted the authorities, and by late April 1944, he received the required papers to send the children and me to Kisrakos. Although I clearly understood why I needed to leave Budapest, I did not want to go. I had lived in Budapest since I was three years old, when we moved there for Edesapa to accept a teaching position at the Teachers College. I had such wonderful and warm memories in the house where we were living. After all, this had been my parents' home before we moved to the apartment at the Teachers College. It was the home in which I had been raised; it was the home in which Gyula and I had planned to raise our children. Our wonderful life was changing ever so drastically, and the safe haven we had created for our family was now very vulnerable.

This house was even the place where Gyula and I had first met. It was right after Christmas in 1931, the day that my parents began moving to the apartment at the Teachers College. Edesapa had asked Gyula, who was nineteen and in his last year at the Teachers College, and another student, who was also staying in the dormitory for the Christmas holidays, if they would help him move some items from our home to the apartment at the college. Neither student had enough money to go home for the holidays; both were stuck at the school with little to do. Gyula and the other student seemed more than pleased to help Edesapa move. I guessed it was not often that students received the opportunity to help the college president move to an apartment. While the boys were moving some items, I overheard

Edesapa talking to Edesanya about Gyula. Edesapa said that he had taught him in several classes, that he was the top student in the school and the best student he had seen in all his years at the Teachers College. He went on to say that Gyula had a very bright future. I had never heard Edesapa praise any student in the manner that he praised Gyula. He not only talked about his academic excellence, but he also told Edesanya that he had a strong character and high personal values. I recognized that with this kind of praise from Edesapa, this person had to be somebody very special.

I began to watch him work. He was a handsome young man with excellent manners. He was most polite and friendly. Even though I was only twelve going on thirteen years of age, I determined that I would to get to know Gyula better. However, I certainly had no idea that eight-and-a-half years later we would marry!

After we married, my parents offered us this house for our new home. Only after they agreed to Gyula's insistence that we pay rent did we accept the offer. Now, after living here with my parents and then with my husband and our children, I was about to leave these familiar, comfortable surroundings, leave Gyula, leave my parents and other relatives to begin a future of uncertainty.

As the time approached for me to leave, my anxiety increased. I did not know if I would ever return to Budapest. I did not know if I would ever see Gyula again. I did not know if I would ever see my parents and other relatives again. We were separating, and somehow I had to trust that this was the will of the Lord and that the Lord would look after us and bring us safely back together again.

CHAPTER 2
THE ROD AND THY STAFF THEY COMFORT ME

Q uickly, yet methodically, I gathered clothes and belongings that I thought the children and I would need for our stay in Kisrakos. Since it was spring, I packed mostly summer clothing. In spite of my concern, I was optimistic that by August, when I was to deliver our third child, the bombings and the war would be over, order would be restored, and we could return home to Budapest.

Gyula was able to take time off from his work so he could accompany us to Kisrakos, located about 240 kilometers from Budapest and only about thirty kilometers from the Austrian border. We took the train to the closest village, Pankasz, only three kilometers from Kisrakos. Gyula's father was waiting for us with an oxen-drawn wagon. Although we usually walked the distance up the hill to the Zsohar farm, Gyula had written ahead and had asked his father to meet us at the train station because we had so much luggage.

Kisrakos was a very small farming village of just over one hundred houses, a population of about five hundred people, and numerous cows and pigs. The village had no electricity, and no one owned an automobile. Not only were the living conditions in the village a cultural shock to me, the family situation was totally foreign to anything I had experienced before. These conditions made it a difficult adjustment for me.

I first had to become accustomed to the family situation in Kisrakos. Gyula's grandfather, who had owned the farm, had died before Gyula was born. When he died, the estate, according to the laws of Hungary, went to the surviving children—not to the spouse. The law further stated that the spouse must be allowed to live on the estate as long as she lived. Consequently, Gyula's father now owned the farm, and his grandmother, as required by law, was allowed to live on the farm with his parents. A very strong-willed, domineering person, Gyula's grandmother was not the easiest person with whom to live! Over the years the relationship between Gyula's mother and her mother-in-law deteriorated to the extent that Gyula's mother simply moved out and left the family. This had occurred soon after Gyula had left Kisrakos to attend the Teachers College in Budapest.

So now, as Gyula brought our children and me to the safekeeping of his family, I, the city girl, had to adjust to life in a small village. His family had to adjust to understanding the city girl! The family lived in a small, thatched-roof house, which was where Gyula was born. The house had one bedroom with only two beds. Gyula's father slept in the bedroom. One other room in the house was a combination kitchen, living room and dining room. Gyula's grandmother slept on a bed in that room. His brothers and sister slept on straw sacks in the same room when they were home. When we arrived, there was no room for us in this small house.

Gyula knew that living space would be a problem, so he had written to his father explaining when we would be coming. This allowed his father to look around for a place for us to stay. Fortunately for us, the schools in Kisrakos already had been closed, and the teacher had left; therefore, the small one-room apartment at the school was empty. Gyula's father went to the school authorities, and they agreed to allow us to stay in the school apartment rent free until the teacher returned. We only slept there. The school was a five-minute walk from the Zsohar house. Each morning we would dress, walk to the Zsohar house and spend the day.

Gyula could stay for only the weekend. He had to return to Budapest because the schools would soon close, and he knew he would be assigned to a civilian job as soon as that happened. After helping us get settled, Gyula said his goodbyes. How lonesome I felt when he left. I was in strange surroundings with people I did not know very well, pregnant, and with two small children to care for and protect. How different my life had become!

I was very nervous about staying with Gyula's family. I knew when I first met them just after we were married that they had not wanted Gyula to marry a city girl; they preferred that he marry a good local country girl. I was not the image of the person they had expected to be added to the family. During earlier short visits, I had managed to get along with them and the visits were generally friendly, but not yet had I been accepted as a member of the family. Now I was not a visitor in the community, but rather a resident! I realized that things were going to be different, and I knew that I had to make the best of the situation. All in all, both the family and the community received us warmly but with the usual apprehension one would expect when outsiders move into a village.

Gyula's father, a very quiet man, wanted the children and me to call him "Papa." He was easy to get to know, and he and I had always gotten along well. On the other hand, Gyula's grandmother, who always wanted us to call her "Mama," was a much more difficult person with whom to gain acceptance.

When I had first come to Kisrakos after we were married in the summer of 1940, I had met Gyula's brothers and sister; we all had gotten along very well. Since my first visit, Zoltan, who had been drafted into the military, had been killed in battle in early 1943. Mihaly had moved to Szombathely; and Ilona had moved to Budapest. Laci, who was twenty-one, and Geza, the youngest at seventeen, were still at home.

Geza made it his job to look after the children and me. He was a great help, especially when we first arrived in late April. He escorted me everywhere. None of the roads in the village were paved, and when it rained, the roads and paths were very muddy. Being so very young, Gyuszi particularly had trouble walking around the mud holes. One time as he was having great difficulty negotiating the mud holes, I was about to pick him up when Geza offered to carry him. Since I was pregnant, this small gesture was especially appreciated. It seemed that Geza was always there at every turn to help me in any way he could.

Mama, accustomed to running everything her way, made it known that she did not care for any fine city girls, and I was certainly included in that group! She made it clear that she did not like the fact that Gyula had married me instead of one of the local girls. When I first arrived, I definitely felt the tension; it was obvious that she viewed me as being an uppity, spoiled girl who thought she knew everything. I had been raised to respect my elders and especially my grandparents. My maternal grandmother had lived with us in Budapest the entire time I was growing up. She, too, was a strong-willed, domineering person. I was determined that since I was going to be here a while, I would do everything I could to gain Mama's acceptance. (Ironically, my grandmother and Gyula never got along.)

I had not learned to cook until after Gyula and I married. When I lived at home before we were married, my grandmother did all of the cooking, and she did not want anyone in the kitchen with her. Gyula was actually a better cook than I was when we married. Early in our marriage, I had many disastrous attempts at cooking. To help me develop some cooking skills, I used cookbooks and learned from friends. Finally, I began to experience a few successes; however, when I arrived in Kisrakos, my cooking skills were still somewhat limited.

One day soon after I arrived, I was in the kitchen with Mama when she was about to bake some bread. Mama usually baked several loaves of bread at a time. She was up in years a bit, and working the dough was very hard for her to do alone. She asked me, "Do you know how to knead dough?"

I answered, "No, but if you would be willing to teach me, I would very much like to learn."

That was certainly the correct response! Mama liked the fact that I was willing to learn and be helpful. She also viewed my response as a recognition that she knew more than I did. From that time on, Mama wanted to teach me, and I was always willing to learn. I really appreciated the opportunity to learn cooking skills, because I always had been frustrated that my grandmother would not teach me or even allow me to watch her when I was growing up. Mama taught me to cook many traditional Hungarian dishes. We quickly became very good friends, and from then on we were always on the best of terms.

Once I won Mama over, everyone else seemed to become more warm and friendly toward me. Not only did the rest of the family grow to accept me and show their affection toward me, but also everyone in the village became much friendlier toward me. Everybody was amazed that the young city girl was willing to work hard and help every chance she could. I did not think it was that exceptional, because that was the way my parents and grandmother had raised me, but the people in Kisrakos just had expected that I would be a lazy person and wanting everyone to wait on me. I always tried to show dignity and respect in everything I did.

One of the big turning points in my relationship with the Kisrakos family and the community occurred one evening when a cow was giving birth to a calf. Although I did not participate in helping with the birth, I was there available to help, and I watched the whole process. Of course, the family was extremely curious; how would I, a fine girl ignorant to farm life, react to seeing a calf being born? They watched my face very carefully as I watched the birth. They noticed that I stayed very calm during the whole process and did not display any unusual facial expressions. This amazed and impressed everyone there. After this incident, they knew for sure that I was far more than just a city girl. Now I was clearly one of them.

I had no way of knowing whether Mama was more mellow at this time than when Gyula's mother lived there. I do know that Mama and I developed strong chemistry, and we worked together amazingly well. Mama was clearly accustomed to running everything, and I respected that. However, I also proved my willingness to share in the responsibilities of maintaining our family, our home, and the needs we all shared during these very difficult times.

Gyula and I communicated by mail. He wrote that he had been assigned by the government to patrol the neighborhood at night. His job was to make sure that everyone obeyed the laws regarding blackouts during actual bombing attacks or when bombing attacks were expected. All lights were to be turned off during these periods. He also wrote that many of the villages near Budapest had so many women and children evacuees from Budapest that the shelters, public buildings and churches were overcrowded with people. They had run out of beds, and they were experiencing food and clothing shortages. Upon learning this, I felt very fortunate that the children and I had been able to come to Kisrakos. We had plenty of food, and although we had to be creative in our arrangements, we did not feel overcrowded. In addition, and perhaps more important, we had the love and support of Gyula's family. We were not living among strangers who had been forced to share their living quarters with us. We had our family.

Another time Gyula wrote that he had received a military draft notice in the mail. Fortunately for us, they were exempting college students and married men with children. Not only was Gyula spared, but my twin brothers who were attending the University of Budapest were also spared from the draft.

August finally arrived, and I was so excited because I certainly was ready to give birth. At the same time, I was somewhat apprehensive. I did not want to give birth in Kisrakos because the practice in the rural area was to give birth at home with the help of a midwife. If the midwife encountered any problems with the birth, she would send for a doctor. This could take an hour or longer; as a result, the mortality rate was much higher in the rural areas than it was in the city. I really wanted the same doctor who had delivered our first two children to deliver our third child. I liked this doctor. He knew me, and I knew him. I also wanted to deliver at the same hospital. The hospital care in Budapest was excellent and far superior to anything available in the rural areas. I felt the safety risk of the bombings in Budapest was far less than the possibility of a problem in childbirth in the rural setting. Furthermore, I wanted to see Gyula and my parents very much. I had not seen them since late April, almost four months before. Gyula and I decided the best thing for me to do was to come to Budapest for the delivery.

I took Erzsike and Gyuszi with me to Szekesfehervar, a town about sixty kilometers outside of Budapest and a major hub for the rail system in Hungary. My parents had been staying the past three months at their summer home at Balaton; Szekes-fehervar was easy for them to reach by train. Szekesfehervar was also very easy to reach from Budapest. I was delighted to see Gyula and my parents waiting there for me. I had missed them so much, and it was wonderful to see them again. After a short visit, I left the children with my parents, who took them to the Balaton. Gyula and I took the train on to Budapest.

It was so nice to be back in Budapest. Although the bomb-ings were still occurring on a regular basis and the danger still existed, seeing my home again was wonderful. Once I settled back into the house, Gyula and I were able to spend some nice quiet time together and occasionally take leisurely walks through the neighborhood. We had been apart for so long. These few days before the birth also gave me some time to gather the baby clothes that had been stored away.

It seemed as though I had been home almost no time when it was time to go to the hospital to give birth. Our second daughter, Ilonka, was born August 16, 1944. I stayed in the hospital the customary ten days before being allowed to return home. Just one week after being released from the hospital, we had Ilonka baptized in the same Presbyterian Church where Gyula and I married and where we had Erzsike and Gyuszi baptized.

The day after the baptism, we began preparing for my return to western Hungary. The war and the bombings had lasted much longer than anyone had thought possible. I knew I should take additional items back with me just in case the war did not end soon, as everyone was still hoping and expecting; therefore, we decided to pack a few extra items to take with us on our return to Kisrakos. We packed some dishes, silverware, serving bowls, additional clothing, sheets, blankets and some other belongings that were scarce on the farm.

After gathering as much as we dared carry back, with our new daughter, Gyula and I boarded a train in Budapest to go back to Szekesfehervar. On the return train trip, we had a very frightening experience. The engineer on the train received word that bombers were coming. Knowing that trains were often targets of the bombing attacks in order to disrupt the rail system, the engineer stopped our train and instructed everyone to get off the train, to run as far as we could away from the train, and to lie down beside a tree or bush. The main thing was not to show any movement in hopes that the bombers would just fly by. Everyone rushed to get off the train and seek shelter. Gyula and I, carrying Ilonka, ran as fast as we could. Only a few seconds after we reached what we hoped was a safe distance away, the planes passed overhead. If they saw the train, it was of no concern to them. They passed us by in favor of dropping their load on Budapest. Still frightened and anxious, we quickly reboarded the train to continue our journey.

When we finally arrived in Szekesfehervar, my parents were at the train station with Erzsike and Gyuszi to meet us. We introduced the children to their new sister, and we all went to a hotel near the train station to spend the night. The next morning after a much too short visit, we said goodbye to my parents, not knowing when we might see them again. This was so difficult for me. The war was splitting families, and regardless of how optimistic we were trying to be, we feared the unknown. Saying this goodbye proved to be a pivotal moment when the uncertainty of the future raised its ugly head. Prior to now, hope had always won when despair appeared in the form of bombings, displacements, etc. But now, since the war had gone on so much longer than anyone had expected, after experiencing the bombings in Budapest again, and after having the encounter with the planes on our train trip, the reality of the possibilities became quite clear. Our lives were obviously changing; our futures were uncertain; the war was taking its toll in many ways.

Gyula, the children and I took a train to Pankasz and from there continued on to Kisrakos. After a stressful and emotional trip, we all finally arrived safely; however, Gyula had to return to Budapest immediately to his civil service job. This was another very difficult goodbye for both of us. We had no way of knowing how long we would be forced apart by these war conditions; Gyula wanted to be with us and protect his family, yet his government position required other responsibilities. He did not want to leave his family, especially the newborn baby, and I wanted him to stay and not return to the dangerous conditions in Budapest, but we both knew that he had no choice; we had no choice.

Returning to Kisrakos, I realized what a peaceful and serene place it was. I recalled when Budapest was the same way. The contrast was now almost overwhelming. I felt so safe in Kisrakos, but now in Budapest the eminent threat was that a stray bomb would hit our house where Gyula was or hit the college where my parents and grandmother lived or hit any one of the neighborhoods that we often visited. The thought was very frightening!

I yearned to return to the peaceful, carefree, happy times in Budapest. I recalled the times after Gyula and I had first met when we would see each other on the streetcar. At the time, he was a student at the University of Budapest, and I was in high school, preparing for the university. We were very much in love. Gyula knew my schedule, so every opportunity he had, he would go out of his way to try to meet my streetcar to ride home from school with me. This gave us an opportunity to talk to each other in a socially acceptable way. We did not date, because in Hungary at the time, dating was simply not done. Young people in love normally only saw each other at the home of one of their families or in chaperoned situations, such as going to church together. But by meeting on a crowded streetcar with many other people around, we could talk with some privacy. Everyone else on the streetcar just thought we were two people who just happened to see each other there! We very often exchanged love letters that we had written during the day. My memories of those times warmed me as the fall season approached Kisrakos. It was as though the Lord himself were touching and comforting me. This was His way of taking care of me and mine.

The fall months passed slowly. The school in Kisrakos reopened, and the teacher and his family returned. This meant that the children and I had to move out of the small room at the school. A nice, sweet lady who was like a member of the family lived two houses down from the Zsohar house. Her house had two small bedrooms and a kitchen. She only needed one of the bedrooms, so she rented us the other bedroom. As we had done when we were in the school apartment, we stayed there only during the nights; we spent the days at the Zsohar house.

I continued to get to know and appreciate Mama. Not only was she an excellent cook, but also she was very handy with tools and very artistic. She loved to work with wood, and she carved the most beautiful wooden chairs I had ever seen. She would paint the chairs white, and then she painted beautiful designs that she created from her head.

Papa was a fix-it man. He could repair almost anything. People would bring all kinds of things to him, and usually he could mend the item so that again it was useful.

Mama and Papa made the caskets for the whole community. When someone died, word spread quickly in the small village. As soon as word about the death reached them, Mama and Papa began making the casket. No ice and no embalming were available at the time, so it was customary to have the funeral and the burial the day after the person died. As a result, Mama and Papa often would make the caskets late at night for the funeral the following day.

As winter approached and the days became shorter, I began to reflect occasionally about the walks I had made with Edesapa when I was a young girl. I began to wonder more about the Lord's will for my life. What would happen to us? How would the war change our lives? I had many questions, but I had no answers. Recalling Edesapa's words provided the only comfort I could muster: "Trust in the Lord. In life you can lose everything, but I emphasize to you, never lose your faith. Remember, never lose your faith! Often it is only through faith that people survive."

With winter weather coming and the temperatures turning much colder, I wrote Gyula to ask him to bring more winter clothes. I had brought some winter clothes when I returned in September, but I had not brought all of the winter clothes we had. Gyula had told me that he had three days off for Christmas. I was hoping that if in fact he could get the time off, maybe he could plan to bring the clothes and be with us at Christmas. The mail service was becoming very slow and unreliable, so I could not be sure that he received my letter. Although he had always responded before, this time I did not receive any response. Needless to say, when I did not hear from him, I became quite concerned for his safety and for the safety of other family members in Budapest.

Since we did not have electricity in the village, we did not have a radio on the farm. The teacher at the school had a battery-operated radio that he turned on once a day in the evening at ten o'clock to listen to the news. I was very interested in what was happening in Budapest and the rest of Hungary, so I asked the teacher if I could come over every evening and listen to the news with him and his family. He agreed, so Geza would accompany me to the schoolhouse, which was less than a kilometer from the Zsohar house. Most of the other villagers were not really interested in hearing the news on the radio that late in the evening. Their thinking was that if anything was important to know, they would hear it in the morning! But I wanted to hear the news firsthand from the broadcast.

It was from one of those radio broadcasts that I first heard that the Russians were invading Hungary and heading westward; another broadcast informed us that the transportation system throughout the country was breaking down. Even if Gyula could get the days off for Christmas, I now wondered if he could get to Kisrakos and back to Budapest in three days. Because I had not heard from him, I assumed he was unable to be with us for Christmas. Although this was a disappointing thought, I prayed for his safety and for that of my parents.

The Hungarian Christmas tradition begins on December 6. On the night of December 5, the children place a boot or a shoe in the space between one of the double windows in their homes in hopes that St. Nicholas will soon be there. (Hungarian houses were built with double windows that easily opened in the summer for a cool breeze and then could be latched in the winter to keep the cold air out. In this space between the windows the children put their footwear.) In traditional fashion, at this time during the night, if the child had been good, St. Nicholas would put in a piece of candy, or if the child had been really good, an orange might also be included in the boot or shoe. The only oranges available in Hungary came from Italy; they were considered a real treat. If the child had been bad, St Nicholas would not put anything good in the boot or shoe; instead, the mean Krampusz would put switches in them. This event was the beginning of the Christmas season. Up to this time no Christmas decorations were displayed anywhere. After December 6, all decorations were displayed except for the Christmas tree.

On Christmas Eve the Angels brought the Christmas tree and the presents for the children. The tradition was that the Christ child sent his Angels down on Christmas Eve night. The Angels brought the presents for the children and the Christmas tree and the spirit of Christmas to the families.

On Christmas Eve, while the children were detained away from the house, usually at a neighbor's house, the Christmas tree was decorated and the gifts placed under the tree. After dinner on Christmas Eve, the candles on the tree were lighted and the gifts were opened. Traditionally, this was the only night that the candles on the tree were lit. The trees were decorated with real candles, and after the candles burned down, they were not replaced.

It was late in the afternoon on Christmas Eve. Geza was taking care of the children at the neighbor's house, and Mama and I were in the midst of baking cookies, which we would use to decorate our small Christmas tree. I was trying very hard to be happy and festive for the occasion; after all, Christmas for the children was most important, but deep down I was heartbroken.

SURVIVING THROUGH FAITH

Not only would this be the first Christmas that Gyula and I had been apart since we met and fell in love in 1932, but it would be the first Christmas I had been apart from my parents and grandmother. The true spirit of Christmas seemed very hard to find with so much uncertainty about their safety.

Suddenly, the door opened, and there stood Gyula. I was surprised and overwhelmed with joy. The Angel of Christmas had brought us the most wonderful gift. Gyula's face was red from the outside cold, but he looked wonderful. Of course, he wanted to see the children immediately, so we ran over to let the children know their father was home. We felt so blessed to be back together as a family. At a time when so many families were being devastated by the war, we were together safely celebrating the joyous season of Christmas. I had experienced many wonderful seasons before, but none could compare to this one. We felt the spirit of the true meaning of Christmas. We were so thankful that the Lord had brought Gyula to us just in time so that we could all celebrate the birth of the Christ child together as a family. In spite of the uncertainty of our future, the comfort of being together for this special season refreshed our souls and our faith. The Lord had supplied our needs.

CHAPTER 3
IN THE PRESENCE OF MINE ENEMIES

The children were extremely excited to see their father. They could not wait to tell him everything they had been doing. While they were visiting, I went back to the house where we were sleeping to decorate the small Christmas tree and place the gifts for the children that Gyula had brought from Budapest. No stores in Kisrakos carried gifts appropriate for small children, and I did not have the time or money to travel to another town for gifts. The only gifts I was able to provide for the children were some candy and pieces of fruit. When it appeared that Gyula would not be with us for Christmas, I had felt so bad that the children would not receive any other gifts. It was so wonderful that Gyula had arrived and had brought small gifts for the children that I could place under the tree. After decorating the tree and placing the gifts, I returned to the Zsohar house for Christmas Eve dinner.

What a glorious Christmas Eve! Our family was together; Kisrakos was peaceful and serene, far removed from the activity of the war; we had food to eat, but more important, we had each other. Who could ask for anything else? We all felt and shared the true spirit of Christmas.

That night we had a wonderful visit. Gyula related how he had longed to be with us at Christmas. He had received my letter about needing winter clothes, but he had not attempted to respond. Although he had earned the time off, he was very uncertain as to whether he would be allowed to leave Budapest for the holidays. He did not want to excite us and lift our hopes for fear the officials would deny his request; he knew we would all be devastated if he were unable to celebrate with his family.

Gyula then began his story of how he had been able to leave Budapest and be with us by Christmas.

Events had been occurring in Budapest and throughout other parts of Hungary that had intensified Gyula's determination to leave the city and come to Kisrakos. Our need for winter clothes was only a minor consideration. Word had spread in Budapest that the Russians had invaded Hungary and were advancing toward the city. The fears of so many now had been confirmed. The war zone would soon encompass their surroundings, and the bombings were as frequent as ever. Gyula was even more determined to leave Budapest for Kisrakos.

For days rumors had been rampant that the Russians were inching closer to Budapest, but no one actually knew how close they were. In an effort to keep the people from panicking, official policy was to publish no bad news. The news media were not given truthful information; as a matter of fact, rarely did they receive any information at all. This was probably a good policy because as the general population became increasingly more nervous, the truth likely would have caused widespread panic and chaos. As a result, no one really knew anything officially, and rumors continued to circulate and escalate. The rumors were enough to concern the people because they knew what the Russians had already done. Everyone now realized that the Russians would not be stopped anyway. The Russians moved their war machine regardless of what lay in their way. Although most of the bridges had been bombed, blown up, or severely damaged at a minimum, the Russians were still crossing the rivers. They simply drove as many tanks in the river as needed to create a bridge for the remaining tanks. The remaining tanks would drive over the tanks in the river, and when these tanks had crossed the river, the Russians used the tanks that were on dry land to pull the tanks that had been used for the bridge out of the river one by one. The tanks that had been in the river were restored, and the war machine continued on its way. Although destroying the bridges did not stop the Russians from advancing closer to Budapest, it did slow them down.

The rumors obviously disturbed the people in Budapest. Although they had no way of knowing just how close to the city the Russians had advanced, the citizens realized they must be very close when the government ordered the road signs destroyed. By destroying the signs, the authorities hoped to make the trip into and within Budapest as difficult as possible for the enemy.

As he heard all of these stories about the movement of the Russians, Gyula decided that he did not care how close the Russians were; he would leave Budapest in time to see his family in Kisrakos for the holidays. The only way Gyula could leave his civilian job and travel out of Budapest was with an official permit. Although he had earned a vacation permit, he still needed official permission to use it. Gyula told the authorities that he wanted to take some more warm clothes to his family who had evacuated Budapest for the country. He showed the authorities the letter I had sent him stating that the clothes we had were not adequate for the long cold winter in western Hungary, and that we needed more clothing from our home. He explained that he had two small children plus a newborn child, and that he wanted to schedule the trip so that he could be with his family for Christmas. After much discussion, the authorities finally agreed to the request and gave Gyula an official permit to leave Budapest for a full week for the holidays.

As the day for his departure was approaching, Gyula packed up the warm winter clothing we needed in two large suitcases to bring to us. In addition to clothing, he packed a knapsack with the important documents he might need. He packed the birth certificates he had collected three years earlier, his diploma, our marriage license, baptismal papers and various other important papers. Although his intention was to return to Budapest after his week's visit, he thought perhaps he could very well need these papers. Furthermore, it was just safer to have these papers with him rather than leave them behind. Budapest had become the most dangerous place in Hungary to live. Because it was the heart of the country, if the Allies attempted to destroy any place, it would be Budapest.

Before noon on December 23, 1944, Gyula left the house in Budapest to begin his trip to Kisrakos. He walked to the train station, carrying the two suitcases and with the knapsack on his back. The suitcases were extremely heavy, but he was young and strong and could easily carry 100 pounds or more. When he arrived at the train station in Budapest, he discovered that the railroad system was absolutely disorganized and in chaos. By now it had become commonplace for the railroads to be bombed; thus, the trains just could not move. At best an occasional train would travel, but schedules were nonexistent. When the railroad personnel had enough people on a train and when an opportunity to leave presented itself, they simply allowed the train to leave, hoping it might arrive at the next station. Although riding a train was a very big gamble, it was Gyula's only possibility for public transportation. No buses were operating anywhere in Hungary.

When he realized what the situation was with the trains, Gyula knew he would have to make other arrangements. He had heard that with the trains in chaos and the buses idle, the resourceful Hungarians had already worked out a method to get around, and that everybody was cooperating. The people had created designated makeshift bus stations all over the city. Travelers would go to one of these stations. If a truck, military or civil, had space and was willing to carry passengers, it would stop at the station. The truck driver would tell the travelers where he was going. The travelers going the same direction could pay a small fee, climb in or on the truck, and be on their way. This was becoming a very well-accepted way to get around. The people had improvised and created a very functional transportation system within the chaos. This method was working very well, and everyone was benefiting.

Gyula decided to walk to the highway to one of these makeshift stations. He found a truck driver who was going toward the west and who would allow him to ride for a small fee. He rode with this driver until the driver stopped, and then he simply got on another truck to go further west. He repeated this routine several times. Most of the time he had to travel in the back of the truck in the open air because no other place was available. The extreme windchill created by the strong December wind and the very cold temperature made riding in the back even more uncomfortable. Because of the heavy traffic and poor road conditions, the trucks moved very slowly. One of the trucks that Gyula was on broke down and had to be repaired alongside the road. He traveled all day and all night until he finally arrived at Szombathely the following morning. He was now about two hundred kilometers from Budapest, but he was still ninety kilometers from Kisrakos.

When Gyula arrived by truck in Szombathely, he heard that a train was going to Kormend, which is only twenty kilometers from Kisrakos. The train station was two kilometers from where the truck had dropped him off, so he walked to the train station and boarded the train that would take him to Kormend. Nobody asked for tickets or any money on the train. This was one of the few railroad segments still operating, and everybody was trying to help each other as people attempted to deal with the inconveniences of war. The railroad certainly did not care about collecting any money at this point.

Once in Kormend, Gyula began walking to Kisrakos when a man with a truck stopped and asked him where he was going. Gyula explained his situation and told the man where he was going. The truck driver said that he was not planning to go to Kisrakos, but because it was Christmas Eve and it was very cold, he would go out of his way to take Gyula the last twenty kilometers to Kisrakos. He told Gyula that he needed to be with his family on Christmas Eve. Gyula was delighted to know that he now was going to arrive in time for the celebration with his family. Although the trip had been long, exhausting and difficult, the reward of being with his family for this most holy season was well worth it.

When he arrived near the Zsohar house, Gyula had the man drop him off a block away so that he could surprise me. He offered to pay the man, but the man refused any compensation. The man just said, "Have a merry Christmas!"

We were overjoyed that Gyula had successfully made this long and difficult journey to be with us for Christmas. After we finished dinner and had a nice long visit, Gyula, the children and I went back to the house where we were sleeping. The children were surprised and thrilled with the gifts that Gyula had brought for them. The small Christmas tree on the table looked so beautiful, with the cookies and the few lit candles we had. This had been an incredible day and a most memorable Christmas Eve!

The next day we had visitors almost the entire day. Friends and family came around to wish us a merry Christmas. Mama and I were glad that we had baked extra cookies. It was customary to offer coffee (a mixture of three-quarters milk and one-quarter coffee) and something to eat, such as cookies, to all visitors. We had such a wonderful day to celebrate Christ and His coming into our lives.

On Christmas night, we went to the teacher's apartment at the schoolhouse to listen to the news on the radio; we heard that on Christmas Eve the Russian fighting troops had surrounded Budapest and that fierce fighting was occurring in the streets. Gyula had only been out of Budapest for about twenty-four hours before the Russians sealed the city. We were overjoyed that Gyula had escaped; however, we were very concerned about my parents and other family members. We had no way of learning what was happening with them. At least Gyula was safe with us, and because of the fighting, we were certain that he would not return to Budapest in a few days as planned. We felt truly blessed that he had escaped Budapest just ahead of the Russians. Now, rather than being stranded in Budapest without us, he was stranded outside of Budapest with us. Again, Providence had played a hand in our lives. Our future was uncertain, but we were together to face our future, whatever it might be.

On the day after Christmas, Gyula began to feel sick. I immediately put him to bed and sent for a doctor. The doctor came and diagnosed him with pleurisy, an inflammation of the lungs. He told us that Gyula was very ill; he said that this was probably caused by the long hours Gyula had spent in the back of open trucks on the trip from Budapest to Szombathely in the cold, damp winter wind. Although Gyula had thought he was dressed warmly for the trip, the long hours in the severe winter winds had taken a toll on his already weary body. The doctor did not have any medication to give him. He prescribed bed rest and patience, for it could take a long time for the lungs to heal.

At about this same time, just after Christmas, the Hungarian government, at the insistence of the German leadership, changed the draft laws and initiated an emergency military draft. All physically able men from ages eighteen to sixty were to be drafted into the German-controlled Hungarian army. The earlier drafts had taken young men over twenty-one years of age who were single or married without children. Because this was considered an emergency draft, almost anyone who could walk was to be drafted. The government felt this reinforcement was necessary in order to fight the Russians.

A few days after Gyula became ill, he received his draft papers notifying him that he was being drafted. He was ordered to report immediately. Because Gyula was in bed with a high fever, a terrible cough, and having much difficulty breathing, he simply was in no condition to report to the military. He was a very sick man. The doctor gave him a written statement that he was not physically fit to go into the military. I went into the village and took the doctor's statement to the commanding officer.

Gyula's pleurisy, even though a very serious disease, proved to be a real blessing. Everybody knew that the Germans were losing, and that the war was effectively over. These had to be the last days of the war. Everything was in complete chaos. The Germans, wanting to make a last stand against the Russians, were willing to sacrifice Hungarian lives to do so. If Gyula had been drafted, he would have been drafted into the army led by the Germans. Who knows what would have happened to him on the front lines facing the Russians. Gyula felt lucky to be so sick! As much as I hated to see him lying in bed suffering, I, too, was thankful that this illness occurred when it did. I could care for him as he lay sick in bed; had he been on the Russian front, I would have been helpless. Sometimes, things that initially appear to be really bad actually turn out to be really good. We felt this was certainly the case with the pleurisy. We were convinced that Providence had once again played a major role in our lives. We were still together as a family, and for the time being, we were out of harm's way.

Since no medication was available to treat the pleurisy, Gyula had to suffer with the disease. Gradually he became better, and after about six weeks he had almost completely regained his strength. By this time the Russians were beginning to advance west from Budapest. We heard on the radio that Budapest had surrendered to the Russians after fifty-six days of violent fighting. The dangerous Russian army was now moving in our direction.

Later in February, about the time that Gyula had fully recovered from the pleurisy, his father became ill. At first

Papa thought he simply had a bad cold, even though he was coughing badly; however, the doctor diagnosed him as having pneumonia. The only way the doctor had to treat him was by giving him aspirin. The whole family realized that Papa was very ill. The following morning, on February 19, just after six o'clock, Papa died. Mama made a casket for her son, and the next day we had his funeral and buried him. Everyone loved Papa. He was a very quiet, hardworking man. He was gentle and kind to us from the first day I met him. After he died, we missed his serenity. He had had such a calming effect on everyone during this highly stressful time.

After Gyula recovered and after his father passed away, he reported to the government authorities, who told him that the draft had ended but that he still had his job for the civilian government. Gyula felt an obligation to complete this assignment. He learned that the ministry for which he had worked had moved out of Budapest to Szombathely, approximately ninety kilometers from our home in Kisrakos. He was told to report to duty at the ministry office to learn what his civilian responsibilities would be. It was now the end of February 1945. Train travel even in western Hungary was completely paralyzed. Very few people owned any type of motorized vehicle in these rural areas. The only way he could get there was to begin walking and hope someone would offer him a ride. With his knapsack on his back, Gyula left Kisrakos and began walking to Szombathely. He had no luck catching a ride. He walked twenty-three hours straight until he finally arrived at his destination ninety kilometers away. When he arrived at the ministry office, he was assigned to serve his duty in Kormend, which was only twenty kilometers from our home in Kisrakos! He had gone all this distance to discover that his civilian assignment was very close to home! As he walked back to Kisrakos, Gyula was very excited! Not only could he fulfill his services for the government, but also he could live at home with his family! Fortunately, a neighbor loaned him a bicycle to make the twenty-kilometer daily trip to and from Kormend. Again, fate had brought us a blessing!

Everyone continued to monitor the location of the Russian troops. News reports were rarely accurate, and rumors were certainly not very reliable. We could never be really sure how far away the Russians were, but we were constantly receiving reports that they were still coming and getting closer.

On March 29, 1945, Gyula came home from Kormend several hours earlier than usual in the afternoon. Several people from villages east of the area had arrived in Kormend, reporting that Russian troops had attacked their villages and the defenseless civilians. The Russians were committing unthinkable atrocities everywhere they went. Because they were drugged, the Russian soldiers were not afraid of anything. They showed no emotion. If a gun was pointed at them, they would merely continue forward trying to destroy whomever or whatever might be in their way; if the soldier's comrade were shot next to him, the soldier showed no emotion whatsoever. The troops were like machines. They did what they were ordered to do. Russian soldiers were raping females regardless of their age, from eight to eighty. If a man tried to stop them, he was shot.

When this news arrived in Kormend, ministry officials realized that the government was powerless to maintain any kind of control in the country. Gyula's superiors released him and the other employees from government service and told them that they were free to stay or go. It was up to the individuals to take care of themselves and their families because the government was no longer able to keep order. Clearly, the Russian communists would now control the Hungarian government. Gyula informed us that we needed to leave that night. He did not know where we were going to go or how we were going to get there. He just knew Kisrakos would not be safe when the Russian troops arrived, and the war machine was coming in our direction and getting closer. We could not take the chance of confronting the Russian troops. We had to leave Hungary.

Once again we were faced with great uncertainty; in fact, the greatest uncertainty so far. We did not know where we were going; we did know we had to escape the threat of Russian invasion. We knew one definite fact: Russian fighting forces were an enemy that we did not want to confront. Now, their presence could almost be felt by the anxiety of the people who were familiar with their brutality. We did not know where safety awaited us; we did not know what the Lord had in store for us. We did know that we had to do anything and everything we could to escape the impending danger, and we had to do it now, tonight. The only other thing we knew was that we must trust in the Lord, and, as Edesapa had counseled me years before, we must "Remember, the Lord's will be done."

We had made no prior preparations for leaving. It had never occurred to us that we might need to flee the peacefulness and serenity of Kisrakos. Now, our very lives and the lives of our young children were at stake. We had little time to gather our belongings and prepare ourselves for uncertain travel. A wooden footlocker, which Papa had used during the first World War, would serve well for packing, but it certainly was not sufficient for the needs of five people. Gyula decided that what we needed were crates in which to pack everything we needed—especially food. To build crates, he needed lumber. Papa never stored much lumber at the farm, and finding lumber on such short notice in the early evening in the small village was very difficult. Mama had some lumber that she had set aside for her coffin. At seventy-nine years old, she knew she would need a coffin at some not-so-distant date, so she had collected the lumber and had stored it behind the house. She insisted we use this lumber to build the crates. Mama laughed and said, "Surely they will find something to bury me in when I die. Furthermore, it won't matter to me at that time. What matters now is that you get your family to safety." Gyula used Mama's coffin wood to make the crates needed for the trip.

Gyula quickly made two crates. The workmanship was not as precise as he wanted, but time was of the essence. Although he was accustomed to making very fine wooden items much like the ones Mama made, he just cut and nailed the boxes together and then built tops for each that could be nailed down once the crate was packed. Opening each crate required prying the top of the box open. One crate was about a meter wide and a meter tall and about a meter and a half long; the other crate was about two-thirds that size. Although they were not the items of craftsmanship normally produced by the Zsohar family, the crates were very sturdy and would certainly withstand uncertain travel conditions.

While Gyula built the crates, I gathered our belongings for the trip. I did not know how long we would be gone, but we decided we would take everything we possibly could just in case it was for an extended time. We believed that we would probably be gone for only a few days, but uncertainty ruled! We gathered clothing, blankets and everything that we owned and needed from the house in Kisrakos. I took the metal dishes I had brought with me from Budapest. Mama gave me a cast iron pan and a cast iron pot for cooking. Mama and I gathered the food for us to take. We had bread, flour, sugar, salt, eggs, bacon, ham, sausage, potatoes, apples and various other items. Mama filled one of my favorite bowls with butter. Mama insisted we take most of the food she had. She said Geza, Laci and herself did not need much, and what they needed, they could get from the neighbors or from the market later. Mama went so far as to carefully wrap each egg in newspaper to make sure it did not break.

Once the crates were finished, we began to pack each one quickly but methodically. The larger crate had the clothing and various other necessities. The smaller crate was completely packed with food. In Papa's World War I footlocker, we placed the dishes and remaining food items. We packed carefully to avoid putting frequently needed items in the bottom of a crate.

We worked frantically all night, and by early morning we had finished packing and crating everything. We included a baby buggy and a baby bed that Gyula had made. He cut the legs off the bed for easier handling. With the legs cut off, it folded together into a small bundle. We put it on top of the other things after they were loaded onto a wagon. In addition, Gyula and I each packed a knapsack. Gyula packed his knapsack with the important papers and documents he had brought from Budapest. By packing the birth certificates, marriage licenses, diplomas and other documents in his knapsack, he could always have them with him in case something happened to the other belongings.

Our goal was to get across the border to a safe place in Austria. When the fighting stopped and order was restored, we would return to Kisrakos. The entire time we were packing, we thought about how soon we would be able to return. It never occurred to us that we might not return.

We asked a farmer who lived nearby if he would take us to the border of Austria in his horse-drawn wagon. For a fee, he agreed to take us but not across the border. We thought just getting to the border was the most important thing to do now; after we arrived at the border, we would then find a way to get across.

Geza, Laci and Gyula loaded the crates, footlocker and baby buggy onto the wagon. They tied the baby bed on top, and the wagon was loaded and ready to go.

The time had come to say goodbye. Never had we been subjected to a more emotional experience. We had never dreamed that the peaceful little farming village would become a target for the war machine. But the enemy was coming. It was closer than it had ever been, and we could lose no time if we hoped to save our family.

We said goodbye to Geza and Laci. Geza, who had just turned eighteen, said he also was going to leave later that day. Laci was planning to stay, but he did not know how long. None of us had any idea when or if we would see each other again.

The most emotional and most difficult goodbye was with Mama. She and I had grown so close in the past year. With everything that was happening, we just knew we probably would not see her again. Mama really did not want us to leave. She had become not only very close to me, but also very close to her great-grandchildren. We had been together for less than a year, but we had developed a lifetime of love for each other. We had experienced so much: She had helped me take care of the children and had taught me to cook. She had helped me care for Gyula during his illness, and, together, we had cared for Papa, her son, before he died. Mama said she understood that we had to leave, but I could never forget her last words to me. She was crying as she said, "I know the boys will leave as well, and I will die alone here in the house." We learned later that her prediction came true. The evils of war had taken their toll on our family.

CHAPTER 4
HE MAKETH ME TO LIE DOWN IN GREEN PASTURES

By two o'clock in the morning, we had everything loaded onto the wagon, had completed our good-byes and were ready to begin our journey. We had worked frantically throughout the night, selecting items, packing crates, and enlisting someone to take us to the border. In less than twelve hours after Gyula told us we needed to leave, we were completely packed and ready to go. Just a few hours earlier, we had been enjoying the peaceful country setting, and now we were already hearing sounds of the war in the background. We knew danger was imminent; we needed to find a safer place as quickly as possible. Because of its location, we decided to go toward Szentgotthard, a town located about twenty-five kilometers from Kisrakos, within three kilometers of the main highway from western Hungary into Austria, and about four kilometers from the border.

The two horses labored as they pulled the wagon loaded with all our possessions and us. We could travel only about five kilometers per hour. As we traveled through the night, we could hear occasional explosions and cannon gunfire. The children were very tired and fell asleep almost immediately after we left. On the other hand, Gyula and I were wide awake and very anxious about everything that was happening. We knew that the Russians were coming from the east toward us and getting closer by the minute. We could hear occasional explosions, and we could see that the night sky had a red tint toward the east.

With each explosion, our hearts pounded a bit faster. Here we were in the dead of night, our three children asleep in a wagon containing all our belongings and desperately trying to outrun a military machine that had literally taken over our homeland. In spite of our fear of not knowing what was ahead of us, we were certain that we were doing the right thing by leaving as quickly as we could.

We arrived at Szentgotthard at about six o'clock in the morning. According to the agreement, the farmer who brought us dropped our crates and other belongings. As Gyula paid him for taking us to the border, the man wished us well and hurried back toward Kisrakos.

When we arrived in the town, we were amazed at the number of people waiting to leave the country. People were everywhere. Many had horse-drawn wagons, and a few had oxen-drawn wagons. However, like us, many people had no transportation at all. Everyone was frightened and panicky. We all realized that the Russians were close, and all of us had the same goal: to flee the country. The scene was chaotic. The only positive thing was that it was now daylight instead of dark.

We now had all of our belongings stacked near the border and no transportation. We had no plan of what to do next. The rail system here, as in the rest of Hungary, was totally paralyzed. The situation around us was the most miserable that I could imagine. Everything was frenzied and disorderly. No one appeared to be in charge or attempting to keep order; as a result, no semblance of organization existed whatsoever. Obviously, everyone had to take care of his own security and basically take care of himself. Both Gyula and I sensed and shared the clear sense of panic in the air.

By now everybody had heard the stories, and all they wanted to do was to escape the brutality of the Russian fighting troops. Everyone had one thing in common: they all feared the Russians. In the distance, we could hear the cannons, and we knew the vicious war machine was inching closer.

Even among the confusion and chaos, we knew we must locate some means of transportation and get across the border into Austria, where we felt we would surely be safer than in Hungary. We began to look around for any possible solution. We questioned everyone and anyone who might in any way possibly help us cross the border. Everyone who had wagons said theirs were fully loaded and that they did not have any space for us. Our faith had sustained us to this point, and we continued to rely on that support. We thought surely there had to be some way to get across the border, but everything appeared very bleak and hopeless. Our faith was beginning to wane.

What happened next was almost unbelievable and totally unexpected. Two men with an oxen-drawn wagon approached the area where we sat with the children and our belongings. They said, "Our employer is a wealthy count nearby, and this wagon and oxen belong to him. He asked us to bring the wagon to the border to see if anyone would like to use it to escape into Austria. The Russians troops are very close to his farm, and the count knows the Russians will either kill the oxen or use them, and he does not want to help the Russians at all." The men then asked, "Is there anyone here who knows how to handle these oxen and who would like to have the oxen and wagon to use?"

These oxen were enormous animals with long spiraling horns. Most of the people waiting there, who did not already have a wagon, were from the city and had never worked on a farm. The huge animals intimidated them. Gyula, on the other hand, had grown up on a farm; he knew how to work the animals and care for them.

Gyula immediately spoke up, "I very much would like the wagon and oxen." The man came over to Gyula and gave him the wagon and oxen. Gyula said, "I would like to pay you."

The man answered, "I do not want your money. The count would like for you to use it to escape. It is yours to keep. The count just wanted somebody to use the wagon and did not want the Russians to get it."

Gyula thanked the two men, and they ran away toward the border and disappeared. We could not believe this good fortune. God had furnished us transportation to leave Hungary. The two oxen were outfitted with a yoke and were attached to a very large, heavy, sturdy wagon worthy to be owned by a count.

After we loaded the wagon with all of our belongings, we discovered that we still had some room on the wagon. Several families nearby were without transportation. We now had an opportunity to do for someone what nobody had been able to do for us a few minutes before—we could offer someone space on our wagon. We invited a couple with a teenage son to join us on the wagon. They had just a few bags that would fit nicely on the wagon. Their name was Kerekes, and they gratefully accepted our offer to join us for the trip.

Once fully loaded, we started toward the border. When we reached the main road, which was about three kilometers outside of Szentgotthard and about one kilometer from the border, we were stopped. The road was closed, and a large number of wagons were waiting for the road to open. We learned that the German army had closed the highway to allow the German troops who had invaded Hungary to retreat into Austria. As far as the eye could see, what seemed to be an endless stream of trucks approached on all four lanes of the highway. These Germans knew they were defeated. As far as they were concerned, the war was over, and they were heading back to Austria and Germany.

Once again we were stopped with nowhere to go. We were so close, but we could not proceed. It was March 30, 1945, Good Friday.

As we continued to wait, we met and visited with many people who were also anxious to cross the border. A Hungarian man named Feher began to talk about organizing a group to travel together. He volunteered to lead the group. A lawyer who spoke excellent German and who had lived in Austria, Feher knew the Austrian people, and, perhaps more important, he knew how to communicate with officials. Feher went on to explain that the impending end of the war had left the Austrian government powerless and, as a result, no law or order now existed. Crime was rampant. He felt that only by banding together would we be safe from criminals. Rumors were that wagons by themselves were always stopped, and everything would be stolen. Feher also had heard that if anyone resisted the bandits, the bandits would simply shoot everybody on the wagon. As people heard these rumors, considered their options for travel and discussed their uncertain futures, a group began to form. Soon, the drivers of seventeen wagons organized to travel together into Austria with Feher as their self-appointed leader.

We waited for hours. German troops had first priority, and officials were not allowing any civilians on the road in order that their troops could make their way back into Austria and Germany. We were becoming increasingly concerned about the Russian advance because as each hour passed, the gunfire and explosions grew louder and louder. Finally, as nighttime was approaching, the Germans opened one of the four lanes of the highway to allow large civilian motorized vehicles such as trucks to leave Hungary. The Germans still maintained the right of way and controlled access to the highway. They were not yet allowing any wagons to use the highway, and it did not matter whether horse or oxen were pulling the wagons. People wanting to use the road had to wait until the Germans were ready to open the highway to all traffic.

As we were anxiously waiting for some indication that the wagons would be allowed on the highway with the trucks so that we could continue our flight into Austria, Gyula noticed that some of the trucks were stopping to pick up women and children and were putting them on top of each truck. For a negotiated price, the truck drivers were helping to evacuate the women and children by utilizing any extra space they had.

Gyula quickly made a decision. Once again, as he had done in Budapest a year earlier, he was determined to send his family to safety ahead of himself. He saw a truck that still had some available space on top and waved for it to stop. Gyula asked the driver where he was going, and the driver said Graz, a city in Austria about seventy-five kilometers by road from the

Hungarian border. Gyula had been to Graz twice before. Since he knew the city, he reasoned this would be a good way to get the children and me out of immediate danger and to safety as quickly as possible. No one knew when the highway would open for all travelers. We could hear the cannon fire getting louder and louder. We knew the Russians could not be too far away. Gyula intended to protect his family at all costs.

Assuring me that he would find a way to meet us in Graz, Gyula insisted that we go with the truck driver. He promised that if the Russians got too close before he could take the wagon across the border, he would abandon everything except his knapsack that held all of our important documents. If necessary, he said, he would take what he could carry and simply run through the fields across the border into Austria.

Gyula agreed to give the truck driver thirty eggs in exchange for taking the children and me to Graz. Erzsike was almost four years old now, and Gyuszi was two. They were thrilled to ride on top of the truck! It was all an adventure to them! I climbed up with Ilonka, who was only seven months old. Other women and children already occupied space on the truck, so we just squeezed in with the others. As the truck pulled away, we waved goodbye to Gyula who called out, "I will find you in Graz." I don't know why, but I felt confident that we would see each other soon.

The truck pulled away and began its journey into Austria. As we crossed the border, I looked back from atop the truck a long way into Hungary and saw the dark sky lit up with fires from the burning villages as the Russians troops advanced. We could still hear the bombings and shootings. It was about seven o'clock in the evening on Good Friday. We were leaving our homeland to seek safety from the intruder. Suddenly, it occurred to me that I was extremely hungry, and I was sure the children were also. At that moment, I realized we were riding atop a load of smoked hams that were covered with a tarpaulin. In the anxiety of the day, we had been so focused on trying to escape the Russians and get out of Hungary that we had never taken the time during the entire day to stop and eat. Now that the children and I were out of immediate danger, I had become very hungry. The smell of smoked ham was not helping my hunger pains! What a wonderful smell! The truck driver had not allowed us to take any baggage with us except my knapsack, which contained a few diapers and a few other items for the children. In our anxious haste, food had not crossed our minds. All our food with everything else was back with Gyula and the wagon. After we were in Austria for a while, Erzsike and Gyuszi asked about something to eat. I had to explain to them that we did not have any food with us, but I was sure we would find some soon. The children accepted the situation and being so tired from the day, they soon fell asleep.

After we crossed the border, the road narrowed to two lanes, both jammed with Germans and Hungarians leaving. Some people had managed to cross the border on foot and were walking on and just off the road. Somehow, other people with horse-drawn wagons had also already crossed. They, too, were adding to the crowded, narrow roadway. It was a mass exodus like nothing I could have imagined. The truck on which we rode traveled very slowly all night through the maze of people, wagons and other vehicles. It was cold on top of the truck, but we had our coats, and we huddled and bundled up together to keep warm.

Travel was so slow that we did not arrive at the outskirts of Graz until Saturday afternoon. The truck driver dropped us off on the side of the road. Other people were gathered in this area, so I decided this would be a good place to wait for Gyula. Within a couple of hours, I spotted Feher and his family. They were ahead of the other wagons, and Feher began to search for a place for us to rest and wait for the others. He noticed a nice green pasture just off the road up a hill, where we could meet and also see the road. He talked to the farmer who owned the pasture, and he explained that we would like to use his property just for a short while to organize our group of travelers. The farmer agreed. It wasn't long before other refugees gathered at the same location. Feher asked if we had eaten, and when he learned that we had not, he gave us some food. We really appreciated his generosity because we had not had anything to eat for more than a day.

Just after we settled at the pasture, the farmer's wife saw me with the young children and offered to allow us to sleep on the floor of the farmhouse that night. We accepted her offer because the nights were still very cold, and we had little protection from the elements.

The following morning was Easter Sunday, April 1. The pasture where we were waiting for Gyula was on a hill outside of Graz. From this hill, we could see the entire city of Graz. Sometime during midmorning while the Easter church services were still going on, we heard Allied planes overhead. Suddenly, we saw them dive and begin to drop bombs on Graz. I noticed that they were American planes similar to those I had seen in pictures in newspapers and magazines in Budapest. Once they dropped their bombs, they quickly accelerated back into the sky.

First, there was one wave of planes. After they delivered their loads, another wave of planes came. Not only could I hear the bombs clearly, but also I could see the explosions. Because we were located away from the city, however, we did not feel that we were in any danger. I watched the planes closely, and I began to notice that there did not seem to be any special target for the bombings. The planes seemed to be dropping their bombs indiscriminately on the civilian population. No military targets appeared to be in the area. They were bombing anything in sight, including the churches. From time to time, some of the planes actually looked like they were targeting churches. Horrified at what I saw, it tore my heart to see churches burning that Easter morning. Everybody knew the war was over. The Germans were already retreating. These demolitions obviously were meant to break the morale of the people, but at the same time they showed a certain blindness to the needless destruction, which seems to come with war.

Sometime later the bombing stopped for about an hour, and then we heard more planes coming. This time English and Russian planes came, but they were not nearly as effective as the American planes. The Germans' antiaircraft guns quickly drove them back. Finally, the planes retreated and the noise stopped, but the damage had been done.

On Easter Sunday afternoon, many of the wagons began arriving. Feher's teenage son and other young people stood by the road. When they saw some of our group coming, they would direct them to the pasture where the others were waiting. Finally, just before dark, Gyula arrived with the Kerekes family.

Again, our family was together, and Gyula related the story of his trip. He said he had waited patiently for the highway to open so that he would be allowed to cross the border into Austria with our belongings. He said that about an hour after we left on the truck, the officials opened the highway to allow all of the fleeing refugees to use the road to escape Hungary.

When they arrived at the border, Feher talked to the border authorities, and they allowed the seventeen wagons to cross the border together as a group. Gyula said they crossed the border with the wagon only about an hour and a half after we crossed in the truck. Through the darkness they slowly plodded with wagons and animals along the highway. Horses were pulling all but two of the wagons in the wagon train, and oxen were pulling the other two wagons. The whole group could travel only as fast as the oxen, but since so many people were already on the road, travel was slow, so the group was not delayed too much.

Gyula said they felt they were in danger only once during the journey. This happened sometime soon after they crossed the border. They knew the Russians were getting very close to the group, as they were traveling through one of the villages. Some kind of missile exploded nearby, and Gyula felt the shock wave of the air pressure on his trousers. With the Russians that close behind them, they decided to try to move a little faster and take fewer and shorter rest breaks. They stopped only when the animals needed food and rest.

As they traveled, the Germans still had the right-of-way, so from time to time the wagon train had to pull onto the side of the road and allow German troops to pass with their trucks and tanks. Once the faster vehicles had passed, the group moved back onto

59

the road and continued their slow journey west into Austria. They stayed as close together as possible for security reasons.

Everyone in the wagon train had the same goal: to escape the Russians. To keep moving away from the danger, they traveled all night and all the following day. The progress was terribly slow. They stopped every few hours to allow the animals to rest and graze. After the animals and people were fed and rested, they once again began their slow progress toward Graz.

Although this group had not known each other at all when they began their journey, soon they were sharing whatever food they had with others. Some of the refugees who were walking on the highway had fled with absolutely nothing. In some cities, rationing prevented people from having any additional food. Most of the people who had food were those who had come from small farm villages. Others just left in a panic and left without taking any food with them at all. Gyula had more food on his wagon than most of the other people, so he shared ham, bread and everything that he had with other people who had less. He made many good friends, as he shared with those who had no food.

The group continued traveling very slowly all Saturday night and all day Sunday. Finally, by midafternoon Easter Sunday, they were nearing Graz. As they approached, they were met by the scouts who knew the whereabouts of the families. One of these scouts told Gyula where we were. Because Gyula knew the town and the area around the town, he quickly found us. We were together again, but we still had no idea where we would go from here.

As Gyula and I began to reorganize our family on our wagon, I noticed that the baby buggy was not on the wagon. Because it contained many of the baby clothes we had, I asked Gyula about it.

Gyula explained that a few minutes after the children and I had left on the truck at the border, a man came up from another group. He was a teacher, Szatai, whom Gyula knew from Budapest. Szatai said that he had a horse-drawn wagon, and the horses could move much faster than the oxen. Szatai told Gyula that he could see by the items he had on his wagon that he had a baby and that he would surely need those baby items in Graz. He knew Gyula would not want to abandon them if he had to flee on foot. Szatai offered to take the baby buggy to Graz so that we would have the things we needed for the baby. He said he could get to Graz faster than Gyula because he had the horses, and Gyula would be slower with the oxen. Szatai could get the buggy to me faster. Since Gyula knew he did not need those items until Graz, and because Gyula knew Szatai and trusted him, he gave him the items and told him how he really appreciated the kind gesture and thanked him for helping out. The baby buggy was a top-quality buggy and was full of clothes, most of which were new baby clothes, diapers and everything else that the baby needed.

Gyula asked if I had seen Szatai. I told him I had not, and that none of the scouts had mentioned anything about anyone asking about us. The way the communications were being handled with the refugees, Szatai easily could have found us if he had wanted.

We checked everywhere and talked to everyone we could to determine if anyone had seen Szatai or might know where our baby buggy and clothes were. We checked all of the areas where refugees were gathering. No one had seen him. On the other hand, we found other people who had done something similar— they also had given Szatai items to take to Graz. He had used the same story with them about wanting to help. Obviously, this man was not as honest as Gyula had thought. For some reason, he had chosen to take advantage of the situation to steal from his friends. This man had conned several people who were all seeking safety. Gyula finally realized that Szatai must have been collecting the items to sell or trade for food or money.

Of course, the baby clothes were important to us. Now all we had was a few diapers and a few clothes for Ilonka in the knapsack and handbag I carried with me on the truck. The rest of the baby clothes were in the buggy. So here we were in Austria, living in a makeshift refugee camp, with no local currency, almost no baby clothes or diapers, and no way to get them. The situation was discouraging, but we were together, and that was the most important thing. We knew that we had to keep our faith and move forward from here. We had to trust in the Lord to protect and guide us.

CHAPTER 5
YEA, THOUGH I WALK THROUGH THE VALLEY

Finally, all of the wagons arrived. Feher suggested that we assess our situation and decide upon the best approach to take from here. He asked various people around the area their ideas about where we should go. He learned that the Russians had slowed down after they had crossed the Austrian border and, as a result, we might have a few days to rest and reorganize. Feher thought this was what we should do. Although everyone was still very nervous, we decided it would be better to follow his advice rather than to take off alone without knowing where to go or where the Russian troops might be.

While Feher was out gathering information, Gyula decided to convert our wagon to a covered wagon. Even though it was early spring, the weather conditions could be winterlike and severe. Occasional snowstorms, rain and constant cold temperatures were the norm. A covered wagon would provide much more protection against the elements. Hungarians had made covered wagons for generations, and Gyula had seen paintings depicting covered wagons from a thousand years before. Gyula cut some willow shoots and branches to build the frame for the cover. As he was looking for something to use for the cover, he noticed that another refugee was throwing away a rug in order to lessen his load. Gyula asked if he could have the rug, and the man was happy to let him have it. Gyula placed the rug over the willow branches and made a very nice covered wagon in which the children could ride.

In the meantime, Feher learned that as the Allied forces were taking over in various parts of the country, the government in Austria was collapsing. The Allied forces had divided the German-occupied countries into four zones, and Austria was one of the countries divided. Graz and much of eastern Austria was the Russian zone; an area north of the Russian zone was the French zone; the southern part of Austria was the British zone; and the area farthest from Graz and toward the west was the American zone. Although he had tried, Feher was unable to determine clearly where the exact boundaries were for each.

With the Austrian government in disarray, no law enforcement existed in the area. Everybody was on his own and had to create his own security. Feher was convinced that the only way we could ensure the required security was to continue to stay together. The road bandits did not know who had guns and who did not, and they just assumed that in a large group surely someone was armed. For this reason, robbers never bothered large groups. To our knowledge, the only one in our group who possessed a gun was Feher.

Knowing that the threat of the Russians was ever present, we all recognized the need to move toward the west as quickly as possible. Even the Austrians began to flee Graz when they heard that Russian troops were coming. Nobody wanted to encounter the brutality of the Russian forces.

The group, with Feher as our leader, spent three days meticulously organizing so that we could continue our trip away from the Russians. The wagons and animals were checked, and supplies were checked and reorganized. Throughout our time in Graz, Gyula had stayed with the oxen all day and night to make sure they were safe. He knew that without the oxen, we were not going anywhere. As we were nearing the time to leave, Gyula reloaded the wagon to make it as secure and as comfortable as possible for the children.

We left Graz with the same seventeen wagons that had crossed the border together. The Kerekes family joined us again on our wagon. We began our journey to move further northwest into Austria to escape the Russian soldiers. Although we were not sure exactly where the Russians were now, we did know that we were in the Russian zone, and that we must leave as soon as possible. We decided to head toward Leoben, about fifty kilometers from Graz. We thought that Leoben might be close to the French zone and safety. With the oxen and horse-drawn wagons, we tried to stay away from heavily traveled roads and inner cities. For this reason, we traveled around Graz, as we proceeded westward. We also stayed on country roads as much as possible.

We traveled very slowly, approximately seven to ten kilometers per day. Perhaps because we were not in immediate danger, this part of our trip proved to be a very emotional time for me. Each kilometer we went was another kilometer away from our homeland and our families and further into an uncertain future. This created loneliness and a yearning to be near my parents and my brothers. Although I had my own family now, I had always been close to my family, both physically and emotionally. Now, we were going farther and farther away from them. I longed for their company, their counsel, their caring, and their companionship. They had always been a central part of my life.

Uncertainty had never been a concern for me in the past. My life had been serene and peaceful prior to the war. The past couple of years, however, had turned my life from one insecure experience to another. I was totally unprepared for everything that was happening to us. I always had been in secure, safe surroundings with no strife or discord. The most insecure time I had had up to this time had occurred when Gyula and I were trying to receive approval for our engagement announcement.

Gyula and I always had planned to be married after I graduated from college in June 1940. About a year before my planned graduation, Gyula approached my father and asked for his approval to marry his daughter. It was customary that the engagement would not be announced until the father had given his consent. When Edesapa mentioned to Edesanya and my grandmother, whom we all called Mamsika, that we were planning to be married, a major problem arose. From the very first time they met, Gyula and Mamsika, a very strong-willed and opinionated person, had not agreed on anything! A subtle friction developed between them from the time Gyula began showing up to walk to church with us every Sunday. But now, after the planned engagement, the discord really became serious.

It all began with Mamsika's insistence that she give us a monthly stipend after we were married. She had been widowed at a young age, forcing her to struggle to make ends meet while raising my mother. Furthermore, other members of her family had cheated her out of her inheritance. As a result of the hard life she had lived, she became a tough and sometimes bitter person. She wanted to protect me from the kinds of hardships she had experienced, so she wanted to be sure we had enough money to meet our needs. This offer highly offended Gyula, and under no circumstances was he about to take a handout from anyone, and especially not from my grandmother! He did not need any help to support a family. He was already teaching and earning a reasonable living. But Mamsika kept insisting that we take the money, and she would not back down. Edesapa could not give his approval for the marriage until Mamsika went along with the union. Edesanya always sided with her mother; as a result, Edesapa could not act one way or another.

For a while, the discussions were so loud and angry that I thought Gyula might call off the wedding plans. To make matters worse, Edesapa, whom Gyula loved and admired, offered to let us live in their house rent free. Gyula made it clear to Edesapa that he would not live in the house rent free and that he would not take the monthly stipend. Finally, Gyula presented a compromise that eventually was approved by Edesapa, Edesanya and even Mamsika. He would accept the offer of the house if he were allowed to pay a modest rent to cover taxes and some expenses. Everyone agreed, and, finally, Edesapa announced our engagement. During this whole disagreement, which took months to resolve, I thought that my world was falling apart and that my future was very uncertain. Now that we were on the road traveling farther and farther from Budapest, to places unknown, fleeing from the Russian troops, the anxieties of our engagement seemed very trivial.

As we slowly but surely continued on our journey, we became accustomed to spending long hours outside. We spent hours and hours walking along the road or trail. The children usually stayed in the wagon while Gyula, the Kerekeses and I walked along with the oxen. We wanted to minimize the load on the oxen as much as possible because we did not know how far or for how long we would be traveling. We knew we needed to take good care of the animals because our progress depended on them.

We stopped early enough each evening to prepare a meal for everyone. The weather was still very cold and sometimes snowy. From time to time, we would have to dig out small branches from under the snow in order to light a fire for cooking or just to heat some water. I was thankful to God for the year in Kisrakos that had prepared me a bit for the rustic conditions I was now encountering on a daily basis. The luxuries of life in Budapest seemed so very far away and so very, very long ago.

Because we had no hay for the animals, we had to stop from time to time to allow the oxen and horses to graze. We tried to stop in places where snow had not covered the grass. On several occasions, we had to dig the snow away just to get to some grass for the animals. Fortunately, the Hungarian oxen, primarily work animals, were very hardy animals and could work hard with very little food. During the first few days, we often had a difficult time finding a place where the animals could graze. Our travel was painfully slow. After a few days, we arrived on the outskirts of Leoben. In a meadow outside the village, we camped as a group and rested for two days.

Again, Feher went to talk to the villagers and travelers about where we should go. He learned that if we traveled to either the British or French zone, we would be returned to Hungary. Obviously, we did not want to take that chance. As much as we missed Hungary, the Russians were still there, and we had experienced far too much to take a chance in arriving at any place where the Russians were. We learned that the safest place to go was the American zone. First of all, we would be safe from the Russians, and second, the Americans were the only Allies that allowed the refugees to decide if they wanted to stay or return to their homeland. The Americans would not force anyone to go back. All the others: the English, the French and the Russians were forcing the Hungarians to return to their homeland. Feher was confident that the information was accurate because he had heard the same thing from other groups who had come from another zone and were turned back.

Feher also learned more about the boundaries of the zones. The Russian zone included Vienna and was bordered on the north by the Danube River and on the west by the Enns River. The area to the west of the Enns River was the American zone. We were still in the Russian zone. Even though we had not seen or heard any Russian troops since the day after we crossed the border, we knew it was only a matter of time before they came further into the area. Again, we found ourselves in the position of needing to move on as quickly as we could.

Based on the information given to us, we decided the safest measure was to head west toward the American zone, using the back roads and paths rather than traveling on any of the main roads. The Germans were still retreating, using the main roads. Realizing that Allied planes might try to bomb the retreating German forces, we did not want to take a chance that we could either be near such an event or that we could be mistaken for retreating forces. Also, we were concerned that since we were still in the Russian zone, we could run into the Russian troops along the road. In addition, Feher also had heard that criminals were working along these main roads. With all of these concerns, we determined that the back roads must be safer.

Feher was developing into a very good leader. He seemed genuinely interested in the welfare of everyone in the group. As a Hungarian, he handled the German language very well, and as a result, he could explain things to the Austrian officials better than anyone else in our group. Gyula and I spoke German, but not nearly as well as Feher. In addition to being able to speak the language, he had developed personal relationships with the Austrians, and he could relate to them as well as he did with the Hungarians. Even on the road from Graz to Leoben, our group was stopped several times and questioned by different people. Feher always served as the representative. He spoke on behalf of the group to any of the people who happened to stop us for any reason, whether they were officials or not. Although we rarely knew who the people were, Feher always was able to explain what we were doing, and each time they let us continue our journey without any problems.

Feher was also talented for getting things done! For example, in Leoben he went to the railroad office and negotiated with the Austrian railroad authorities for transportation for some in our group. He successfully got the Austrians to agree to allocate space on a few empty railroad boxcars free of charge for those in our group who were just walking and were somewhat of a burden to the rest of us. These people had very few belongings, and they did not have any food. The train would only accept those people who did not have any large baggage. As a result of Feher's initiative, those people traveling with us who were walking or had few belongings on their wagons were able to take a train west toward Schladming, away from where we thought the Russians were.

One of the people who boarded the train was an artist with whom Gyula had become friends on the journey. An old man in poor physical health, he could not travel well with the group. He had his daughter with him, and they decided to take the train. He had a large, heavy roll of paintings on canvas that he could not take on the train. Another man had been carrying the paintings for the artist on his wagon, but this man, too, decided to leave his few belongings behind and take the same train. The artist asked Gyula if he would take the paintings with him in his wagon. Gyula agreed and assured the man that he would return them to him as soon as he possibly could.

After two days in Leoben, we were ready to move west toward the American zone. We did not know the distance to the Enns River, but we had heard it was several kilometers. Travel proved to be even slower than it had been from Graz to Leoben. Nobody in the group knew the area roads at all. In the mornings, if the sun was shining, we headed away from the sun, and in the evenings, we headed toward the sun. If it was very cloudy, we tried to guess the best way to go. It seemed that much of what we were doing was guessing. Each day we were not sure where we would go or where we would end up. Soon, we realized it had been a week since we had left Leoben.

Gyula may have known where we were, but I most certainly did not. Each day, the place we stopped at did not look much different from the place where we had stopped the day before. I wondered if we were actually making progress or if we were going in circles. We usually camped in a pasture. Feher always tried to receive permission from the landowner to camp for the night. Usually, the farmers were very nice and accommodating, allowing us to stay on their property; in some cases, no landowner could be found, so we camped on the property anyway.

Because the animals needed to graze, we stopped frequently. Occasionally, some people were able to get some hay for the horses. Although no one in the group was carrying hay, some of the horse owners always seemed to have hay for their animals. We never knew how they got the hay or where. Actually, we really did not want to know. Gyula never had any hay. We just let the oxen graze wherever and whenever we could. Fortunately, the oxen did not need to eat as often as the horses.

In the afternoons, we stopped early enough to find wood for the fire we used to cook food. Not having any gloves, my hands became very cold when I had to dig out the sticks and twigs from under the snow. Because the weather was usually cold and damp, starting a fire each evening was a struggle. Almost always the wood was wet. We did not have newspapers or anything like that to help. Very few matches were available, so we had to be very careful not to waste any matches in starting the fire. In addition, only a few of us in the group had pots or skillets with which to cook the meals.

Because Gyula and I had brought a lot of food, we shared from the beginning with those who did not have any. Some people did not have any provisions when we started the trip; others had a little but ran out soon after we started our journey. We could not be together and have food and see others who were hungry. As long as we had food, we shared what we had. But as the days became weeks, we, too, began to run low.

Whenever we stopped, Gyula often asked farmers if they had some chores he could do in exchange for food. Anytime we had the opportunity to work, Feher had no problem with stopping. Those in the group who had farming skills would help

Gyula with chores for the farmers. We realized that because our food supply was dwindling, we should take every opportunity to gather additional food. If the farmer had enough work and had enough additional food, we would sometimes spend a couple of days at one location. Those who did not have farming skills did what they could to help support the group. Everyone in the group always did what they could. These stops also allowed us to rest from the long days of walking and in the wagon.

As we continued to travel westward, we tried to stay in the valleys where the terrain was flat and where we could stay close to creeks and rivers for water. We always had plenty of water, even though the only water available came straight from the river or mountain streams. The water appeared clean and clear, and we used bottles to keep fresh water in each wagon as we traveled. The animals drank the same water. Fortunately, we were never far from good, fresh water, because that was all we had to drink except for the little bit of milk we occasionally could find for Ilonka.

As we traveled on the back roads, from time to time, we came to creeks or brooks that did not have a suitable crossing for the wagons. When this happened, we had to stop so that the men could build a passageway across the stream. On these days we did not make much progress at all.

My focus was always on the children. Caring for three toddlers is a great responsibility at any time, but under the circumstances we were experiencing, it was awesome. I focused on trying to keep them as comfortable as possible. Because they always traveled inside the covered wagon, Erzsike and Gyuszi were very eager to get out of the wagon and run and use up some of their energy when we stopped for the evening. The days inside the wagon seemed to become longer and longer.

Each night everybody slept in the wagon together. When it was time for everyone to go to sleep, the children made room for the four adults on top of the crates and other baggage in the wagon. Since the Kerekes family was still traveling with us, eight people slept in the wagon. We positioned ourselves any way we could. Sometimes, we could get comfortable lying down, but frequently we slept sitting up or half lying down. Most of the time we were so tired it did not matter. The early spring temperatures were still cold but not as cold as we were accustomed to during the middle of the winter in Hungary. As a result, we were able to stay warm with only a few coats and blankets.

The days became weeks. Everyone grew increasingly tired and frustrated as we traveled toward the American zone. Food became scarce, and conditions progressively seemed to worsen. No end appeared in sight to the daily wandering through the valley toward the west. Although we traveled each day, we did not seem to be making any progress. The uncertainty and anxiety continued to increase. Nobody knew for sure what was ahead, and everyone feared that the Russian troops were gaining on us and were close behind. This uncertainty added to the already harsh physical conditions and emotional turmoil.

As time passed, some people simply could not handle the severe conditions and gave up. Many said they would return to Hungary to deal with the Russians. Because they were so eager to return to their homeland, they convinced themselves that the conditions could not be that bad and especially no worse than what they were experiencing. They felt that if they continued on under these conditions, they would surely die, and, therefore, they decided that whatever was waiting for them in Hungary would be better than dying. Each time a family left the group to go to a camp or to return to Hungary, I gave them my parents' address in Budapest. I asked them that if they were able to get to Budapest, to please contact my parents and tell them that we were all safe and that we would contact them as soon as we could.

We heard rumors of refugee camps in various places. Some of the refugees who left our group said they were going to try to find one of these camps. As each wagon left our group, we wished them well and prayed for a safe journey. We never heard what happened to any of the people who left our group. We do not know if they safely reached their destination or if they encountered any of the potential hazards in the area, such as road bandits or Russian troops.

By the latter part of April 1945, only eight of the original seventeen wagons remained as a group. The harsh conditions had taken a toll. Gyula and I, too, were frightened and exhausted by the uncertainty and the day-to-day living conditions; on the other hand, we believed that the Russian communists who were in control of Hungary would not be very tolerant of those of us who had fled when they occupied our country. Also, we did not want to leave the security of the group we were with to travel alone and expose ourselves to the road criminals that were rampant at the time. Therefore, each day we decided if we could just make it another day or two, we would finally reach the American zone, where we could wait until we were sure it was safe to return to Hungary. We had trusted the Lord to get us this far. In spite of the hardships, we still had faith that the Lord would lead the way to a safe place.

CHAPTER 6
HE LEADETH ME BESIDE THE STILL WATERS

As we had begun our flight from Hungary under the cover of darkness that night in March, we had thought that we had plenty of food. The crate was filled with food, and a few additional items were in the footlocker. Ordinarily, this easily would have been enough for our family for several weeks. However, as we fled from Hungary and into Austria, we gladly shared our food with our fellow travelers who had little. As a result, we were now running out of food, as we were approaching the end of April. Our concerns were real and our circumstances were grave, but throughout our ordeal, regardless of how bad our situation became, we never regretted sharing with others less fortunate.

Although we had plenty of Hungarian money with us, no one would accept it. As a matter of fact, no one accepted the Austrian currency either. The Austrian government was collapsing, and the Allies were taking over the country; consequently, people knew that the currency would probably be worthless. Gyula had approximately three thousand Hungarian Pengo, the equivalent buying power of three thousand dollars. This was not on the basis of the exchange rate but on the value it had for buying goods and services in Hungary. Although this seemed to be a significant amount of money, because of the war, it was worthless.

Nothing was sold or bought with money during this time in Austria. Everything was traded and bartered. Food had the most value. We began to take advantage of every opportunity to secure additional food. As our supply continued to diminish, I began trading things I had brought with me for food. I had some nice dishes from Hungary. Austria had a shortage of dishes at the time, so mine were easy to trade in the small villages. I also had some very nice undergarments and lingerie that I traded. These items did not have much value, but whatever food I could get for them was a big help. I also had some beautiful Hungarian clothes. The Austrians did not have clothes such as these, but they liked them very much. I traded these clothes, as well as some sweaters that I had knitted. As time passed, not only were we running out of food, but we were also running out of items to trade.

It was late April, and we had been traveling for weeks. We were in the Enns Valley near a place called Schlattham when we decided to stop and rest for the night. We were completely out of food, and our situation had become very desperate. An incident occurred near Schlattham, which revealed just how desperate people were becoming. Some of the refugees saw a hawk attack a pigeon in flight. The crippled pigeon fell to the ground, and everyone ran toward it, hoping to be the first to reach the wounded fowl. The little bit of food that the pigeon provided was all the food that the fortunate refugee had to eat that day. All the refugees were in the same predicament.

Because Gyula and I knew we were running out of food, we had eaten very little the past few days, saving what we had for the children. That night we gave the last of it to the children. We had no idea how we could possibly explain to Gyuszi and Erzsike, who were two and almost four years old, that there was nothing left to eat. They had never experienced hunger. We had always provided for them, and they would not be able to understand why they would have to go hungry. And even worse, we were completely out of milk for eight-month-old Ilonka.

That night, before we went to sleep, Gyula and I held hands and prayed. As I was praying, I remembered what Edesapa had said to me as a child: "Trust in the Lord. In life you can lose everything, but I emphasize to you, never lose your faith. Remember, never lose your faith! Often it is only through faith that people survive." I was trying to hold onto my faith, but what frightening circumstances we found ourselves in! We had been trusting in the Lord, but we found ourselves miles from our homeland, traveling with people we had not known until some four weeks before, going we knew not where, and now we had absolutely no food to give our children nor any likelihood of finding any. How were we to explain to our children the next morning that there was nothing to eat? Because I knew of absolutely nothing else I could do at this point, I told the Lord that I trusted Him to do His will, and that I knew somehow He would help us through this crisis.

As we finished our prayers, Gyula began reciting his favorite Bible passage, the twenty-third Psalm:

"The Lord is my Shepherd; I shall not want."

As we continued to hold hands, I joined him, and together we finished reciting the Psalm:

"He maketh me to lie down in green pastures; He leadeth me beside the still waters. He restoreth my soul; He leadeth me in the paths of righteousness for His name's sake. Yea, though I walk through the

valley of the shadow of death, I will fear no evil; for Thou art with me; Thy rod and Thy staff they comfort me. Thou preparest a table before me in the presence of mine enemies: thou anointest my head with oil; my cup runneth over. Surely goodness and mercy shall follow me all the days of my life; and I will dwell in the house of the Lord forever."

As we completed the Psalm, the silence was deafening. We did not speak, but somehow we each knew that we shared a total and complete calm, something we had not felt in a long, long time because of the stress of our escape. We relaxed, and for the first time in many, many nights, in spite of the fact that our circumstances were more desperate than they had ever been, we both fell asleep immediately.

Gyula left the wagons the next morning, heading toward a farmhouse nearby. As he was approaching the house, a woman came out. Since Gyula spoke fluent German, he had an advantage over most of the other refugees in dealing with the Austrians. He explained our situation and asked the woman if she needed any work done in exchange for food. Gyula told her that he had grown up on a farm, and that he knew how to do all kinds of farm work.

The woman told Gyula that her husband had been in the war, and that now he was a prisoner of war. Because her husband was away, she needed someone to plow the field for spring planting. She said she did not have much food, but she would share her food and some milk with us if Gyula would plow her field for her. He told the woman he would be glad to help her. In turn, she would be helping us.

Gyula connected his oxen to the woman's plow. When he began to plow, the most incredible thing happened. As the plow moved through the dirt, potatoes began to pop up out of the ground. First one, then two, then many more potatoes were greeting us. To Gyula's pleasant surprise, he was plowing a field of potatoes that had not been harvested. The farmer had planted the field a year earlier, and since he was away at the war, no one had harvested the potatoes. The woman either had forgotten about the potatoes, or she may not have realized what was planted in the field, but she, too, was pleasantly surprised.

As Gyula plowed and turned up potatoes, he threw them aside. We stayed in Schlattham for three days, and each day Gyula plowed the fields for this woman, and each day he gathered more potatoes. There were far more potatoes plowed up than the woman needed. Gyula ultimately harvested nine large sacks of potatoes. The woman said she only needed two sacks. She asked Gyula to take the rest and divide them among the other refugees. These potatoes were like candy to everybody because we had not had anything like that for a long time. We had not even had bread for weeks. In addition to the potatoes, the woman gave Gyula the food and milk that she had originally promised to give him for plowing her fields. Our prayers had been answered. Somehow, the Lord had directed us to this exact place near the Enns River, where there was an abundance of food at a time when we were in desperate need for food.

While we were at this same campsite, Ilonka became very ill. Because we had gotten very little milk in the past few weeks and because most of the food we had was not suitable for a young child, Ilonka had not received the nourishment she needed. As hard as I tried, I could not seem to give her what she needed to keep up her strength. The milk we were given by the woman at the farm lasted only a couple of days. One of the horses had recently had a colt and, as a result, was producing milk. In order to get Ilonka some nourishment, Gyula decided to begin milking the horse for Ilonka.

Even though Ilonka was ill, we needed to break camp and continue toward the American zone. We still had no idea where the Russians were, but as long as we were in the Russian zone, we were always afraid that we could be overtaken or trapped by them. We again regrouped and continued to our unknown destination.

A few days later, we were traveling a narrow road high in the mountains leading up to the small village of Kleinsolk. We camped in a meadow near the village, thinking to ourselves that this must be the end of the world. In spite of our prayers a week before, in spite of our submission to God's will, we found ourselves in absolute despair. The six weeks of constant, underlying fear, the anxious travel, the uncertainty of our destination, the inability to care and feed for our children the way we always had made us feel we were wanderers in the wilderness with no direction, no guidance and no hope. Nothing could possibly be beyond this place.

We arrived in Kleinsolk on May 8, ironically the day a cease-fire was declared in the war. All of the German soldiers had been ordered to turn themselves in as prisoners of war. That afternoon, German officers, who were camped nearby in the same mountains, still in the Russian zone, came to us saying that they thought for certain the German army and the American army would join together to fight against the Russians. These

Germans simply could not believe that the Russians and Americans were allies and fighting together. They could not imagine this "love affair" would last, so they felt that the Germans and the Americans would become allies against the Russians. These Germans already knew that the German army had failed in the past when fighting Russian troops, and without help they would be defenseless against them. Somehow, they surmised that with the help of the Americans, they could conquer the invading Russians forces.

The German officers knew we were refugees, and they asked the men if they would go to the German camp and help them move some ammunition to a safe place. This was ammunition that the Germans wanted to use against the Russians. They not only needed the manpower, but they also wanted our horse-drawn wagons to help them. The Germans said if the men would come with their wagons and help, they would give us some food. They knew that we needed food, so they were sure we would help. Of course, they were right! The Germans gave the men directions to their camp and the time when they should arrive with four or five wagons. They needed to haul the ammunition from the camp to the hiding place in the mountains. Gyula was one of the volunteers who went with the men. In no way did he want to support any effort to extend the war or support any more fighting, but Gyula could not pass up an opportunity to secure food for his family.

When the men arrived at the designated place, the German commanding officer was not there. The men were told to wait until the commanding officer arrived. In the meantime, one of the young refugees asked the German officer on duty, "Do you have some coffee?" The officer replied, "Yes."

All of the refugees, including Gyula, decided they wanted some coffee because they had not had coffee in a very long time. They took out some cups, and the German took them to a big milk can identical to those used by a farmer. He opened up the can and with a ladle scooped out the coffee and poured it into the cups. Gyula drank one sip slowly. Even though he had not drunk any coffee in a long while, he thought this was very peculiar-tasting coffee. He sipped a second time and determined that the drink really did not taste like any coffee he had ever drunk before, but since the German said it was coffee, he assumed that it was coffee. He and all of the others drank it as though it were coffee. The whole time Gyula drank, he was suspicious about what he was drinking because of the taste; however, some of the men commented that this was very good coffee. Everybody wanted to believe it was coffee. The Germans finally smiled and admitted that they were not serving coffee at all! The drink actually was German schnapps, the strongest of the alcoholic beverages. The Germans laughed heartily. They had played a trick on the Hungarians.

After they were told that it was schnapps, Gyula took another drink and recognized the taste. As we discussed later, Gyula pointed out to me that this incident very simply shows the strength of the power of suggestion. Because the Germans had told the men that they were drinking coffee and because the Hungarians desired coffee so much, they actually thought they were drinking coffee, and even though some of the men thought it was strange-tasting, they were willing to acknowledge the drink as coffee.

Soon, the commanding officer arrived and told the refugees that they were not going to be needed to move the ammunition after all. He had received some clear information that the Americans and Germans were not going to unite; thus, the entire effort would be useless. Since our men had come to help, the Germans gave us the food as they had promised. The Germans gave the men canned beans and peas as well as some other food. Even though we still had some potatoes left from earlier, any food we could get was very important.

The men left the German camp and started back to our camp on a narrow road that was actually nothing more than wagon tracks through the woods. Soon after the men started, darkness fell, and being in the woods, they could not see very well. Several craters, probably created by bombs from Allied planes, lay along the way. The bombs probably had been intended for bridges on the river or for other targets in the area, but instead, had missed their targets and had fallen in the fields or in the woods. These craters were full of rainwater and mud.

One of the men driving his horse-drawn wagon had been drinking too much "coffee." Because of the darkness, as well as his stupor, the man could not see anything. Instead of letting his horse use its natural instinct to avoid the hazards, the man held the rein and guided the horse straight into one of the bomb craters full of mud and water. Once the horse got into the water, it did not want to come out. The men worked several hours in the deep mud trying to pull the horse out. The horse seemed to be totally helpless and did nothing to help get itself out of the hole. The men pulled the rein together to encourage the horse, but it would not budge. The animal lodged in the mud and water. It was very late into the night. All of the men were cold, miserable and covered with mud and water. They knew they had to save the horse because a wagon without a horse is useless. The worst part was that the man who had directed the horse into the mud hole in the first place had no sensibilities at this point, and he declared that because he was cold, he was going to walk to the camp without his horse or wagon. He decided he would not help get his own horse out of the hole. Finally, after hours of working, the other men got the horse out and salvaged the wagon.

When Gyula returned to camp from this escapade, he was covered with mud. It took me hours to get all of his clothes clean again. The following day, once the man sobered up and realized what had happened, he thanked the other men for their help and apologized for the whole incident.

Ilonka continued to be sick. The horse produced enough milk for Ilonka to drink, but she was not getting enough other food that was suitable for a nine-month-old baby. At six months she could hold up her head, but now due to malnutrition, at nine months she had lost the strength to hold up her head.

I talked to some of the local people in Kleinsolk about what was happening to Ilonka, and they became very concerned for her. They invited us into their home so that we could try to nurse her back to health. Gyula and I were very frustrated and felt helpless, but the local people in this village were very nice. They even went to the drugstore and bought us some medicine to give to her. After about four days of staying with Ilonka in their home and eating good food and taking medication, she finally showed signs of regaining her health, and we felt she was well enough to travel.

About the time Ilonka was healthy enough to travel again, a man from the village approached us very early one morning, with a very scary rumor. He told us that the Russian troops were nearby. He explained that by noon the Russians would occupy the territory where we were camping, as well as all of the land up to the Enns River. In order for us to be safe, we must cross the Enns River by noon that day.

We were all frightened because we had come so far for so long, and now it appeared as though the Russians were going to trap us. We had to assume the rumor was true. We had escaped Hungary and had traveled for several weeks under very difficult conditions to stay far enough ahead of the Russians to be safe. We definitely did not want to be trapped by the Russians now.

Most of the bridges across the Enns River had been bombed and destroyed. Some of the villagers informed us that there was only one bridge we could cross with our wagons. It was about six kilometers away from where we were. With noon as the deadline and thinking the Russians were very nearby, we knew that we needed to move quickly to get across the river to safety. We threw everything on the wagons and started as fast as we could toward the river and the bridge. The oxen were slow-moving animals, but Gyula was able to make them run like horses. We wanted to save everything and get everybody across the river before noon.

Absolutely determined not to be captured, we were doing everything we could to escape. Everyone was going as fast as they could down the mountain toward the river, running alongside the wagons. One man became so panicked that he recklessly drove his horse wagon down the narrow mountain road toward the river. He lost control of his wagon and it turned over. Everything he had in the wagon scattered onto the road. We would have left all of his things there except that the road was too narrow, and nobody behind him could pass. Everyone stopped. The men straightened the wagon, put everything back very quickly, and we continued our race against time. The whole scene that morning was total panic and chaos.

Soon after we crossed the river before noon, we learned that the rumor was not true. For whatever reason, someone had spread an irresponsible, unsubstantiated tale that caused panic. Nonetheless, we were safely across, and everyone relaxed and breathed a deep sigh of relief.

Feher had learned in Leoben that the American zone was on the west side of the Enns River, which was where we were, and the Austrians confirmed that we were now in the American zone. For the first time since before we had left Kisrakos, we felt we were relatively safe from the Russians. Now that we were in the American zone, Feher called us all together to decide where we should go from here. The majority of the families decided that although we felt relatively safe now that we were in the American zone, we would feel much safer when we reached the American Occupation Forces. Feher had been told that the Americans would eventually occupy the territory where we were, but we decided to continue toward the area already occupied by the Americans in Austria. Although we were weary from six weeks of wandering through the Russian zone, we were now very eager to be in the territory where we could actually see Americans. This became our new goal.

Families on three of the wagons said they had traveled enough; they were not going to go any farther. They felt safe enough, and they would stay and wait to see what developed.

We said goodbye to the other families, but this was not easy. After all, we had traveled together through incredible hardship and anxiety, and we had become very good friends with all of the people in our group. Originally a group of frightened people trying to escape Hungary, we had joined together and worked together to meet our common goal of safety for ourselves and our families. None of us had wanted to leave our homeland, but because of the Russians, what we were leaving behind was not the homeland we had known. None of us had ever experienced a nightmare like we had been through. We knew somehow that had we stayed behind, our destiny would have been much worse. However, each family had to make the decision it felt best for its members. We had to respect those choices, so we said our farewells and continued on our journey. Now only five wagons traveled together. We continued westward through the river valleys, now feeling safe on the more important roads.

Gyula and I had walked the entire time we had been traveling. The soles of our shoes had been worn out for days, so we had used whatever we could to increase the life of our shoes. Each day we placed cardboard or anything else we had or could get that would work in them.

After a couple of days, we arrived at a town called Mittendorf. We stopped again in a farmer's pasture and rested. We learned that there was a German warehouse nearby that had been raided by the Austrians after the cease-fire had been announced. We were told that the warehouse was open, and that we could have anything we wanted that was left there. We went to the warehouse and found that the Austrians had taken everything but some bags of yellow peas and some old German army boots. We decided we could use both. We took several large sacks of peas and some lard. Gyula found himself a matching pair of army boots that he could wear, and I found myself a nonmatching pair of boots, but they were still much better than the shoes I had with the cardboard in the soles. At this point, I would take what I could get. We thanked God for the food and footwear regardless of quality.

At first, we wondered why the villagers had left the yellow peas behind. After a while we learned why! The villagers knew that these peas were not very tasty. Because we were short of food again and were very hungry, the peas just represented food to us, and we did not pay much attention to the taste. Later, this changed!

We spent only one night in Mittendorf. The next day we sent some of the men to find the shortest, simplest way for us to get farther west into Austria to where we were told were Americans troops.

The scouts came back with a report that there was a shortcut over a mountain pass to an area thought to be occupied by the Americans, but the road was a steep, narrow logging road and washed out. The men decided that to get to the safety of the American-occupied territory, nothing was going to be too difficult to overcome. They had shovels, picks and their own hands, so they decided we would go up the mountain and determine if it was feasible to repair the washed-out road so we could cross.

We started with our five wagons up the narrow road toward the top of the mountain. We soon arrived at the washed-out section only a short distance up the mountain. The men immediately began repairing the road. With their tools, they moved some of the large stones and filled the holes with dirt. They also put enough dirt in the washed-out places so that we could cross if we moved one wagon at a time. After almost a day of very hard work, the men were ready to start moving the wagons over a long section of the repaired road. They moved one wagon at a time, using what animals and manpower they needed to get the wagons across the repaired road. The children and I stayed out of the way because the work was difficult and dangerous. Finally, by late in the evening, the men had all of the wagons through that portion of the pass. We immediately made camp for the night.

Early the next morning, we started again. It took us all day to cross over the top of the mountain. We went down the other side through a long, winding pass. When we reached the bottom of that pass, we again made camp for the night.

The following day we began to climb another high mountain through a high, even narrower and steeper pass. We thought the climb two days earlier had been hard, but this climb was far more difficult. It took every available man working with the animals to pull or push each wagon one at a time up the mountain. No one was allowed on the wagons except in some cases the small children. The women and older children walked. Finally, we reached the top of the mountain pass. On the other side, we could see the valley below. It was such a beautiful sight until we realized we had to go down a much steeper road that was also washed out in several places. This road was much more treacherous than any we had crossed earlier, and traveling appeared impossible.

The men discussed the situation; nobody wanted to turn back. We had come too far to stop or give up now. The last few days had been the most difficult part of our journey, but through perseverance, resourcefulness and teamwork, we had negotiated the mountains. We also knew that we could not have gotten this far without the help of the Lord; in addition, we knew it would take His help to overcome this obstacle. None of the men had any experience with handling wagons on such steep areas. Fortunately, no one had been injured on any of the earlier dangerous climbs and descents. We decided to move cautiously a short way down the mountain to get a better look at the most dangerous portion of the pass. After arriving at this spot, the men carefully surveyed the area and found there were huge rocks and boulders, which had been exposed by erosion during the winter months. I could see what they were studying—the rugged path was frighteningly steep. Furthermore, it was very narrow. If the men were to lose control, a wagon would certainly plunge down the side of the mountain, hit a tree and be completely destroyed. The men walked around the area and devised a plan that they all agreed might work to get us down this steep and dangerous pass. They knew they had to be very careful. I knew that the only way they were going to get the wagons down this trail was with the help of God. I prayed to God that He would give these men the strength and wisdom they needed to safely get the wagons down the mountain to the valley below.

Instead of repairing the road as before, the men decided to chop big holes at certain locations in the road to create a kind of stair step arrangement or terraces so that the wagons could only go a short distance at a time. Working together using ropes and large poles, they slowly lowered one wagon at a time a short distance from each of the terrace levels to the next until they finally got past the steepest section. This took the men a full day, but all of the wagons made it safely down this dangerous portion of the mountain.

The remaining road down was still in very bad shape and made travel slow. Fortunately, the lower section was not nearly as steep as the higher sections of the road. We finally reached the bottom of the mountain into the valley below to a village called Obertraun, with a population of about 500 people. We passed through the village, and after crossing a bridge over the Traun River, we decided to stop for the night in a nice, flat, wooded area. We were very tired after the difficult travel through the mountain passes, and we needed to rest for a couple of days.

The setting was magnificent. We were on the bank of a beautiful, fast-moving river. A pristine lake, which we had seen from the mountains, was nestled in some trees a short distance away. The majesty of the surrounding mountains was incredible. Spring flowers were beginning to peek out of the ground, and the land was lush with trees and vegetation. Now that we could relax a few minutes, we could soak in the incredible scene around us. Looking back up the mountain, we marveled at what our group had accomplished in crossing over the mountain. We knew that it could not have been accomplished without the hand of God giving the men the strength and support they needed. I remember saying a prayer thanking God for safely getting us over the mountains to this beautiful place. Only five wagons of the original seventeen that had left Hungary had withstood the hardships and made the entire journey to Obertraun. The Kerekes family had remained with us for the entire trip.

The next morning we saw another group of refugees with some fifteen wagons pass our camp heading west toward

Hallstatt, about five kilometers away. We had not seen them earlier, so we assumed they had taken a much longer route around the mountains to arrive in Obertraun. Within a few hours, the group returned. They were not allowed to pass on the road to Hallstatt. The American occupation troops had already arrived there and would not allow anyone to move on the road without a permit, and the Americans were the only ones who would issue permits.

The Americans troops simply were not letting anyone go through. The war was over, and they were in control of the area. They decided that keeping the road closed to through traffic would help them reestablish law and order in the area. It did not matter whether the travelers were refugees or what they had on their wagons, the Americans were not letting anyone pass through. Our group did not know what we were going to do next. Although not in American-occupied territory, we were as close to being there as we could be without actually being there. It appeared that we were at the end of our journey, at least for a while. But what a beautiful place to stop! The mountains, the lake, the river, and the lushness of the countryside provided spectacular surroundings. The peaceful village and the still waters of the lake supplied the serenity we needed to restore our spirits after weeks of dangerous and treacherous travel, always stressful because of uncertainty. For the first time on our trip, we could actually feel completely secure and safe from the Russians.

CHAPTER 7
I WILL FEAR NO EVIL

I was actually very happy when we learned that the Americans would not let us go any farther. I was so very tired and so very weary after traveling for seven weeks. Of course, we had no choice, but I definitely was ready to settle in one place for a while. Gyula never indicated one way or the other, but I think he was probably ready to settle down as well. He, too, was tired and had been under much strain as we had fled the Russians. In reality, I think the whole group with whom we had traveled felt as we did. The seven weeks had been a terrible experience for all of us. Now that the Russian troops were no longer a threat to us, we could actually relax somewhat, which meant if we stopped traveling we could get some much needed rest. The continuous uncertainty of where we were going to be and what we might encounter on the road had taken its toll on all of us. We were always concerned about possible illness or injury as we traveled through Austria. We were very thankful that except for Ilonka's malnutrition, no one had become ill or injured during the entire trip. Many dangerous situations had arisen as we crossed the waterways and mountains, yet no one had received so much as a scratch. Being forced to stay here for at least a few days would give us time to rest, regroup, and decide what we should do next. We arrived in Obertraun on May 17, 1945, two days before Erzsike's fourth birthday. We were not starving, but our meals had consisted primarily of the yellow peas. Needless to say, we had limited resources for birthday gifts, but I thought that since our diet had been so limited, Erzsike might really enjoy bread for her birthday.

On the morning of Erzsike's birthday, I went into the village to see if I could buy some bread for her. I knew everything was on a ration card, but I thought this special occasion warranted the effort to try to buy some bread. By this time, the only thing of much value I had left other than my wedding band was a little gold necklace. I went to the bakery to see if I could exchange the necklace for a piece of bread for Erzsike's birthday. As I approached the bakery, I could smell fresh bread baking. It had been so long since I had smelled this wonderful aroma. I spoke very good German, so I explained to the baker what I hoped to do. I told him about Erzsike's birthday and I told him that I did not have any money, but that I would like to exchange my gold necklace for some bread. He was a very honest man. He replied: "I cannot take your gold necklace, and even if you had money, I could not sell you any bread. You do not have a ration card, and without a ration card I cannot sell you any bread. The ration laws are so strict that I cannot give you any bread either. The government authorities carefully watch the allocations of all items on ration cards. I am sorry, but there is nothing I can do for you."

He turned from the door and started to walk away, but he suddenly turned back and called to me. "Wait a second." He then went into the kitchen to the table where his family and helper had just sat down for their breakfast. The baker took his ration of bread that his family had planned to eat at breakfast and handed it to me. "You take this bread. Give it to your daughter. It is a gift." I was overwhelmed by his kindness. I graciously thanked him and went on my way. Again, the Lord had provided! And the kindness and generosity of people willing to help others less fortunate had once again occurred.

Erzsike's birthday cake on her fourth birthday was bread. I divided the bread between Erzsike and Gyuszi. The smile on Erzsike's face was heavenly as she thoroughly enjoyed each bite of the soft, fresh-baked bread. I'm sure Erzsike has never had a birthday cake that tasted as good as that fresh bread on her fourth birthday.

I had a totally new appreciation for the phrase in the Lord's Prayer, "Give us this day our daily bread." Five weeks had passed since we had eaten any bread at all. Since that day, I have never thrown a piece of bread away.

A few days after we arrived in Obertraun, Ilonka once again became very weak and ill due to malnutrition. Again, she was so weak that she could not lift her head. We had to do something to help her, but we did not know what. Gyula decided he would go to Hallstatt to find a doctor.

It was very hard to move between Obertraun and Hallstatt at the time. The road was still closed by the Americans, and no one, whether on foot or bicycle or by any other means, was allowed to pass on the road. To help maintain order, the Americans wanted to limit the movement of people. To get to Hallstatt, people either had to go through the fields and woods or on the lake. The Austrians knew the best way through the woods to get to Hallstatt. Those Austrians who had boats used them to travel on the lake. Gyula did not have a boat, and he was not familiar with the area, so it was very difficult at first for him to travel through the fields and woods to get to Hallstatt without being seen from the road. Hallstatt was about five kilometers away, and if the soldiers along the road saw people traveling, they would stop them and not allow them to continue.

It was absolutely crucial for Gyula to get to Hallstatt to see if he could get some help for Ilonka. Finally, he figured a way around the roadblock through the fields and woods to reach Hallstatt. When he arrived in Hallstatt, Gyula decided to talk to the head of the American troops about Ilonka's health.

The Americans had a German-to-English translator, so Gyula told the American officer about Ilonka's very weak condition resulting from malnutrition. Gyula explained through the translator that we had very little food and that the food we had was not providing the proper nutrition for the baby. She was not receiving the vitamins she needed.

The American officer agreed to travel to Obertraun the following day and investigate her condition. In the meantime, the officer wrote out an order for food that would help provide Ilonka and the other children with the balanced diet they needed. He ordered that we be given certain amounts of powdered milk, rice, chocolate and sugar from a local warehouse. This German warehouse, located next to the temporary military hospital in Obertraun, contained various kinds of food. American troops had captured the warehouse, and the local village government under the direction of the United States military was responsible for distributing food stored there. The officer told Gyula that these items were what the children would need, and that Gyula should take the order to the local city hall in Obertraun. The officials there would give him the food listed on the order.

The translator, who was an Austrian and worked as a local assistant to the American officer, had children herself; she knew what Ilonka needed to improve her condition. She went home and got some vitamins, especially vitamin D, which she had saved from a time when her children were small. She gave the vitamins to Gyula. This way we could immediately supplement Ilonka's diet with vitamins until we were able to secure the promised food.

Gyula returned to Obertraun through the fields, the same way he had gone. He immediately went to the local city hall and left the order with the Burgermeister who was the head of the village. He said that as soon as he could fill the order, he would send the food out, but he did not know how long this would take.

We were completely new to the area, and we trusted and believed everyone. At the time, we did not know that the Burgermeister did not want refugees there, and that he did whatever he could to make life difficult for all of us.

Although the American officer had promised that he would come to Obertraun to check on Ilonka's condition the next day, road conditions prevented his doing so. That night the only road from Hallstatt to Obertraun was closed as a result of an avalanche. A half-mile stretch of the road was covered with about twelve feet of snow. The road remained closed for several days before the snow could be cleared. Since the village did not have any machinery to clear the road, people used shovels to clear the snow, which, of course, took a long time. The only way the officer could travel was by jeep, and with the road closed, he sent word that he was stranded, but that he hoped Ilonka's health improved quickly.

A couple of days later, someone illegally opened the German warehouse and allowed the civilian population to enter. They literally raided and completely cleared the warehouse of all of the food, which was so scarce, even for the Austrians, that when the warehouse was opened, it became a free-for-all for the local residents. People stole anything and everything that they wanted. They were literally walking through coffee beans and sugar, as they gathered the items they wanted. They carried out the most valuable things at the time: sugar, flour, raw coffee beans and cigarettes. With money, people could not buy much of anything, but with raw coffee beans or sugar, people could trade for almost anything. The Austrians took everything from the warehouse.

In the meantime, we were waiting for the promised food. It never arrived. It was only later that we learned what had happened at the warehouse. Gyula waited a few days before he went back to check on the order. When he arrived, he was told that the order could not be filled because no food remained in the warehouse. Gyula later learned that before the raid on the warehouse, the Burgermeister went to the warehouse and took the food that was on the order for Gyula. Instead of sending the items to Gyula, he kept all of them and used them for himself. This was the first of many despicable actions the Burgermeister took against our family while we were in Obertraun. He had no conscience and no heart. He was an evil man. Once we realized the extent of his hatred for the refugees who had settled in the area, the more determined we were to overcome the obstacles he placed in front of us. We understood his power over the community, but we were not afraid of this evil man. Gyula never reported to the Americans that he did not get the food. It was useless because the food was gone. We were refugees and new in the area, and we were slowly learning the realities of being such.

When we first arrived in Austria, the country did not have a currency of its own. Austria had German currency, but now that Austria was no longer a part of Germany, the Austrians were concerned that the money might no longer have any value. Furthermore, the authorities discouraged people from using the old currency until a new currency was established. Because of this, people did not want to accept currency for goods; they feared that it might not have any value. The authorities told the people to hold onto the German currency until the order came to explain how to change the German currency to the new Austrian currency. Meanwhile, everything was handled on a barter system; one item was exchanged for another.

The law required that people register with the local government when they moved into the community. We had already been in Obertraun for several days when we were told we needed to register. We registered both with the local government and with the American forces, which controlled the area. We asked the Americans to not send us back to Hungary, and we asked to be allowed to remain in Austria. The American army major approved our request to stay in Austria and provided us with a temporary exemption from repatriation to Hungary. This allowed us to remain as residents of Austria, but we had to renew the permit from time to time.

In completing the paperwork for the Americans, we were given the option of using the English translation of our names on the official documents. Gyula and I decided that it might be simpler if we used our English names because the Americans would never correctly pronounce or spell our Hungarian names. They were having enough trouble with our last name; to combine that with the first names would be too much for them. Using our English first names would surely simplify everything. Gyula's name translated to "Julius." My name translated to "Elizabeth." Erzsike translated to "Elizabeth" as well, and Gyuszi translated to "Julius." I usually referred to him as "young Julius." Ilonka's name translated to "Helen." We decided from that point on to use only our English names.

Being able to speak fluent German continued to be a huge advantage for us. We could easily communicate with the Austrians. Since the Americans always had German translators, we also could communicate well with them. Refugees who spoke only Hungarian had a very difficult time finding translators for both German and English.

When we first arrived in Obertraun, the city hall had refused to issue us any ration cards. We were not residents of Austria and were not employed in Austria. Without ration cards, we had to struggle to meet our basic need for food and stay within the community's and the country's laws. Julius worked anywhere he could to provide what he could for us. We were definitely tired of yellow peas at every single meal.

Julius located work at a small farm nearby. The old man to whom it belonged was at home, but his young son, who was the primary worker in the family, was still away at war. Early every morning, Julius went to the farm and cleaned out the stalls, swept the barns, chopped and split the wood, cut the hay or grass and fed the cows. He did whatever work was needed in exchange for food. The farmer usually gave us some food for breakfast and a little milk for the children. Other times he gave us a piece of bread or potatoes or eggs.

Initially, when we arrived in Obertraun, we continued to live out of the wagon, as we had done before on the road. We camped outside during the day and slept in the wagon at night. Since we had no idea how long we were going to stay there, we did not unpack the large crate. We did not know if we were going to eventually have to move on or just what would happen. Until we learned more about our situation, we did not want to completely unload our wagon. Because the weather was becoming more pleasant, being outdoors for the day was now very comfortable.

Once the town realized that they were stuck with the many refugees and that we would not be leaving soon, most of the townspeople tried to be as humane as they could afford to be or were allowed to be toward us. The temporary military hospital issued us a tent because no temporary housing was available. They also gave each refugee family a single folding army bed so that we could have a bed inside the tent. Julius and I set up our tent near the wagon on the bank of the Traun River where we had been camping. Julius slept on the single army bed in the tent. Elizabeth and young Julius slept on the folding bed Julius had made, the one we had brought with us. The bed was small and without much room, but a four-year-old and a two-year-old could fit just fine. Helen slept on a straw bag next to me in the covered wagon.

Life was neither simple nor easy, but we tried to establish some kind of normal routine. Julius worked as much as he could, I watched and cared for the children, and the children played around our camp home. We tried to provide as much normality and stability for the children as we possibly could. An amusing incident occurred one afternoon, while we were living in the tent along the river. The Kerekes family had set up their military-issued tent a little ways down the river. We had just finished lunch, and young Julius had sneaked away from our wagon to the tent where the Kerekes family was living. Mrs. Kerekes had just made some fresh cookies. I don't know where or how she had secured the ingredients because everything was so scarce, but somehow she gathered the ingredients and had baked cookies, which had a wonderful aroma. Young Julius came up to her and started crying profusely. Mrs. Kerekes asked him, "Why are you crying? You just ate." He responded by saying: "I am crying for one of those cookies. I will cry for my supper again later." He accomplished his goal; Mrs. Kerekes gave him a cookie!

We had been eating yellow peas almost exclusively since leaving Mittendorf. At first, we could tolerate the taste because we were so hungry. But as we ate the same peas day after day, we became very tired of them, and their true taste began to come through. We had been eating those yellow peas for three meals a day every day by the time we arrived in Obertraun. Only on occasion would we have anything other than yellow peas. Although I prepared the yellow peas in every conceivable form, I could not change their taste. I cooked them for lunch, and then I cooked them again for supper. We reached the point that we could hardly look at the peas any more. Since Obertraun had salt mines, we had plenty of salt. As soon as we arrived in Obertraun, we began salting the peas, but the salt did not help either. The yellow peas still tasted like soap.

We did not see many opportunities to vary our diet in the near future. But, regardless of how distasteful the peas became, we were thankful to have them and glad the Austrians had not wanted them. Had they not left the peas, we would have had almost no food at all. At least the peas provided some nutritional value; they were high in protein.

The biggest problem we had with the yellow peas was that they did not provide the necessary balanced nutrition that young Helen needed, and she remained very weak, though she gradually showed some signs of improvement, which probably resulted from the vitamin D we had been given. Julius always looked for work, and he took whatever jobs he could secure in the area. When he was not paid in food, he was usually paid with cigarettes, which we could use to trade for food. I met a farmer who would trade skim milk for cigarettes, so we had milk for Helen. The farmer explained that skim milk was not included on the ration card because skim milk is a leftover product after making butter. He said he would sell me all the skim milk I needed. I would not need a ration card. With this skim milk, the vitamin D, and some other food Julius was able to secure, we were slowly able to improve Helen's health, although she was not as strong and as healthy as she should have been.

One of the jobs Julius received was at the temporary emergency veteran's hospital. He cut hair! This German army hospital was very near where we camped along the Traun River. The hospital was like a German version of a MASH unit. All the patients in the hospital were soldiers who had been injured in the war. They had a wide variety of injuries. Some did not have hands, others did not have feet, and others might have holes in their abdomens. Although they were recuperating in the hospital, they still remained in pretty bad shape aesthetically. No one in the hospital had been cutting the soldiers' hair. One of the refugees with us was a professional barber, and he was hired to cut hair in this hospital. When he realized that there was more work than he could do, he asked Julius if he would help out. As a student at the Teachers College in Budapest, Julius had made a little extra money cutting his classmates' hair. The barber knew of Julius's experience, and he knew Julius had his own clippers and shears. The haircuts were not fancy, usually a burr cut, but nonetheless a good haircut. Julius would cut patients' hair in exchange for whatever they could give him. He usually got paid in the most popular currency at the time: cigarettes, coffee beans or sugar. With those items, we could buy food. Occasionally, Julius was paid money. We could still buy a few things with money, but we could not buy food.

Within a couple of weeks of arriving in Obertraun, it became evident that we were not going to be traveling again for a while. After the stress of seven weeks on the road, literally fleeing for our lives and two weeks with makeshift living still in the covered wagon but with the added "luxury" of a tent down by the Traun River, I was more than ready to try to find a house that we could rent. I wanted to settle into more livable conditions, but more important, I especially wanted to provide the children with more stability.

I began to look around the village for a house or an apartment. One morning as I was out looking around, I noticed a young woman pushing a cart filled with freshly cut hay from a nearby field. I could see that the woman was struggling to push the heavy cart, so I offered to help her. The woman thanked me and said that she lived just up the road a short way. When we arrived at her house, the woman invited me to come in, to have some coffee, and to visit for a few minutes. She introduced herself as Maria Kieninger.

As we visited, I told Maria of our experiences over the past few weeks. Maria was obviously interested in our family and our situation. I told her about Helen's illness, and that the cause had been the lack of the right food to eat. We still did not have a ration card and primarily all we were eating were the yellow peas. Maria said she had a friend who was the cook at the German army hospital in Obertraun. She said that maybe she could do something to help the family. This was the same hospital where Julius had been cutting hair from time to time.

Maria appeared at our tent that evening with a pot of food that she had received from her friend at the hospital. She also brought some skim milk for Helen to drink. She explained that after I left, she went to the hospital and asked her friend, the cook, what she was doing with the leftover food that had not been served to the patients. The cook said that they threw it out. Maria asked her not to throw it out and explained to the cook that there was a family that could really use the excess food. The cook gave Maria the food to bring to us. Maria told her that she would bring me to the hospital the next day.

Maria took me to the hospital the next day to meet the cook. I explained my situation and told her that we could use the food that was being thrown out at the hospital. We agreed that if I would come in the early afternoon after all of the food had been served and after the cook knew what was left, she would give me the leftovers. Since the main meal in Europe is served at noon, this was the only cooked meal at the hospital. In the evening, the patients were served a light meal, usually only a cold sandwich. Leftovers would only be available after the noon meal.

Beginning that very day, I went to the hospital after each noon meal, around one to one-thirty in the afternoon, after everybody had already eaten. The cook gave me the food that was left in the pot after serving the patients. I did not accept any food that had been left on the plates. The quantities of food varied from day to day, but whatever we received always helped, and it was always good. We could finally change our diet from yellow peas and were so thankful for having this precious food. Our major concern had been the proper and adequate nourishment for our children, and especially for Helen, who had been so malnourished. Helen's health began to improve almost immediately, and soon she was completely healthy.

Although nobody had much money at the time, the cook refused to accept any money for the food. Although the food would have been thrown out, I did not feel that it was right for me to accept it every noontime without some form of payment. I still had a few nice things that I had brought from Hungary and had not yet traded—slips, blouses, etc. These items were much too fine for the way we were living at the time. I had no use for them any longer. Although the cook did not ask for anything, occasionally I took her an item or two as an expression of my appreciation for helping us. We usually received enough food for the whole family at noon, and from time to time we even had enough left for supper. We received food from the hospital almost every day until they closed the facility about six months later.

Maria became a very good friend. She was the perfect person for me to meet because of her kindness and generosity.

Maria was a member of one of the very few families who were not opposed to having the refugees in their village. I wondered how I came to meet such a lovely and caring person whose father was equally as caring. They immediately accepted us into their lives. I felt that somehow God had guided me to Maria at that particular time and at that particular place. At first, it was I who needed Maria and her family. As time passed and as our friendship became stronger, Maria and I, as well as our families, realized we needed each other.

Soon after we arrived in Obertraun in early June, Julius learned from someone that the artist who had given Julius his paintings for safekeeping had settled in Schladming. Julius had worried about the safety of the paintings from the beginning and was eager to return them to him as soon as possible. Julius was an artist himself and had painted numerous pictures, which we left behind in Budapest. He knew how much the artist would want his paintings back. Julius was determined to fulfill this commitment of returning the paintings as soon as he could. Travel was still very difficult and in many cases restricted, so Julius finally decided to walk to Schladming, carrying the very heavy roll of paintings on his back. Schladming is a distance of over forty kilometers by road from Obertraun. Along the way, a farmer's wife saw that he was carrying these heavy paintings on his shoulders and back and gave him a child's wagon to put the paintings on so that he would not have to carry them. Once he arrived in Schladming, he asked around until he located the artist. He felt he would never see his paintings again and was delighted with having them back. He gave Julius two of the paintings in appreciation for returning them. Julius did not spend any extra time in Schladming because he knew he had to return to Obertraun as quickly as possible. It took him five days to deliver the paintings and return. Later, the artist sent another painting to us in Obertraun. These beautiful paintings are treasured keepsakes in our family.

For several weeks, we were very restricted as to where we could go because people had to have a permit to travel on the roads. We could go from one village to another if we walked through the fields and woods and bypassed the road. We continued to live day to day, trying to make the best of each one. In some sense, we felt trapped. We did not have any particular place to go. Our goal in leaving Hungary was to reach safety, and we felt very safe in Obertraun. What we did not have was a home. We did not know what the situation was in Hungary, so we did not want to chance going back until we were sure it would be safe to return. We finally began to realize that we would probably be in Obertraun for a long time.

By mid-June, the soldiers were very slowly beginning to come back from the war. All of the German army, including the Austrian soldiers had been declared prisoners of war. Each soldier was processed through the American, French, British or Russian forces before he could be released from service. This was a time-consuming process, so the number of young men in the village remained quite small.

Jobs were scarce. The two industries that provided the main sources of income in the area were the salt mine and the forest service. Because there were so few men in the village as a result of the war, jobs were available with the forest service. The salt mine was not hiring employees at the time.

In late June, Julius heard that he might have a chance to work for the forest service, and that they would pay him in currency. We were beginning to need currency to buy certain items in the stores. In addition, if Julius could secure a job, the government would issue us ration cards.

Julius and twelve other men from the refugee group went to the forest service to apply for a job. The forest ranger hired all of the men to work in the woods as lumberjacks. Julius and the other men reported to work the following day. They went with two foremen to work in the woods near the mountains. The work was very hard, backbreaking and dangerous. To cut the wood, the men usually used one of three different saws. For cutting the largest trees, they used a two-man saw that was about two meters long with handles on each end. For cutting smaller trees, they used one of two large one-man saws. One of these saws was about two meters long; the other was about a meter and a half long. These saws had large, sharp teeth that could cut through a large tree very quickly. The workers were also issued axes for trimming the tree branches. Most of the men were not accustomed to such hard manual labor and working under the harsh conditions in the woods. Some of them did not even wait until the end of the first day before they quit. The next day only seven men showed up. The day after, only five, and within a week, only two men were left: Julius and one other.

Three weeks later only one man remained from the original group of thirteen that had been hired on a trial basis by the forest service; that was Julius. He was the only man who could overcome the hard work. Determination to provide for his family allowed him to look beyond the pain and soreness he experienced day after day. In addition, he had an advantage over the other workers. Because he had grown up on a farm where he had worked from the time he was a young boy, he was not afraid of hard manual work. Although he had not used saws like the ones used by the forest service, he had cut wood on the farm and had used many different farm tools. Before he had moved to Budapest to attend school, he had done much hard work on the farm. He also worked on the farm during the summer, when he was not attending classes in Budapest. He had worked long days cutting hay with a sickle out in the fields. He knew he would become accustomed to the manual work, and he knew this was his best chance of providing money for his family. He was determined that he would not quit. Before long, he was rewarded for his efforts by being hired by the forest service as a permanent employee. Furthermore, the forest service work suited Julius through his educational background as well. He had always liked the out-doors and nature. He had a doctorate in natural sciences, and he knew the Latin names of the plants and trees in the forest. Under the circumstances and considering this was the only regu-lar paying job in the area, Julius felt very fortunate to have a job that he could relate to in a professional and educational way.

Julius reported to work each day at seven in the morning. When the location for the woodcutting was within an hour's walking distance from the forest service hut, he walked to the work location on his own time. Since he had to be at the loca-tion ready to work no later than seven in the morning, he had to start much earlier to be on time. He quit working at five in the evening. Again, if the work location was less than an hour's walk-ing distance from the forest service hut, he had to walk back on his own time, not on the company time. If the work location was farther away than one hour's normal walking distance, then the time started down in the valley at the forest service hut. The walking time to and from the work site in this case was on company time; therefore, Julius received pay for the time.

Regardless of where Julius was cutting wood that day, he had to walk to the forest service hut every day, carrying his tools with him. These tools (primarily axes and saws) were assigned specifically to him, and they were very valuable; the tools were his livelihood. He did not dare leave his tools in the woods or at the hut. People could not readily acquire quality steel tools, and Julius could not take the chance that they might be stolen. If he lost them or if they were stolen, he had to replace them himself. Even though the tools were extremely heavy, he carried them everywhere on his shoulders, including home every night.

Even though Julius knew how to cut wood, it had been a very long time since he had done this kind of manual labor on a regular basis. He had a difficult time becoming accustomed to the long workdays. When he first began working for the forest service, our tent was about one and one-half kilometers from the forest service hut. For the first few days on his walk home each evening, Julius was so tired from cutting wood that he had to sit down and rest every two to three minutes. It took him over an hour to walk the one and one-half kilometers back to the tent. When he arrived home, I always had supper ready for him. Because we had no chairs, the only place to sit was on the army bed that had been issued to us. At the time, the army bed served as a chair, a table and a bed. He would sit down on the bed, and I would step away to bring him his food. By the time I turned back around with the food, I would find Julius lying on the bed sound asleep. I would set the plate down and shake him so that he would awaken and eat. Then when I turned to lift the plate again, Julius would fall sound asleep to the other side of the bed.

I worried about his being so tired. I would work with him to keep him awake long enough to eat, and then he would fall sound asleep until morning when the routine of the day would begin again. Seeing Julius this tired and exhausted, I could not help but reflect on how much our lives had changed since the days when we first met. He had been nineteen years old and so strong and full of energy. I had not been quite thirteen years old when I decided to meet the man about whom Edesapa had spoken so highly. Julius had been as handsome as he was smart. It did not matter to me that he was over seven years older than I. I still had wanted to know him better.

The winter we met was very cold. Each night the janitors at the Teachers College sprayed a flat area of ground with water. During the night, it froze solid, and by the next day a nice skating rink had formed. The rink attracted many people from the surrounding area, along with the students and teachers of the Teachers College. On January 6, 1932, I noticed Julius skating around the rink. I had already met him briefly when he helped Edesapa move us from our house to the president's apartment on campus during the Christmas holidays. I thought this would be a good opportunity to meet him and to get to know him. He seemed to glide on the ice. I was not nearly as good a skater as he was, so I somewhat waddled out onto the ice and asked him if he would skate with me. I could tell he did not want to skate with me, this young clumsy child, but he did anyway—probably because Edesapa was the president of the school he was attending! We skated around a little with him holding me up most of the time. Even though I was not at all graceful, I enjoyed skating very much that day because I was skating with this strong man.

The next day I saw Julius skating again. I could tell he did not want me to approach him about skating, but I did anyway. Again he agreed, and by the end of the day, he did not seem to mind skating with me as he had the day before. The following day I came out again, and we skated together. My persistence was paying off! Each day, Julius seemed a bit more receptive to our skating together. I even began to notice that he seemed to be expecting me, and he seemed excited to see me when I arrived. Each day we enjoyed being together even more than the day before. We continued to meet to skate. Julius and I were very happy that this was a cold winter, and that the ice rink stayed open until the end of January. We were able to skate every afternoon after school was out.

On January 16, I celebrated my thirteenth birthday. Edesanya gave me the most beautiful dress I had ever seen. I immediately made plans to wear the dress to the annual Scouts Ball on February 1. February 2 was a Catholic holiday, and all schools in Hungary were always closed on that day. On the evening of February 1 before the holiday, the Teachers College had a dance called the Scouts Ball, which included a short program in the evening and then a dance until midnight. Since the Teachers College was an all-boys school, the college invited the students from an all-girls school located not too far from the Teachers College. Edesapa, as president of the college, always attended, and I went with my parents to the dance. As I had planned, I wore the new dress I had received for my birthday. I felt like a princess at a king's ball. It was the first long gown I had ever had, and it was elegant.

At the Scouts Ball, a very good Gypsy band always played dance music. Julius and I danced the entire evening, and Julius teased me that I could not dance any better than I could skate. This did not matter because we enjoyed dancing together! We talked about how much we had enjoyed the ice-skating, and we agreed that it would be nice if the weather would stay cold and freezing so that we could continue to see each other at the rink. In this very short time, we both knew we already had fallen in love.

That evening while we were waiting to go home after the dance, Julius and I declared that we loved one another. Julius then asked if I would marry him. He said he would wait until I finished my education to marry. I, of course, said yes. That night, slightly more than a month after first meeting, Julius and I made a commitment that would last a lifetime. Although I was only thirteen and Julius was nineteen, we knew we had found our soul mates in each other.

Now it was 1945, thirteen years later, and that night seemed eons ago. No longer did I feel like a princess, and my prince was an exhausted man who could hardly stay awake to eat a meal. How different our lives had become. The events of the past few months certainly had not been a part of our dreams and hopes, as we realized that our love was meant for a lifetime.

It took Julius about three weeks before he adjusted to the hard, punishing work and could stay completely awake for a meal. He became stronger and more accustomed to the work and the long hours. Soon thereafter he could do the work without any strain at all.

Not only was the work very strenuous, but it was also dangerous. After the trees were cut down, the lumberjacks cut them into large logs. The workers would remove the bark to make it easier to slide the logs along the ground. The logs were then hauled to a logging road and collected there until the winter snow. Vehicles could not drive on the logging road because it was nothing more than a wide trail through the woods used for hauling logs by sleds in the winter. When the snow came during the winter, the forest workers would put the logs on a sled and chain the logs down. Only one forest worker rode the sled. He would sit in the front of the sled, carefully guiding and controlling the sled on the haul road to the bottom of the mountain. Accidents did happen. If a large deer or bear jumped in front of the sled and the worker braked too quickly, the logs, because they were stripped of their bark, could break loose and injure or kill the worker. The worker had to be very skilled at braking the sled. All the workers learned they could not be too careful. To complete the process, at the bottom of the mountain the lumberjacks would off-load the logs in a gathering area. Later, a wagon or truck hauled the logs to the lumber mill.

Julius was always very careful and became so accustomed to the hard work that he took Saturday and Sunday jobs cutting extra wood. The local people came to him with special-order jobs, and he worked for them. Sometimes, he would even work at night with a lantern. When he first started working in the evenings, the villagers wondered what the noise was up on the mountain. They would look out and see the light and soon learned that it was Julius chopping wood up on the mountainside. They had never seen anyone cut wood after dark before. They began to call him the "crazy Hungarian." Nonetheless, he earned the respect of the villagers because he proved to be such a hard worker day or night. They appreciated the fact that he worked hard to support his family.

Only after Julius began working as a forest service employee were we eligible to receive ration cards for food. Once Julius got the job, he immediately went to the American military authorities and received a permit that allowed us to receive regular civilian ration cards from the Austrian food and supply authorities. The Burgermeister absolutely refused to give us ration cards until he was required to. The forest service was a state business; employees working for the state had to be issued a ration card for food. The Burgermeister had no choice. With the ration card, we could get more and different foods to eat; as a result, we could cook a little more. We no longer had to eat those terrible yellow peas. With the food I was getting from the hospital and now being able to buy food, we finally were able to quit eating the yellow peas every day and could eat what we chose to eat. For the first time since Elizabeth's birthday, we had bread, which we could now buy with a ration card.

We also requested a ration card for clothes. Now that Julius was working, we had money to buy some of the most necessary things, especially shoes. The Burgermeister told us that since we were not Austrian citizens, we were not allowed to obtain a ration card for clothes. We later found out that the Burgermeister had lied. Nonetheless, we were unable to buy any clothing.

Mr. Kieninger, Maria's father, was an older man who worked hard and accepted us as part of the community, even though we were refugees. He had some old clothes from his younger years, which he gave to Julius. They were not fancy, but Julius could work in them.

Julius and I shared the responsibility of providing the needs for our family, and life was very difficult for us, but even though they were very young and did not have huge responsibilities, life was also not easy for young Julius and Elizabeth. They were old enough to realize that their lives had changed drastically. They had sensed the dangers we had encountered and had realized that we were not living in the luxury we once had, but they coped as best they could. Many times during the day, they would sit in bed and play and laugh. Other times they would fight and end up crying. They usually stayed close to the tent to play. I was always worried when they played too close to the Traun River, which flowed very swiftly and was deep. If they were to fall in, we would have had a very difficult time saving them. Occasionally, the children would find some other local children with whom to play outdoor games. The children never seemed to have any trouble finding things to keep themselves occupied, despite not having any toys with which to play.

It seemed that every day as one particular woman walked by our tent, for some reason, young Julius and Elizabeth would be crying. Finally, one day the woman came by and noticed that the children were playing and not crying. The woman made a comment to the children that they were being so good and then asked, "Why aren't you crying?"

Young Julius answered back, "We are playing now; we will cry again later."

Young Julius and Elizabeth shared the same bed. One day Elizabeth was in bed screaming. Julius and I asked what was going on. Elizabeth did not say anything. She just continued screaming. Finally, young Julius answered: "She is screaming because I am kicking her." Shortly thereafter, we placed a board diagonally across the bed to keep the two of them separated.

During that entire summer of 1945, we lived on the riverbank, in the army tent and on the wagon. The whole group, which had traveled together, was together for only a short while there. Like us, others had tried to find a place to rent, but no one would rent to any of the refugees. Other people slowly began to go to other places. Each time a family or person left, I would always give them the address of my parents in Budapest, just in case for any reason they happened to return to Budapest. I would always ask them to tell my parents that we were all doing well and that they could write to us at the Kieninger address in Obertraun.

The Americans finally lifted the travel restrictions during that summer, but they continued to maintain a strong presence in the area to ensure that order was maintained as the country transitioned from war to peace. The Americans continued to work with the refugees to provide the necessary documents we needed to stay in Austria. They also provided opportunities for the refugees to go to camps where they could live until a permanent home was found for them.

Some of the other people with our group found jobs in other places, but most of them went to refugee camps. Going to camps was really the easiest way to go because in the camps the refugees did not have to work; in fact, they did not have to do anything. As part of the Marshall Plan, the government fed and clothed the refugees in camps, but we did not want to have any part of the refugee camp experience. Julius and I decided we did not want to live off any taxpayer's money or program as long as he was able to work. We decided we would rather stay in Obertraun and struggle to survive until we could return to our homeland once again.

Slowly, the friends we had made during the frightful flight from Hungary began to move on. The Kerekes family who had shared our wagon stayed in Obertraun only for a short while. They decided to go to a camp rather than seek a job. The man and son were two of the men who had started work at the forest service but quit almost immediately. We later heard that they immigrated to Australia.

Feher, our leader, the one who had served as our spokesman and who had organized our small group throughout our flight, was an older man and could not work for the forest service. His son, like the others, thought the lumberjack work was far too hard. Feher and his family also decided to go to a camp. By the end of the summer, our family and one other family were the only refugees from the group left in Obertraun. The other family, who had a ten-year-old daughter, lived out of their wagon for a while, and then they quietly moved in with the Bender family as domestic help. The Benders lived across the street from our friends, the Kieningers.

Julius continued to work hard with the forest service. I continued to make the tent and wagon as normal a home as I could for our family. We still had no idea when or if we could return to Hungary, but we were determined to care for our own family as best we could. Our life was not easy, but we did not have to fear the Russians. Many of the Austrians did not want us there, but we did not have to fear for our lives. We had our friends, the Kieningers; we had our family and each other; but, most of all, we had our faith that God would see us through as He had done thus far.

CHAPTER 8
THOU PREPAREST A TABLE BEFORE ME

In September, the days began to shorten, and the weather turned colder. We knew that sometimes in September the area around Obertraun could receive its first frost, especially in the area where we lived because it was at the bottom of the north slope of a very steep and high mountain. We learned later that because of the shade of the mountains, we would not see the sun from October to April. With the harsh Austrian winter rapidly approaching, we knew we could not live in the tent much longer.

We had tried to find a place all summer to rent that would protect us from the weather. We had not lived in a regular house for over five months. We had been living in the wagon and the tent for three and a half months on the Traun River. The Kieningers told me that the house across the street from them belonged to the Benders and was for rent. It was a small house, but at least it was a house that would be warmer than the tent and wagon. Downstairs was a kitchen and a small room. Upstairs was a nice bedroom. It was empty and available. I went to the Benders, who lived next door to the house that was for rent and asked to rent the house, but they said it was already rented. Once again, I went throughout the village searching for signs for an available house or rooms for rent. Each time I received the same story: the house or room was no longer available. Nobody would rent to us.

The Benders, who were actually very nice people, finally confided in me why neither they nor anyone else would rent to us. The Burgermeister had warned the people in the village not to rent to a refugee family. If anyone rented to a refugee family, the Burgermeister would retaliate in some way and, in fact, would dismiss the person if he worked for the city. The Burgermeister was the village boss, and nobody dared to cross him. Very intimidating, he looked like an overstuffed bulldog, and he had proven in the past that he could be very vindictive toward anyone who crossed him or made him angry. He was clearly the most powerful man in the village, and he knew it!

We realized that many of the Austrians did not want any of the refugees in their country. Who could blame them? The war had drained the resources of the country. The Austrians had a very meager living themselves. In the area around Obertraun, unless someone had a job either in the forest service or in the salt mine in Hallstatt, not much else was available. The area had no industries and, because of the lack of land, commercial agriculture was nonexistent. Kieninger and most of the other residents had small vegetable gardens, and some people had a few fruit trees. The Austrians did not have much for themselves, so they certainly did not want to share what little they had with strangers. Even though we needed a place to survive, I could understand why the Austrians did not want the refugees there. It was difficult, however, to understand the almost evil feelings of those like the Burgermeister who did not want us in their community under any circumstances. Fortunately, some people overcame those feelings and helped.

We were becoming very concerned about how we were going to survive the winter. I was constantly looking for any place to live that would provide more protection than the wagon and tent. Each day I did not find a place was another day closer to the cold winter winds and snow.

I had been buying milk from Mr. Kieninger and had become well acquainted with him. His family had become our most reliable friends. While visiting with him one day, I noticed an old, small, abandoned stone building nearby; it sat next to the side of the mountain. I asked him if he owned the building or if he knew who owned it. Although the building was adjacent to his property and the building was only a few meters away from his home, Mr. Kieninger knew he did not own the building or the land that the building was on. He said he thought it might belong to someone in Bad Ischl, which was the closest large city and was about thirty kilometers by road from Obertraun. He suggested that I go to the local city hall and find out who owned the property.

Officials checked the records and found who owned the property with the building, but they had no current address of the owner, who had not been seen in years. They considered the property to be abandoned. They informed me that the building was very run-down and had been condemned and considered unfit for human habitation. Since the property was considered abandoned, I asked if any law existed that would prevent our moving into an abandoned building. The city official told me no such law existed and that the officials could not keep us from moving in if we wanted to, but it would be at our own risk. They made it clear they wanted nothing to do with the building or our moving into it. It was our decision. I am confident that the officials thought that once we took a closer look at the condition of the old building, we would abandon the idea of moving in and would instead move away from their village, seeking shelter elsewhere for the winter. If, indeed, they thought that, they were incredibly wrong!

The old stone house sat at the base of the mountain. Obviously, someone had used the building for storage in the past. It did not appear that anyone ever had lived in it. The building had one room downstairs and one room upstairs. The upstairs room was approximately four meters by five meters; the downstairs room was slightly larger. The wall on the upstairs was one layer of stone; in several places the mortar was missing between the stones. This created several cracks in the wall, and we could easily see outside through them. The doorway to the upstairs room faced the mountain and had no door. The two upstairs windows were opposite the door and faced away from the mountains and toward the road; they had no glass. The floor upstairs consisted of thick wooden planks. The bottom room had only a dirt floor and a wide opening for a doorway. No stairs led to the second floor. Regardless of all its shortcomings, however, the old stone building provided shelter, and we needed shelter.

A few good people helped us to get the place ready so that we could at least move in. Mr. Kieninger, as usual, supplied significant help to Julius and me. For example, Mr. Kieninger had an extra solid wooden door that would fit in the doorway; not only did he give it to us, but he also helped Julius install it. Because Mr. Kieninger knew the people of the village, he knew to whom he could go to find other items needed to make the house livable. Many people had the standard sized-window openings on their homes. Mr. Kieninger went from house to house and collected windows that could be used for the upstairs room. He installed these two double windows in the upper room, and we could open and close them as we chose. We now had two windows and a door, and we felt the house was beginning to be livable.

Julius's boss, the forest service foreman, arranged for him to obtain some lumber. As a goodwill act, the forest ranger took Julius to the sawmill. The forest ranger made a deal with the mill that he would give them a whole tree if they would give Julius lumber that he could use to build some stairs and some furniture. Julius received a wagon load of lumber, and used the oxen and the wagon to haul the lumber from the mill to the house.

After Julius brought the lumber home, Mr. Kieninger loaned him some tools and gave him a coffee can full of old nails. Because all hardware required a ration card, just like milk, meat and bread, Julius could not buy nails. Mr. Kieninger had saved the nails. Because everything had been so scarce for so long, it was common practice for people to pull the nails out of old, unusable lumber and save them. Again, Mr. Kieninger was very helpful.

Julius used the nails and lumber to build a ramp from the side of the mountain to the second floor of the house. The lower room was bigger than the upper room because there was about a half-meter wide landing on three sides of the upstairs. The roof had a very steep slope, and the roof overhang created a protected area on the sides of the house where the second floor landing extended beyond the upstairs wall. The bottom floor had a dirt floor and was not habitable at all. The cracks in the lower floor walls were even larger than the cracks in the upstairs walls. The lower room may have at one time been a stable or a tool storage room, but it was certainly unlivable for people. Julius decided to keep the two oxen in the downstairs room for a while.

Needless to say, our next problem was to furnish our newly found home. We did not have a stove or oven for warmth. A blacksmith in Obertraun, who did plumbing and, it seemed, almost everything else, including building stoves from sheet metal, heard we needed a stove. This man took an old stove from his junk pile, repaired it and gave it to us. Not only did he give us the stove, but he also came to the house and set it up safely and efficiently in the small room. He placed the stove immediately to the right of the door, made a chimney and connected the stove to the chimney. We had a safe, reliable, steel flat-top stove suitable for both cooking and heating. Since it was a wood-burning stove and since we had access to plenty of wood, fuel was not a problem. Julius offered to pay the blacksmith for the stove, but he would not hear of it.

As the army hospital was sending patients home, they began to have extra beds available. Mr. Kieninger convinced the hospital to give us a hospital-type bed and a bunk bed for us to use. We put the two beds, one against the other, along the left wall from the doorway. On the other side of the room was the baby bed, which was on the floor because the legs had been cut off to fit in the wagon when we left Hungary. Beside the baby bed in the corner of the room were Julius's work tools.

Julius had some cut lumber left over from building the steps. He used this lumber to build a tabletop for a combination kitchen and dining table. Mr. Kieninger found some old table legs and gave them to Julius to complete the table. We put the table midway down the right wall from the doorway. We used the crates that Julius had made from the lumber for his grandmother's potential coffin as storage places for clothing. We put the large crate in the far right-hand corner of the room, and we put the smaller crate along the right wall near the large crate. At the time, we could not afford chairs, so we sat on the crates and the beds.

With the house furnished, the five of us could move from the tent and wagon near the river to the house. We gladly returned the tent and army bed to the government surplus. This was not the house we wanted, but it provided considerably more shelter than the tent. After all the work Julius and Mr. Kieninger had put into the house, it was now at least livable and would protect us from the wind and the snow.

Elizabeth and young Julius slept on the hospital bed with a board diagonally across the bed between them so that they could not kick each other. Elizabeth had her head on one end, and young Julius had his head on the other end. Helen slept on the baby bed. Julius slept on the top bunk, and I slept on the bottom bunk. At meals, Julius and I sat on the crates to eat; Elizabeth and young Julius had to stand to eat.

Living was not easy. Our home was far from what we had in Budapest or even on the farm in Kisrakos. We certainly had no conveniences, but at least we were protected from the elements, and we were safe. We had no electricity, so our only light came from a kerosene lantern. We did not even have an outhouse; we simply went into the woods when nature called us. We did have a potty seat for the children to use when they were young. We used an area above the ceiling in the attic for storage. This was where we stored the footlocker.

Securing water was no problem. A natural stream came down the mountain like a waterfall. Year-round the crystal-clear water came from melting snow on the mountain. Long ago a big wooden trough had been built for the cows to have something from which to drink. The trough had an outlet that maintained the water at a full level. Excess water would pass over the outlet and continue down the mountain to a stream. Since the water trough was located just a few steps away from the house, we could go out, place our container under the stream and fill it with clean, fresh, cold water before the water ran into the trough.

Sometimes in the winter when the weather became extremely cold, the natural stream would freeze before the water came down the mountain. At these times, we would have no water. We usually kept some fresh water in the house just in case. Fortunately, a major freeze usually lasted only a few days. The Kieningers had a deep artesian well that always had water. We did not often go to them to ask for water, but we knew we could if we ran short.

Usually after one of these cold spells, a sudden shift in wind would occur, and the wind would come from the south. We were happy when the wind shifted because that meant that we would have water again the next day. However, this warm wind also tended to melt the snow quickly and often caused an avalanche. Although we were happy to get water again, we always were a bit apprehensive. Since our house was so close to the side of the steep portion of the mountain, we knew we were located in the path of any potential avalanche.

As winter approached, I began to become very home-sick for Hungary and for my family. I had made it through the summer pretty well because I was so focused on trying to get us settled and deciding what we were going to do. Now that the prospect of spending the long, cold winter in this miserable, tiny house was upon me, I became extremely homesick. I missed Hungary; I missed my parents with whom I was very close; I missed my friends; I missed our home; I missed our old way of life. Sometimes, I thought I could not bear another day. I just wanted to go back to Budapest under any circumstances.

I began to reminisce frequently. The memories and recollections of our life there offered some comfort. I especially remembered our wedding and what a joyous time that had been in our lives. Everything seemed to be working out for us then. Julius was completing his work on his doctorate, and I had just completed the Teachers College and had received my teacher certification. We were happy and full of hopes and dreams for a future together, raising our family in Budapest.

Julius and I married on July 22, 1940. Because in Hungary marriage is a legal contract, couples had to go to a state office for the legal marriage. Afterwards, they had the option of having a ceremonial church wedding. At eleven in the morning of our wedding day, we were officially married in the state office. Our witnesses were my uncle on Edesapa's side of the family and a teacher from the Teachers College. That afternoon at four o'clock, we had the church ceremony. We were proud of ourselves in that we were going to have a marriage ceremony that broke a popular tradition in Hungary at the time. We had the usual formal wedding ceremony, but afterwards the Hungarian tradition was that the bride and groom stayed at the front of the church to be congratulated by all of the guests at the wedding. What usually happened was that the wedding guests, in their excitement to congratulate the couple, would rush up, kiss them, hug them and almost always step on their feet right there in the church. They would shake the groom's hand to the extent that he was not able to hug his wife for two or three weeks because his arm would be so sore or out of joint. We did not like this tradition. When the ceremony concluded, we quickly turned from the congregation and walked out. The church sexton had told everyone who came to the church for the ceremony that the couple would not be congratulated after the wedding. We left our parents behind to be congratulated by the guests. We had no reception after the wedding, so the people who were not invited to the dinner had to wait until after we returned from our honeymoon to congratulate us.

When we left the church, we had a waiting cab that took us to the photographer's studio, where we had our official wedding pictures made. The only photos taken at the wedding were during the ceremony by an associate of the photographer. We were so happy now that we were man and wife that we actually were allowed to go to the photographer without a chaperone! Finally, eight and one-half years after we had realized that we were in love and wanted to spend our lives together, we were now husband and wife!

From the photographer's studio, we took a cab to the wedding dinner. The customary dinner after the wedding usually included only close family, but because Edesapa was so well known, he invited a large number of people from the Teachers College and from the community. The dinner had many wonderful, varied foods. It was held at the president's apartment at the Teachers College. Six connecting rooms were all opened up, with long tables loaded with everything imaginable. All of the people ate, drank, joked and had a most enjoyable evening. When the time came for us to leave to catch our train, we simply, neatly, quietly sneaked out! Nobody noticed when we left, possibly because the wine was flowing freely. Edesapa later told me that long after we left, somebody asked, "Where is the young couple?" By then we were already on the train!

Originally, we had planned to go to Italy for our honeymoon. However, because the war was already causing turmoil in Europe, we decided to go to western Hungary to a resort spa for a few days and then to go to Kisrakos so that I could meet Julius's family. The only person from Julius's family who attended the wedding was his brother Zoltan. The remainder of the family did not approve of him marrying a city girl and therefore chose not to come to the wedding. Nonetheless, when we arrived after the wedding in Kisrakos, his family greeted me warmly. I was pleased because I knew why they had not attended the wedding, and I was concerned that I might be shunned. The visit and honeymoon turned out to be wonderful.

As these memories raced through my mind, providing me with comfort, warmth, and joy, I would be left with such a wonderful feeling. Even though these events occurred only a few years earlier, they seemed so very, very long ago. The life I had spent in Budapest seemed so extravagant to me now, as I looked around this tiny room we called our home with very little to eat and very few clothes to wear. Our life in Budapest had been wonderful with so many friends and so many activities and no concerns for our physical well-being. Now, in Obertraun, we were actually only about four hundred kilometers and five years from that life, but it seemed a world and century away.

Life continued to be difficult. Most of the people in Obertraun still did not want us there, and we were struggling to provide food and clothing for the children. It was getting colder much sooner than we had expected, and I continued to yearn for Hungary. Everything was depressing. Julius knew how much I wanted to go back, but he also felt there would be problems if we returned, so he was very patient with me and encouraged me to stay "just a little longer." He said that we would stay just through the winter; in the spring, we would see how things were then. He was always very careful not to say we would not be returning to Hungary anytime soon. He would focus on getting by for a few months at a time and then reassess the situation later. He always left me with some hope. He always knew how to keep me calm and hopeful of returning to our homeland.

Once we were settled in the house, we tried to establish a routine and normal life as much as we possibly could under the circumstances. Because the weather was typically cold and perspiration was not a problem, the children typically would bathe only once a week. To bathe the children, I warmed pots of water and poured them into a large kettle. Each child went through the same routine: soap, wash, rinse, dry, on the way! Next child! The smaller child could just sit in the kettle, but the bigger children would have to stand to be washed. All the children had to use the same bath water because it took far too long to heat enough hot water to let each child have separate baths. This process provided our only bathing facilities. It was often cold, even in the summertime. During the summer when the weather did become warm, people swam either in the Traun River or in Lake Hallstatter, but even then the water was very cold. Very few days were really warm. The weather was so seldom hot during the summer that nobody ever complained when it was.

During the winter, the house was always cold. Somebody had given us blankets, so we had covers for the beds. I was the first one up in the mornings, and I would start the wood fire. I became quite good at using kindling and paper to start the fire. The forest service gave the lumberjacks working in the forest the leftover wood scraps that were not good for anything except burning. Julius always brought home as much wood as we needed. In the winter, he brought the wood on a sleigh he borrowed from Mr. Kieninger. The wood was provided to us in meter-long lengths, so we had to cut them to the length we needed for our personal use.

I always prided myself on being able to learn new things. When in Kisrakos, I had learned how to work on a farm. In Obertraun, I learned how to use a saw to cut the lumber. Julius brought home large branches that he had not had time to cut and split in the woods. I learned how to cut and split the wood to the size needed for the fireplace.

I washed the family clothes in the same large kettle in which the children bathed. Washing clothes was a very difficult job. Monday was always wash day. To wash our clothes, I first soaped the clothes in a large tub in the small shed by the water trough. I usually did this on Sunday night and left the clothes overnight to soak. The next morning, after rubbing the clothes over a washboard to get the dirt out, I would take the soapy clothes inside and put them into a kettle of boiling water. I boiled the clothes for a short while, and after the water had cooled down, I would take the clothes out of the water and put them across the washboard to let the excess water drip off. The next step would be to take the clothes outside to the water trough, where the stream ran off the mountain, and place them in the cold water coming down. I rinsed the clothes until the water ran clean. Then, I would hang the clothes outside on a clothesline to dry. When it was cold and snowing or raining, I took the clothes into the house. An area where the roof came down created a little space on both sides, and I put a clothesline there to dry the clothes.

Occasionally, when the water in the trough froze, I had to go to the creek to rinse the clothes. The creek was about a ten-minute walk from the house. I would put the clothes on a sled and pull it down to the creek. I had to kneel on the snow-covered ground and rinse the clothes in the creek water. Sometimes, if the creek was frozen also, I first had to break the ice in the creek to reach the water. The ice in the creek was usually not very thick and was fairly easy to break. Once I had the clothes adequately rinsed, I would pull the clean, rinsed clothes back to the house on the sled. In the wintertime, the clothes froze right away after they were hung. Even frozen, the clothes would dry within a couple of days.

One day while I was rinsing the clothes in the creek, I began to feel the first sign of the arthritis that was later to become very painful for me. The ground and water were bitterly cold. I felt arthritis pain in my hands, knees and hips. I tried not to complain about this because Julius was doing more than his share of working long hours in the evenings and weekends cutting wood in the mountains. The pain was just another hardship we had to endure in order to provide for our family.

When the Americans finally allowed unrestricted travel in the area, getting around was not difficult. Although we were on the outskirts of the village, the village was small; we could easily walk to all of the local markets. If we needed to go to any other place, we took the train. Once the war was over and things began to return to normal, the train was the only viable transportation; however, there were plenty of trains. Except during war times, the train schedules in Europe were always very reliable. Everyone learned the train schedule, and we adjusted our needs to the train schedule. The train station was about a kilometer from where we lived. We could walk to the station in less than ten minutes. Train transportation was just as convenient as having a car and sometimes more convenient.

Hallstatt was larger than Obertraun, so we occasionally went to Hallstatt to shop. Because the town was only five kilometers away, we usually walked. It was easier to walk the distance than to ride the train because the train did not go through the town of Hallstatt. The Hallstatt train station was on the east side of Lake Hallstatter. The town of Hallstatt was on the west side of the lake. The people of Hallstatt bought their train ticket and then went to the boat dock a few minutes before the train time. A boat carried them over to the train station that was less than a kilometer from Hallstatt. The people who got off the train took the same boat back across the lake to Hallstatt. The boat ride was included in the price for the train ticket.

Soon after Christmas, the family that had moved in with the Benders found they could immigrate to Canada and left Obertraun. By January 1946, Julius, the children and I were the only Hungarian family still living in Obertraun.

Everything was not drudgery; humorous things happened from time to time, and more frequently than not, the children were involved in these incidents. When Julius originally had made the ramp to the upper room, he did not put a rail on the ramp. One day, three-year-old Julius was playing on the ramp and fell onto the ground below. Many sharp rocks jutted up underneath the ramp, but one very small area had no rocks. Fortunately, young Julius fell exactly on that spot. But as he was falling, he caught his head on one of the rocks and received a small cut on the side of his head.

When Julius arrived home from work, he could see that young Julius had a bandage on his head. As young Julius described to his father what had happened, he didn't want his father to feel bad, so he quickly added to his story: "At least I can sleep good now." Julius knew that if his son had fallen directly on the rock and directly on his head, he could have been killed. Soon after this incident, Julius built a handrail on the ramp for safety.

When Julius was not cutting wood up in the mountains in the evenings, he often worked at night in the house sharpening tools for an hour or two before bedtime. He had learned how to sharpen tools while working with his father on the farm in Kisrakos. Julius always had been skillful with his hands, so while working in the forest, he became quite adept at sharpening tools. As word of Julius's skill spread throughout the village, many of our neighbors brought their tools to him to have them sharpened. Most people did not pay for the work with money because they simply did not have much. The little money they did have they needed to purchase items from the store. They would pay Julius with cigarettes, eggs, flour, coffee, cottage cheese or whatever they had at the time. Even when money was available, a barter system worked very well. Julius never quoted a price or asked how much people were going to pay. He just did the work, and people gave him whatever they had. Some people paid with hay that he used to feed the oxen.

From time to time, Julius worked weekends for the forest service, which managed a restaurant high in the mountains for skiers and hikers. No roads went to the restaurant, so the forest service used their workers to deliver provisions to it. On weekends, the forest service workers hiked up the mountain and delivered food and kerosene fuel to the restaurant. Many weekends Julius hiked up the steep and rugged path to deliver the items. Of course, he was paid extra for this work.

Julius loved being up in the mountains. He loved their beauty and always wished he had the money for art supplies and the time to spend to paint the landscapes and nature he so enjoyed. He did have a sketch pad, and occasionally he would take it with him in the mountains and create pencil sketches of the scenery. Sometimes when the other forest workers were napping at lunch, he would sketch them as they slept in the woods and share the sketches in amusement with them after they awakened.

Julius established a reputation as a skilled hard worker, and many people requested his services. Anytime he could work a job in addition to his forest service job, he was happy to do so because this meant he could take better care of his family. A shoemaker, who had heard that Julius was very good at cutting wood, asked him to cut for him from his allocation in the forest. The local law allowed each landowner in the village to have an allocation of wood from the forest. The landowner could use the wood for whatever purpose he chose until the allocation was fully utilized. The shoemaker needed the lumber from his allocation to build a house on his property. He and Julius agreed on a price. Julius cut and delivered the wood to the specified location so that it could be sent to the mill for cutting. The shoemaker was so pleased with the work that Julius had done that he not only paid him the agreed-to price, he also made and gave him a pair of high-quality, custom-made work boots. This was a very welcome gift, because until then, Julius had not had a good pair of work boots.

After this first winter in Obertraun, we decided we no longer needed the oxen. We were having a hard time gathering enough grass and feed for them during the winter months. Because they were so strong, it was very difficult to take them to graze on the mountainside. We thought it would be best to sell them. Someone offered to buy the wagon and oxen, so Julius sold them.

The winter months had proved very challenging. The weather, the cramped living conditions, the homesickness—everything combined made our life very difficult. Somehow, through faith in God's providing love, we made it through the first winter. Through hard work and long hours, Julius was providing for his family. We finally had secure shelter, as meager as it was. We had food, though not very much and not much variety. Our family was intact, and we had not succumbed to a refugee camp. The Lord had provided! Now, with summer coming, I was excited that maybe, just maybe, we would be able to return to Hungary.

CHAPTER 9
I SHALL NOT WANT

Waiting for the time when we could go back to Hungary proved extremely painful for me. We had no idea exactly what conditions were in Budapest. We had not heard from any of our family, so we had no way of knowing how they had been affected by the fighting in the city. During the entire winter, I was extremely homesick, and, try as I might, I could not stop thinking about my parents and my family. In the spring of 1946, we finally began to receive letters from my family in Hungary. One of the people who had left our group and returned to Hungary had contacted my parents and told them where we were and that we were all right. We received several letters from my parents that spring. The letters confirmed that we had made the right decision to leave Hungary. The letters told us the story of what had happened in Budapest and what was still happening with the communist control of the country.

The letters confirmed the reports that we had heard on the radio while still in Kisrakos of vicious fighting in Budapest from Christmas 1944 to the middle of February 1945. During this time, the Russians perpetrated unspeakable acts against people and property. My parents and my grandmother, Mamsika, had hidden in a bomb shelter in the cellar of the Teachers College soon after the fighting had begun.

My twin brothers, Marci and Emre, had been in their second year at the university when they were drafted into the military as part of the emergency draft. They were assigned to the university brigade to fight the Russians in Budapest.

While my family was still in the bomb shelter in the cellar at the Teachers College, the police suddenly showed up one day, arrested Edesapa and took him to jail. Every time he asked what charges were against him, they beat him. They beat him so severely that they broke his back. Finally, he was told that he was an "enemy of the people." He had absolutely no idea what that meant. Edesapa finally learned that one of the instructors at the Teachers College had wanted his job as president. In a vindictive act, he had made some false allegations against Edesapa so that he might get my father's job. Never had Edesapa mixed teaching with politics. He always had felt that teachers should not be a part of any political party because they needed to teach objectively without any political views. He taught students to think and have their own political views. In order to remain objective, he never had belonged to any political organization. How ironic that after years of teaching students to think for themselves, he became the victim of a spiteful, political accusation.

When the fighting in Budapest ended, no one dared to leave a bomb shelter until assured it was safe to return to the streets. Finally, when Edesanya and Mamsika felt safe enough, they walked back from the Teachers College to the house they had owned prior to moving to the College, the house that Julius and I had rented. When they arrived, only a couple of blocks away, they found it open; a bomb or some sort of shell had hit the house. When they entered, they saw a large hole in the roof over what had been the dining room. A beautifully carved dining table had received a direct hit and had been completely destroyed. Everything on the table had been destroyed except the Bible. The shock of the bomb blast had thrown the Bible behind the stove. The Bible was undamaged. Practically everything else in the dining room was destroyed or badly damaged, including a very nice grand piano. This area of the house was not livable.

As I was reading the letters revealing all of this, I recalled that Julius had always been concerned that a bomb would hit the house because of its location between the military artillery site on a hill and the defense factory that was near the Teachers College. Now, it was evident that his concerns were well founded. Fortunately, it appeared that nobody bad occupied the house when the bomb hit. I again thanked God that Julius left Budapest to come to Kisrakos before the fighting had begun. As a result, he had avoided the potential for disaster had he been in the house when the bomb hit.

Before my family went to the bomb shelter, they had gone to the house and had hidden a few things in the basement. They had been confident that if the Russian soldiers came through the neighborhood, the house would be ransacked. As Edesanya and Mamsika began looking around, their worst fears were confirmed. Either before or after the shell hit the house, someone had gone through the house and had taken almost everything of value. Very little was left. Julius and I had received some beautiful silver and crystal pieces for wedding gifts, but all of it had been stolen.

Edesanya and Mamsika also found that a woman had moved into the cellar of the house while they were away in the evacuation shelter during the fighting. They learned that this was quite common in the area. Many people found that communist squatters had taken over their homes and were living in them as though they owned them. Most of the squatters were people who did not have young children and had chosen not to evacuate during the war. Instead, they had stayed behind and had taken advantage of the opportunity to occupy nice homes that were vacant. Once these squatters occupied a house, they could not be forced to leave. The laws in Hungary stated that if a dwelling were unoccupied for a period of time, someone could move in. If the squatter stayed for a period of time, he could not be evicted.

When the fighting was over, the only place Edesanya and Mamsika had to live was to move back into the bombed house. The apartment at the Teachers College was no longer available because when Edesapa and been thrown in jail and he had been removed from his position as president of the Teachers College. Edesanya and Mamsika lived in the bedroom area on the main floor that was barely livable; the communist woman continued to occupy the basement of the house.

In the meantime, Edesanya and Mamsika had heard nothing from Emre, Marci or Edesapa. Edesanya decided to look for Edesapa first. She went to every known jail, but she could not find him. Finally, at one jail the police told her that he had been taken to the hospital with a broken back, and they told her which hospital. When she went to that hospital, she was told they had never heard of my father. While she was standing in the hospital corridor, someone pushed a patient by on a hospital bed. A sheet covered the patient, but an arm was hanging out from under the sheet. Edesanya noticed that the ring on the hand of this patient was her husband's ring. She knew immediately that he was there and that the hospital staff had lied to her. She confronted them, and they finally admitted that he was a patient, but he was under arrest and could not leave. Edesanya tried very hard to secure Edesapa's release from the hospital, but everything she tried was to no avail. Even though he was in the hospital because of his broken back, he was still a prisoner. Neither the hospital staff nor the authorities were going to release him until after a trial. The staff never allowed Edesanya to visit or see Edesapa while he was in the hospital. They told her that she could not see her husband until he went to trial.

While Edesanya was waiting for Edesapa's trial date, she began looking for Emre and Marci. She went from place to place where there were injured Hungarian soldiers. She was determined to find both of her sons, my two brothers. She was looking everywhere and asking anyone whom she thought might give her some information. She just knew they would be among the injured and that they were both alive. Finally, Edesanya found Marci in what was, at best, a makeshift hospital in the basement of a school. He was lying without a coat on some straw and was very cold and hungry. She also determined that he was badly injured and had received no medical attention. His left arm was badly wounded, he had been shot in the chest, and his left lung had collapsed. The doctors had decided that Marci was in such bad shape that he was going to die anyway; they did not want to waste any medication on him.

No way was Edesanya going to allow her son to die. She was resolute in her efforts to do what she could to restore his health. She began by bribing the doctors to treat Marci. She gave some of her handmade rugs that had not been stolen from the house to the doctors in exchange for their medical treatment of

Marci. Still, the doctors and the medical staff would not feed him, so Edesanya went three times a day and took him food. Slowly, Marci began to regain his physical strength, but he had lost the use of his left arm (he was left-handed), and he had lost the one lung that had collapsed. Finally, after weeks of treatment, Marci recovered enough that Edesanya could bring him home.

Months passed and finally the day arrived for Edesapa's trial. The colleague who had made the false accusations against him and had stated that he was an "enemy of the people" could not show any evidence that Edesapa was ever involved in any political activity. On the other hand, some of the ex-students who had known Edesapa willingly came forward and defended him. The charges were finally dropped, and he was released from custody and the hospital.

After he was released, even though he was totally innocent of all charges against him, Edesapa was not allowed to participate in any of the Teachers College activities. All references to his tenure at the college were removed. Although Edesapa had been an instructor at the Teachers College for ten years and had been president for thirteen years after that, it was as though he had never existed. Only one other man had served longer than Edesapa as president of the college. Edesapa had written books on teaching techniques, and he had been considered an outstanding educator before the war. Now, after the war, the communist government did not recognize any of his accomplishments. Furthermore, the government took away his entire pension. Fortunately, after a long battle with the government, he finally received a portion of his pension, but he never received the entire pension he was due.

When Edesapa was released from jail, his back was still badly injured. He had not been properly treated, and, as a result, he was stooped over and could not straighten up. A doctor who knew Edesapa and knew of his outstanding record as an educator heard about his condition. The doctor contacted Edesapa and volunteered to operate and correct this problem for no charge. Edesapa agreed. After the operation and rehabilitation, he was able to walk upright again.

Edesanya continued her search for her other son, Emre. She had learned from Marci that they had been fighting in the area of the King's Palace on the Buda side of the city. Marci was with the veterinary school brigade, and Emre had been with the engineering school brigade from the university. During the fighting, the two brigades were assigned different sections of Budapest to defend; thus, my brothers were separated. Marci never saw his twin brother again. Edesanya searched all of Budapest, but she was unable to locate Emre or to learn anything about him. She refused to believe that he was dead. Finally, she assumed that he was taken as a prisoner of war to Russia. Later, she assumed that there was either a mix-up in his release papers or he had married and was unable to contact his family. She adamantly refused to even think that he was dead.

At one time, Edesapa wrote that he had received a letter from a Swiss organization that offered financial aid to families whose children were killed in the war. This clearly implied that this Swiss organization had information to indicate that Emre was dead. At first, even Edesapa would not accept that Emre could be dead. He did tell Edesanya about the letter, but he did not tell her that they presumed him to be dead. She was so sure that eventually he would come back. She would have been devastated to learn that Emre was dead. The Swiss organization felt that families whose sons were the main financial providers in the home and were killed in the war needed financial support. Edesapa, at first, would not think of accepting any money. Finally, however, he decided to accept the offer because my parents were desperately short of money.

Later, another letter came to Edesapa that told of a mass grave in Budapest where many soldiers were buried. The letter stated that their son was thought to be in that grave. Edesapa and Marci went to the grave, but they could not recognize Emre's body among the many badly decomposed bodies. A person later told them that he had witnessed Emre's death and that he had been shot in the head. Marci and Edesapa did not have this information at the time they went to the mass grave. Had they known, they might have been able to identify him. My family never learned the truth about what happened to Emre, and Edesanya always continued to believe that he was alive.

In one letter, Edesanya specifically stated that she felt that if Julius returned to Hungary, he would be in immediate danger. She wrote about a woman who had been arrested for ignoring the blackout laws. After this woman was released from jail, she had threatened retaliation against Julius because she held Julius responsible for her arrest.

Julius had told me about this woman. He had been on patrol in our neighborhood just before he left to come to Kisra-kos for Christmas in 1944. One evening he noticed a woman, who lived in a house nearby, was opening and closing the doors several times each night with the light on in the house clearly after the blackout signal had been sounded. The law required that anyone who had a light on in the house must keep all doors and shutters closed. If for any reason someone needed to open a door, he must first turn out the lights. Without lights the aircraft would have a more difficult time finding the city and reaching their desired bombing targets. This woman opened her door repeatedly each evening. It was Julius's job to advise her that she was breaking the law. He went to her house and explained to her that opening the door with the light on was illegal. He went on to explain to her why she should not do this and that she could direct aircraft to the city and endanger everyone. Whether she was doing this on purpose as a signal to the aircraft or not, Julius did not know, but he did know his job and the law, and she was disobeying it. Julius told me that he never reported the incident or his discussion with this woman to the authorities; he had merely warned her.

Edesanya explained in her letter that the woman was Jewish. Someone reported her illegal activity, and she was arrested and taken to jail. Julius was confident that somebody else saw the same activity by the woman and reported her. She just assumed it was he because he had approached her and warned her. After the Russians took over Budapest, the woman was released. Because the woman thought that Julius was responsible for her being placed in jail, she swore that she would get even with him if he ever returned to Budapest. She said that she was well connected in the communist party, and she would tell the communists that Julius was a Nazi. She was confident she could say and do whatever was necessary to have Julius arrested. Edesanya wrote that people with the right connections could make any type of false allegations and create a nightmare for their enemies that might be very difficult to resolve. This had already happened with my father.

In another letter, Edesanya wrote about the squatter woman in their house. By law they could not evict this person. She was a communist, and after my family moved back into the main floor of the house, the woman would spy on them and report to the government anything she felt was not consistent with the communist party beliefs. Edesanya wrote that she constantly listened in on their conversations and made it a point to see who visited my parents. Although the house was practically unlivable because of the terrible damage, the woman continued to stay. All attempts to have her evicted failed.

My parents were reluctant to rebuild and repair the house. They were concerned that if the house looked too good, the communists would take it over and have them evicted. It was a fairly common practice that if a member in good standing of the communist party liked a house, he would notify the communist authorities that he wanted the house. If the acquiring party were awarded the house, the homeowners would be told early one morning to gather what belongings they could carry with them and vacate the house. Most then moved out into the country to live with another family in a village. The communists selected the family with whom they would live, and the family in the country had to accept the Budapest family. Although they did not want to share their home with complete strangers, they were required to make room for the city family. As incredible as it was, my parents felt the only reason they were able to keep their house was because their house had been bombed; consequently, they refused to repair it. The house was located in Buda, the elegant part of Budapest. The communists were taking many homes in the area, but they did not want a house in such disrepair. As ironic as it was, my parents were lucky that their house had been bombed.

The letters were filled with stories of struggles and hard-ships my family was experiencing back in Budapest. The letters spoke of shortages of money and food. Life was far different than before the war. All winter I had hoped that the situation in Hungary would be better and that we could return to the good life we had enjoyed before the war. None of the letters we received from Hungary gave us any encouragement that the situation would improve in the near future.

Nonetheless, I wrote my parents and told them about the miserable living conditions in Obertraun. I told them how difficult the winter had been in the small, crowded, damp house, how homesick I was, and how much I wanted to return to Hungary. I told them how we were struggling to survive and how much I missed them. Until April 1944, when Julius moved the children and me to Kisrakos, I had never been away from my family. Although the bombings were already taking place in Budapest when I was in Kisrakos, even then, I always felt I was only a half-day train ride away from my family. I was not at all prepared for being away from my family for such a long time. I wanted so badly to go back to Hungary that after receiving the first few letters, I felt that conditions there could not possibly be any worse than where we were. I wanted my parents to understand clearly how badly I wanted to come home.

Edesanya responded to my letters by telling us not even to think about coming back because of the bad situation in Hungary. She wrote that all of the teachers were being required to pledge their allegiance to communism; if we returned, Julius would be required to do the same. She knew as well as I did that Julius would never swear that he supported and believed in communism. Edesanya further wrote that if Julius did not pledge his allegiance to communism and agree to everything he was told, he would be sent to a labor camp, which would probably be in Siberia, or, even worse, the communists might shoot him right away. Regardless of what would happen if we returned, the children would certainly have to grow up in state-supported, communist-run schools. Edesanya emphasized in her letters that regardless of the hardship and loneliness we were experiencing in Austria, we were safe and, therefore, were much better off in Austria than in Hungary. As much as I hated to accept it, I began to realize Edesanya was right; the best place for us was in Austria. Going back to Hungary under those circumstances was far too risky. Edesanya and I were exceptionally close, and I knew that the letters telling us not to return home were painful for her to write.

To make sure I understood that we were not to return, Edesanya regularly wrote about instances in which families were separated by the communists, and no one really knew why or what happened to them. She always concluded the letters by making absolutely clear that we were not to consider returning to Hungary. In each letter she emphasized: think of the children and their future. They would not have a future in Hungary. Each letter I received from home helped me to deal with my homesickness.

As I thought about the letters and tried to reconcile myself to the fact that I would be unable to return to my family, it occurred to me that another benefit of not returning (though insignificant in comparison with the other reasons) was not really directly addressed in the letters. Everyone knew that Julius and Mamsika did not get along at all. They had a history of subtle, if not direct, confrontations. Because Mamsika felt that life had not treated her fairly, she was very often difficult and seemed to feel a need to make life difficult for others. As a widow, she was left extremely poor and had to work selling vegetables and flowers in the market, barely providing adequate food, clothing and shelter for her and for Edesanya. This experience not only created a harsh demeanor; it fashioned a person accustomed to doing things her way. The sun did not seem to be shining too often when she was around! I always wondered if Edesapa fully understood when he married Edesanya the consequences of having his mother-in-law as part of the package. Over the years, Edesapa had learned simply to ignore his mother-in-law and to avoid confrontations. On the other hand, Julius let Mamsika get under his skin from the very beginning.

The conflicts began soon after Julius and I made our commitment to each other in February 1932. Edesapa attended a Catholic church; Edesanya, Mamsika and I attended a Presbyterian church on the Pest side of the Danube River. Each Sunday Julius began appearing just in time to walk to church with me. As soon as Mamsika would see Julius coming, she would grab my arm, forcing me to walk beside her. Julius would have to walk beside Edesanya. Julius never said anything to Mamsika, but I knew her determination perturbed him. Of course, later, as we planned our engagement, a major confrontation between Julius and Mamsika arose with the dispute over the monthly stipend. Once we got past that incident, we set the announcement of our engagement for December 24, 1939. Julius and I decided we wanted to put the date that we actually made a commitment to each other inside the engagement ring. That date was February 1, 1932. Again, Mamsika voiced her unsolicited opinion! She was very verbal in her opposition to that date being in the ring. She said it was ridiculous and totally false because it was not the official engagement date. My parents finally persuaded Mamsika to calm down about the date, but the comments still irritated Julius.

I was scheduled to graduate from college in June 1940, so Julius and I wanted to plan our wedding as soon after that date as possible. Once again Mamsika voiced her wishes! She made it clear that she wanted our wedding to be held on her namesday, which was August 18. On the Hungarian calendar, each day of the year has a corresponding proper name with it; the date corresponding to an individual's name is referred to as his or her "namesday." Julius clearly did not want Mamsika's namesday as our wedding day, and we both agreed we did not want to wait until August for the wedding anyway. Julius always had loved Edesanya very much; in fact, she had been more of a real mother to Julius than his own mother, especially since his own mother had left the family when Julius was at the Teachers College. Edesanya's namesday was a month earlier on July 22. We decided we would much rather be married on Edesanya's namesday than on Mamsika's, but, we also knew that Edesanya almost always wanted to do what her mother wanted. As we discussed our plans, we knew that by choosing Edesanya's namesday, we would secure the approval of both Edesanya and Edesapa. We told the family that we wanted the wedding on Edesanya's namesday, and before Mamsika could protest, the remainder of the family enthusiastically supported that date. July 22, 1940, became our wedding date.

We were pleased that we had circumvented an altercation over our wedding date, but Mamsika had other ideas! We could not believe it when she informed us that she wanted to go on our honeymoon with us! We had known that her mother had arranged Mamsika's marriage and that there had been no love in the relationship between Mamsika and her husband. However, we were not prepared for her next announcement: she had not had a honeymoon with her husband, and she wanted to join us! I thought Julius was going to explode! Edesanya helped me to convince Mamsika that her going on my honeymoon was not a good idea.

We were married exactly one month after I graduated from college and received my teaching diploma. Even after we were married, Mamsika managed to irritate Julius. When we moved into my parents' home, Mamsika insisted that we sleep in twin beds in the bedroom. Julius immediately pushed the beds together to create one large king-sized bed. That really antagonized Mamsika. She was so accustomed to having her way that she could not believe someone would actually reject her wishes!

The first Christmas after we were married, Julius bought me a very nice black coat with fur on it. He knew I had never had a nice winter coat. In celebration of our first Christmas and the first anniversary of our official engagement, he bought me this lovely coat. Mamsika found out that Julius had bought a coat, so she went out and bought another coat with fur on the inside and waterproof on the outside. It was a very nice coat also. Julius was very upset. I received both coats and was very careful about when I wore the coats not to offend my husband or my grandmother.

Even after our first child arrived, the relationship between Julius and Mamsika did not improve. Mamsika insisted that she should be the one to take Elizabeth home from the hospital after she was born. When Julius learned this, he made arrangements to have Elizabeth released from the hospital in the morning of the planned day instead of the afternoon as Mamsika had been told. When Mamsika arrived at the hospital, she found that everyone already had gone home. Julius wanted to be the one to take his first child home from the hospital, and he made sure that happened without an argument beforehand.

We visited with my parents frequently, and, of course, Mamsika was always there. She could not resist giving us advice on how we could do a better job of raising our children. She cleverly would address those comments toward Julius. He reached the point that he did not want to visit my parents just because Mamsika was there. Anytime Julius and Mamsika were in the same room, everyone could feel the tension.

Mamsika had a way of creating an atmosphere of unhappiness wherever she went, not only with us, but also with almost everyone she was around. She was my grandmother, and I loved her dearly, but I always wished she could have mellowed a little so that I could have enjoyed being around her more.

From the time we left Hungary, Julius never mentioned anything about being glad he was not around Mamsika; however, I was certain that he was pleased that he did not have to confront her frequently. I knew that if we were ever able to return to Budapest, we could not live in the same house with Mamsika. Julius and Mamsika had trouble living in the same city before the war; living in the same house would have been impossible. In that respect, being in Austria was a blessing in disguise for us. I wondered if this was part of God's plan.

The letters from home were clear that even though we struggled to get away from the Russians and encountered many hardships along the way, our journey had not been nearly as difficult as the struggles people in Hungary were facing. Not only were conditions bad there, but also the lives of the people were in constant danger. Once we had escaped from Hungary and moved toward the west, we had not experienced that level of danger.

A year after leaving Hungary, I realized that we could not return again soon to make a home there. Obviously, what I had wanted was not what was best for our family. We needed to make the best of our situation in Austria and look for a place we could call home again. I never had felt that Obertraun would be our long-term home. Although more people were being friendlier toward us, most people, especially those in the government, did not want us to stay. Our future was unclear, but our strength came from our faith in God to continue to provide for our family and our needs.

CHAPTER 10
HE LEADETH ME IN THE PATHS OF RIGHTEOUSNESS

Once we realized that returning to Hungary was no longer an option, we began to consider where we might go to establish a new home for ourselves. We knew that after we registered with the Americans and after they declared us displaced persons, they would do everything they could to place us in a country that was accepting immigrants. Austria was not accepting applications for permanent residence; the country already was overcrowded and heavily burdened with refugees. As a result, the Americans were working with the Austrians to find homes for all of the refugees in Austria. They were giving our names to various countries that had indicated an interest in accepting refugees. They also gave our names to organizations like the Church World Services, which was a Protestant organization that was helping to place refugees or displaced families in accepting countries. Using a particular skill that was needed in the country was an eligibility requirement, and most countries were accepting immigration applications for single people or for married people with few or no children. Opportunities for immigration of families with three or more children were slim. We were told that requirements for immigration might be relaxed, creating more opportunities after the countries assimilated their soldiers and transitioned to a peacetime economy. Most countries did not want refugees to take jobs that they needed for their own citizens. In addition, fearing that large families would be a burden on their country during a time when they were trying to reestablish a peacetime economy, many countries did not want large families.

We knew we had to be patient and continue doing the best we could with what we had. Following the same philosophy that Julius had expressed in tempering my hope to return to Hungary, we decided merely to make it through the summer and hopefully something would open by fall.

After a year in Obertraun, we were still struggling to meet our basic needs. The house wasn't much, but it provided enough shelter for us to make it through the long, cold winter. Food was still scarce and very expensive. I found myself being very creative to provide the nourishment my growing family needed and, at the same time, to offer a bit of variety in what I could prepare for them. After Julius became a state employee, we received ration cards for meat. Because meat was very expensive, we seldom bought it. We did the best we could to get the most nourishment for the least amount of money.

The butcher slaughtered and butchered his own cattle, and he let the blood set and coagulate into a gelatin or paste-like substance. He would place the blood in a dish that he could sell without charging it against the ration card; therefore, anybody could buy blood. Because it was cheap and provided good nourishment, I went to the butcher every Friday and bought some blood. I used the blood in some of the foods I prepared. For example, after mixing some rice in the blood and cooking the mixture, I would add a little spice to the dish. This mixture turned out to be a palatable meal, especially if we ignored the smell. We had this dish frequently on Saturdays or Sundays.

The ration card determined what we could eat, when we could eat it, and how much of a certain food we could have. For example, the card allowed only one egg per person per month. Even though the Kieningers had chickens, the ration card limited them as well. Because they had chickens, it was easier for them to get the egg, but still they were allowed just one egg per month per person. We actually received more eggs because Julius was sometimes paid with eggs for the extra work he did for the farmers. Even with the extra eggs, we did not have enough to make cakes. We could get soy meal or soybeans that provided some of the same nutritional value as the eggs, but the soybeans were not quite as good as eggs for baking. At one point, I tried to make a cake with the soybeans; it turned out to be big disappointment. I later tried using the soy meal to bake biscuits and rolls, and the results were much better. We did not need a ration card for lard or oil.

Because I did not have enough eggs to make cakes, I created my own desserts, especially on Sundays. I would take a loaf of bread, like French bread, slice it, and then soak the bread in milk. We always had enough skim milk, which we bought from the Kieningers. The skim milk was not counted against the ration card, and we used it to supplement the whole milk that we bought with the ration card. We could buy as much butter as we needed. I melted some butter in the frying pan and put the bread on the hot butter and browned it a little. I then put a little sugar on it, and the result became a dessert. This was similar to French toast. Although it was still bread, it made a very good dessert, which we had almost every Sunday.

Julius sought every opportunity to make extra money. He learned that a French company came to Obertraun each spring and bought fresh snails that were plentiful on the meadows around Obertraun in the spring. Early on the spring mornings, snails would come out onto the grass wet with dew. The French loved to eat the snails. The company had a representative at the same location early each morning, and they paid a nice price for the fresh snails. Each morning before Julius went to work in the forest, he would gather snails from the meadows or lower part of the mountains, take them into Obertraun, and sell them to the French company. We set aside the little extra money he made during snail-collecting season so that we could buy a few items we needed for the house.

The Traun River was famous for its trout. Julius liked to eat fish very much, but we could not afford to buy the trout at the market, and to fish for trout in the Traun was not feasible for us either. In order to fish in the Traun River, one had to purchase a license from the fish warden. Even after purchasing a license, when one wanted to fish, the fish warden had to accompany one. Fishing in the Traun River was considered sport, and the fishermen were not allowed to keep their catch. All fish caught either were thrown back or given to the fish warden. If the fish were given to the warden, the fishermen could buy back the fish from the warden for a designated price that was somewhat lower than the market price. Julius did not have any money for a license, nor did he have any money to purchase the fish if he were to catch any.

One morning while Julius was out collecting snails in the spring, he noticed someone fishing alone in the Traun River. He approached the man and introduced himself. The man was the son of the fish warden. He and Julius visited for a few minutes and became acquainted with each other. The son confided in Julius that he did not have a fishing license, and, furthermore, he intended to keep his own catch. The man said his father did not give him any special privileges regarding fishing in the Traun. The father treated his son just like anybody else who wanted to fish. The son told Julius that his father did not get up early in the morning, and that it was always safe to fish at that time.

Julius and the fish warden's son became good friends. He invited Julius to join him fishing in the early mornings. Julius and the fish warden's son would meet several mornings a week, especially in the summertime when it became light very early. The son would take Julius to the best place to catch trout. Julius did not have any fancy equipment. He only had a stick, string, hook and bait, but with this he caught some very nice trout. If the son thought for any reason his father might be out early in the morning, he did not show up. Julius knew that if the son did not show, it was not safe to fish. They never were caught. The fish provided us with some very nice additional food that we would not have otherwise had. We really enjoyed eating the wonderful trout.

Maria Kieninger became Mrs. Perstl the summer after we arrived in Obertraun. Maria did not move out of her father's house; instead, her new husband, Alois Perstl, moved in. Mr. Kieninger continued to live in the house and was still the respected elder. Shortly after Maria and Alois Perstl married, Maria gave birth to a little boy.

Maria and I became very good friends. We always helped each other in every way we could. I would shop for all the groceries for our families, the Kieningers and Perstls. I also would go to the village office to pick up the ration cards for all of us. This allowed Maria to do things she needed to do at home, especially caring for a very young child. For this assistance, Maria frequently gave me potatoes and other vegetables, apples or whatever extra they had from the small garden to share with our family.

Apples grew very well in the valley, and many farmers, including the Kieningers, had apple trees. In the fall, Julius often was paid for his extra work with apples. Every house had two or three apple trees, and the farmers would harvest the apples in the fall before the first freeze and put them in their basements with newspaper in between each apple. This preserved the apples, so they were available all winter.

In the early summer of 1946, my monthly periods became irregular. This had been happening since we had left Hungary, and I suspected the cause was a combination of stress and not eating a balanced diet. I had been so intent on Julius and the children receiving proper nourishment that I sometimes would not eat properly. When this happened, I would miss an occasional period. This time I had missed three periods in a row. This had not happened before, so I went to the doctor in Hallstatt. Dr. Ballick, a young Austrian doctor who had gone into the military service right out of medical school, had just recently opened his private practice in Hallstatt. He had never treated women before because all of his practice had been treating men in the military.

After examining me, he told me I was pregnant. I was very surprised. Julius and I had been very careful. We did not have room for and could not afford to have another child. Our situation was difficult enough with three children, so we had been very diligent to avoid having another child at the time. But since the doctor said I was pregnant, I assumed that I must be pregnant. He said I should give birth in the first part of February 1947. He put my condition in writing so that I could receive some extra food ration cards.

When February arrived, I had gained some weight, but I did not feel I was as heavy as when I had been pregnant with each of the other children. Since my diet and eating habits had been completely different than they had been in Hungary, even with the additional ration cards, I did not think too much about my size. This entire pregnancy felt considerably different than the other three. Finally, in mid-February, I returned to the doctor and told him that I was almost two weeks past my due date of early February, and that I did not feel I was going to deliver soon. I thought that there must be something wrong with me or with the baby. He examined me again and told me to go to the Bad Ischl Hospital for further tests. Bad Ischl was the closest large city, about thirty kilometers from Obertraun and Hallstatt. When I arrived at the hospital, I explained why I was there, and the doctor examined me. After the exam the doctor smiled and said, "You are very healthy, and the baby is very healthy. The only problem is you are only six months pregnant and not nine months pregnant." As it turned out, I had not been pregnant at the time I went to see Dr. Ballick. Once Julius and I had learned that I was supposedly pregnant, we had stopped taking the careful precautions. It was only afterwards that I became pregnant.

Dr. Ballick, who had not had any experience in treating women, was very embarrassed. Even though he examined me, he did not know what to look for. Obviously, he received a quick education and probably did not make the same mistake again!

Finally, on May 28, I began to feel labor pains in the afternoon. Julius was still working up on the mountain, and I had no way of reaching him to tell him I was beginning labor. I had to hope that I would not have the baby before he arrived home. About seven o'clock in the evening, he finally arrived home. Even though I was in labor, I had prepared a meal for him. I could not eat, but the rest of the family ate. After supper Julius went to the neighbor, who had a phone, to call an ambulance to take me to the hospital. The ambulance had to come from Bad Ischl, which was almost an hour away on a very winding road.

In the meantime, Julius, who hated to wash the dishes, asked me if I would wash the dishes before I went to the hospital. While the ambulance was coming, although I was in much pain, I washed the dishes. I had been in labor since early afternoon. Finally, when the ambulance came, I was in much pain. Julius stayed home with the children, and I immediately but slowly entered the ambulance to begin the long winding trip back to the hospital. The paramedic in the ambulance was very nice and tried to comfort me on the way to the hospital. Before we arrived, I realized that the baby was ready to come. I knew that if I started to push, the baby would not be far behind. I asked the paramedic if he could deliver a baby. He said he had never delivered one, but he thought he could if he needed to. He encouraged me not to push, and I tried desperately not to do so, but I knew that once the baby decided it was time to come, the baby would come.

By the time we arrived at the hospital, I was ready to deliver. They placed me in a wheelchair and literally ran from the ambulance straight to the delivery room. In the delivery room, the doctors and all the nurses were preparing to deliver another baby, but when they saw my condition, they immediately came to me. I delivered almost immediately. I had forgotten to change clothes before I left home. I still had on my cooking apron! They did not even have time to remove my shoes! The baby boy, Zoltan, was born just as the new day began on May 29, 1947.

After ten days in the hospital, I returned home. When I arrived, every cooking dish we had was dirty. While I was in the hospital, Julius cooked and cared for the children, but washing dishes was not his thing!

After Zoltan was born, Julius had to build a new baby buggy to replace the one that Helen had used—the one stolen as we fled Hungary. This new buggy was a work of art. The buggy had four hand-carved wooden wheels, and the axles had springs on them to give the buggy a smooth ride. It also had a plastic window on each side and a retractable sunscreen on the top. We made room in the already crowded small house for the baby buggy. Zoltan now had a place to sleep.

As Zoltan grew, he became an extremely active young boy. He seemed to have a way of getting into anything and everything. Sometimes, I wished that he would just sit still for a few minutes. We tried to watch him continuously so that he would not get into anything or hurt himself. Even before he began to walk, we would sit him in a tub to keep track of him. Although he could not walk, he could crawl. One day we left him sitting in the tub in the yard for just a few minutes, and when we returned to get him, he was not there. Where was he? What happened? How did he crawl out? We finally located him. The next time we put him in the tub, we walked away and watched him carefully. He had learned that if he shook the tub from one side to the other, the tub would turn over and he could crawl out.

Austria, like other countries in the region, was converting its currency to a new postwar currency. The government announced that during a specified period of time, people would be allowed to exchange their old war money for new postwar money. The first set amount per family member was an equal exchange, and the rest was at a fifty percent unit rate. Both Mr. Binder and Mr. Kieninger had a great deal of old money, and both men asked Julius to exchange their money. Since Julius had very little of his own money, he could take their money and exchange the amount allowed by law for our family of six, thus helping our friends to retain as much as possible. Because Mr. Kieninger had been so kind to us in so many ways, Julius decided to help him. Since their family had only three members, using the six members of our family helped Mr. Kieninger save quite a sum of money. We were happy to be able to do something to help the Kieningers in this way. Mr. Binder understood why we wanted to help Mr. Kieninger, and he did not hold this against us.

At about this same time, the Austrian government ordered that all foreign currency brought into Austria be destroyed. Julius burned the three thousand Hungarian pengos he had brought with him from Hungary to comply with the government order. He did not want to burn money, but he took the order seriously and destroyed the money. We could not have used it for anything anyway. If the officials had discovered that we had foreign money, we would have been in trouble.

We became more and more cramped in our small one-room house. The house was so damp that shoes placed under the bed would grow mildew. Dr. Ballick had expressed some concern about our living in this house, because the damp conditions were an invitation for diseases and sickness. A number of cracks appeared where the mortar had fallen from between the stones in the house. If it was light outside and dark inside, one could see out through the cracks in the wall. The house was not structurally weak; it just created an environment for disease. Finding another place, however, seemed out of the question.

The Burgermeister never allowed us to have clothing ration cards. We learned late in our stay in Austria that we had been entitled to the ration cards once Julius began working for the forest service. But because we did not have the required ration cards, we were not allowed to buy the clothing we needed, even though we were eager and willing to buy clothes. As a result, having adequate clothes, especially shoes, was always one of our biggest needs.

Julius and I always walked to various places in the area. Because we walked everywhere, we quickly wore out the soles of our shoes. If we could not get any good shoes, we had to repair the ones we had. To repair the shoes, we would get some cardboard, cut it out, and stick it in the shoe for a new sole. As soon as that cardboard wore out, which was usually very quickly, we would find another piece of cardboard.

Because we could not buy clothes, we often had to rely on others for help. For example, when Mr. Kieninger's older daughter died, the family gave me some of her clothes and shoes. Until then I had no shoes I could wear that fit me. I had long before worn out my shoes I had brought from Hungary, and I had been wearing the mismatched boots I had retrieved from the warehouse. The clothes Mr. Kieninger gave me were good, usable clothes, but they were far too large, very plain and not attractive at all. Nonetheless, I appreciated just having the additional clothes, and I wore them anyway.

We had been living in Obertraun for about two and a half years when we received a very pleasant surprise. A priest in Bad Ischl wrote, asking us to come to see him; he said he had something for us. I could not imagine why we would receive a letter from a priest wanting us to come to his house because we were not Catholic. Out of curiosity, we went to Bad Ischl to meet the priest. He, too, was a Hungarian refugee, and he had been a very good friend of my uncle. Also, he was the priest who had baptized my brothers. By chance the priest had heard our name and had made a connection. Somehow, he had learned the children's ages and had gathered a large box of boys' clothes. By this time, young Julius had grown out of all of his clothes, and we needed clothes badly. The priest gave us pants, shirts, shoes, hats, jackets—everything that we needed and did not have. He only had clothes for boys, none for girls. He also had something for me: a pair of women's high-top shoes. They were a little bit small and not comfortable on my feet at all. But they were shoes, and I always needed shoes. I knew that after time I would become accustomed to wearing them.

As we were leaving, I asked the priest, "You know that we are not Catholic; why are you so nice to us, and why do you give us all of these clothes?"

He replied, "Are you a Christian?"

I answered, "Yes, I am."

The priest replied, "Everybody who believes in God and in Jesus Christ is my brother or sister. Now, go in peace."

It was so interesting to me that the same man who had baptized my brothers would be in Bad Ischl at this very time. It also was interesting that he would contact us at a time when we were in desperate need of clothing. Just this gesture of generosity made me feel so very good. It was all an amazing thing. I felt that clearly this was the work of God.

Although the boys had plenty of clothing now, we were still in dire need of clothing for the girls to wear. Shortly after the visit with the priest, I met a woman from Vienna; every summer she came to stay with the Perstls. The area where we lived was a popular vacation spot for many people from the larger cities. I visited with the woman often, and we became friends. In conversations with her, I mentioned that we did not have any ration cards for clothing, and that we were running out of clothing, especially for the girls. I told the woman about our experience with the priest and his giving us clothes for the boys. I said jokingly to her that I needed to find another priest who had a bag full of girls' clothes.

The woman thought for a moment and said that maybe she could help us. She had a friend in Vienna who was an excellent seamstress. She always had some scrap material left over from clothing she made. She said that when she returned to Vienna, she would talk to this woman and ask her if she would be willing to use the leftover scrap material to make the children some clothes. Just before she returned to Vienna, the woman took measurements of the girls, including shoe sizes.

A few weeks later, we received a large package in the mail. The seamstress in Vienna had made the most gorgeous and wonderful clothes for the girls. Very artistically put together using the scrap fabrics, the clothes looked much like quilts. These clothes were a treasure. The woman also sent socks, shoes, coats—everything that the girls would need. I was so grateful for her generosity. Now everybody had good clothes. Once again, at a time when we most needed help, the Lord worked through people to provide for our needs.

In addition to my normal chores of taking care of the children and our one-room home, I worked around the area to earn extra money. I found that if I stayed very busy, I did not think as much about our situation and my desire to find a permanent home. I knew that we could use the extra money I earned from doing whatever work I could get. I did not tell Julius I was working for other people because he clearly would not have approved. One of the jobs I did was to wash clothes for the Perstls when Maria did not have the time to do her own laundry. I did not do the washing every week for her, but fairly often I helped her. I also ironed for the Perstls.

I also took a job knitting for a store in Bad Aussie, a nearby village. The Austrians wore long knee socks with their lederhosen. Many people did not know how to knit socks, especially the heel, which required intricate and careful expertise. I had learned to knit in school and had become very skillful; as a result, I easily could knit the socks, even the heels. When I learned that a business in Bad Aussie was looking for someone who would take home orders for knitting socks for a set price per pair of socks, I knew this would be perfect for me. The business would take the orders and give me the knitting yarn for the work.

The train connection between Obertraun and Bad Aussie was quite good. I would take the train to Bad Aussie, and the store owner usually would give me the material for three or four pairs of socks. Of course, they always wanted the work done yesterday! I would take the work home and do the work as fast as I could. When I finished, I would take the socks back to the business on the next train. Often, the people who placed the orders did not want just plain knitting but instead wanted unusual, fancy patterns. I would make whatever patterns the business requested. The business owner would give me a description of the patterns that the customers wanted, and I would then knit those patterns. The knitting and clothes washing provided us with a little extra money. For the knitting, I was paid in currency, but the clothes washing was done on a barter basis.

I always did the extra work during the day when Julius was not around. I was careful not to make any mention of my working when Julius was around because he clearly would not have wanted me to leave the children alone for any length of time. Maria was always close by in case the children needed an adult. The children did not seem to mind my being gone for the short time it took to get from our house to Bad Aussie and back. The train trip was only about fifteen minutes each way, so I usually was gone for less than an hour each time. Each time I made the trip, I dropped off completed work and picked up new work at the same time.

Since Julius never actually had told me not to work, I felt that I really was not doing anything wrong! I was just very busy and always failed to mention to him that I was working for someone else! On the other hand, if Julius specifically had forbidden me to work, then I would not have worked. Consequently, I was very quiet about doing the extra jobs, and the subject never came up! The Perstls helped to keep my secret too.

Maria knew that Julius would not allow me to work if he learned about it.

From time to time while working for the Bad Aussie shop making the stockings, I would have some yarn left over from the amount given to me for the job. The store owner said I could keep whatever yarn was not used to make the stockings or other items. Usually, there was not very much yarn left over, but what little I had I used to make little caps, socks and sometimes a small sweater that the girls could wear. This helped us a little with the shortage of clothing.

Mr. Kieninger observed that I was doing the knitting using the light from the kerosene lantern we had in the house. The kerosene lantern was all we had. It provided enough light for most things, but it really did not give enough light for the close needlework I was doing. Mr. Kieninger felt the kerosene lantern was very inadequate, and he told me that we needed electricity in the house. This was out of the question. We certainly could not get electricity through the electric company because it was far too expensive. Mr. Kieninger offered to run a wire from his house to our house so that we could see better. He had a friend who was an electrician who knew how to run a wire from his house to ours. About two years after we arrived in Obertraun, because of Mr. Kieninger's kindness and generosity, we finally got electricity.

Of course, the electricity that we used appeared on the bill sent to the Kieningers, but they never charged us for it. We offered to pay, but they insisted that we accept the electricity without charge. They told us that because we were helping them with so many chores, this was something they could do for us. I gladly helped the Perstls and Kieningers any way I could with various chores, and I was not expecting any money in exchange, and the Kieningers did not expect money for the electricity. It all evened out over time. They were very good neighbors and friends, and we always worked to help each other.

Soon after Mr. Kieninger had the electricity installed, I began thinking about how fortunate we had been to find this house at this location. No place in the area was available for us to live in, but for some reason we found this abandoned building within a few meters of the kindest and most generous people we met throughout our stay in Austria. I felt from the time I met Maria that God had guided me to her. My meeting Maria led to my finding this house, and although not much, it provided shelter for us. By having the house so close to the Kieningers and Perstls, we were able to survive much easier than if we had been near almost any other family in the village. Obviously, God not only had His hand in my meeting Maria, but He also had His hand in my finding the house in which we were living. Without that house next to Maria and her family, I shudder to think what we would have done.

As previously mentioned, the Kieningers were very busy with the cows they had, so I frequently went to shop in the village for them. The stores did not provide sacks to carry the groceries purchased, so I took two satchels with me. I carried Maria's groceries home from the store in one of the satchels. I also picked up Maria's ration cards from the city hall. These tasks were easy for me to do because I needed to do them for my family anyway. In exchange, Maria gave me the milk allowed on the ration card, plus as much of the skim milk as I wanted. Maria paid with various items for the washing and ironing, but for my going to get the groceries and the ration card, she always paid with milk.

Julius also helped the Perstls when he could. Mr. Perstl farmed a small tract of land across the road from his house. On this land he grew hay. When it was time to cut and dry the hay, Julius helped Mr. Perstl with the work. The hay was all cut by hand. As a result, it was a slow process, but when it was haying time, the work needed to be completed in a very short period of time, and Mr. Perstl needed all the help he could find.

After two long years, we finally saved enough money to buy two chairs. The chairs were the first major purchase we had made since we left Hungary. Before the purchase of the two chairs, we sat on the two crates, which we had put in the corner. We bought two new chairs to set on the other two sides of the table. Elizabeth and young Julius were so proud of the chairs because up to that day they had stood to eat; there had been no other option. Elizabeth was so excited that when she went to school the next day, she announced to the teacher with a loud voice so that the whole class could hear: "Guess what? We have two chairs!" In a place where two chairs were nothing and people lived in fully furnished houses, everyone laughed, but at the same time, everyone was happy for her. The teacher informed me later about this incident!

Snow always began to fall in Obertraun in late October. Often in May, snow was still on the ground, having lasted throughout the winter. We always walked on an established path. No one cleared the roads, because no one had a car. Only one neighbor, Mr. Schilcher, who lived across the street from us, had a motorized vehicle, a small truck. Very few people had horses either. Most people had bicycles that they rode when there was no snow on the road.

Until we bought the chairs, we could not even consider buying a bicycle, although we wanted one very badly. After about another year, we finally saved enough money to buy a sparkling new bicycle. It took us a long time to save enough money to purchase a one, but we finally had some transportation. Bicycles were relatively expensive for people who did not have much money. Everybody who could afford one owned a bicycle. People who had a bicycle considered it a necessity and not a toy. Once people bought a bicycle, they kept it, so there were never any used ones available for purchase.

Elizabeth and young Julius learned how to ride the bicycle rather quickly. I had not had a bicycle as a child, so I did not know how to ride one. In Budapest, public transportation had been so good and reliable that no one needed a bicycle. I did not want to walk everywhere, so I decided to learn to ride the bicycle. I arose very early in the morning, as soon as there was daylight, and I practiced on the bicycle. I went to a place where nobody could see me practicing. A short stretch of road nearby made the perfect spot because it had very little traffic early in the morning. The road was flat, so it was easier to learn there than on some of the others. I had seen other people learning to ride bicycles on this section of road. I was so proud when I could stay on for a good ride. Once I became comfortable on the bicycle, I rode it into town. When there was snow or ice on the road, I would not risk riding because I knew I would almost surely fall. Only a few people knew how to ride a bicycle on the snow.

After we had electricity in the house, it was a really big event when we saved enough money to be able to buy a radio. This was the first luxury we had bought since coming to Obertraun. Once we bought the radio, we listened to it at every opportunity.

After a while, we did establish some routine, and we became somewhat more accustomed to the conditions under which we were living. Actually, we had many wonderful times amidst the hardships in Obertraun. In spite of the really rough times, we always found joy in our lives and always had something to laugh about. This was especially true at Christmas. Julius and I made sure that Christmas was special for the children.

We maintained our Hungarian Christmas traditions while in Obertraun. We continued having the children put out their shoes on the windowsill on December 5, in hopes that St. Nicholas would put a treat in the shoe and that the Krampusz would stay away. On Christmas Eve, we sent the children to the neighbor's house for a long visit in the late afternoon. While the children were visiting, the Christmas Angel would visit our house and deliver a fully decorated Christmas tree, along with gifts for the children. The tree ornaments were mostly decorations that we made. I always baked cookies to hang on the Christmas tree, as Julius's grandmother and I had done our last Christmas in Kisrakos. We were able to buy a few pieces of candy wrapped in foil, and we tied the candy together with string and hung it over the branches of the Christmas tree. When the children returned to the house after dark, they would be surprised to find that the Christmas Angel had visited and delivered gifts and a Christmas tree with lighted candles symbolizing the beginning of the Christmas season. The Christmas presents usually consisted of one item for each child, and the gift was usually something that we had made. I made the cutest little dolls from rags. Julius loved to carve, and he would carve small items like a cane or little car with wheels or similar toys. One Christmas Julius made a beautiful sled; another Christmas he hand-carved a pair of snow skis. The children always had something for Christmas, and it was always made with love. We all loved to sing together, and over time we taught the children not only Hungarian Christmas songs but German Christmas songs as well.

Typically, we spoke only Hungarian in the house. Since very few young children lived close by, young Julius usually played by himself or with Elizabeth. For this reason, he had very little exposure to the German language, and he did not speak much German when he began the first grade. Even Elizabeth had a limited knowledge of German when she started school at six years old. The school she attended in Obertraun was about a fifteen-minute walk from the house. Other children in the neighborhood also walked to school, so they enjoyed themselves on their strolls to the school. When it came time for young Julius to begin first grade, Elizabeth, being the protective big sister, was going to help him. They both went to school together, and Elizabeth took him to his class. After the break period at school, young Julius was nowhere to be found. The teacher wondered where he was and became quite anxious and concerned about what had happened to him. She got on her bicycle and went down the road looking for him. Very quickly she saw him with his knapsack, walking down the road heading toward home. She stopped him and asked him what he was doing here. Young Julius told her that she had told him to go home. He had misunderstood something she said in German, and he thought he was to go home. It did not matter to him that no one else was going home. He understood that he should go, so he was on his way!

The school in Obertraun that Elizabeth and young Julius attended was very small at the time, with only two teachers and two classrooms. Grades one through four were together and grades five through eight were also together. With this arrangement, the lower-grade children could hear what the upper-grade children were learning; thus, the first-graders were exposed to the fourth-grade knowledge. This paid off for many students. This allowed those children who could excel to advance faster and pick up additional knowledge.

A very cute little girl lived across the street and down the road from our house. Everybody called this little girl the "French girl." They called her this because her father was a French soldier who had been stationed in Obertraun during part of the war. While her husband was away at war, a young neighbor woman had an affair with the French soldier; the result of the affair was this cute little girl.

One day as I was looking out toward the road, I saw a little somebody pulling another little somebody on the sled that Julius had made the children for Christmas. As I looked closer, I saw young Julius pulling the little French girl to her home. She was a very attractive little girl, and young Julius had decided he wanted to court her. It was quite a sight to see this little boy pulling this adorable little girl across the beautiful winter snow scene.

Although we were far from home and missed Hungary terribly, we had some wonderful times in Obertraun in spite of our hardships. We made some very dear friends, and we were able to establish a somewhat normal life for our children, though it was very meager. It certainly did not compare to what we had planned for our family during those years we were making plans to become engaged and to be married. But the Lord had led us to this place. He had allowed us to care for ourselves. He had provided for us, and He had protected us.

One of our biggest disappointments in Obertraun was that we did not find a church in which we felt we could worship regularly. Obertraun had two churches: a Lutheran church and a Catholic church. Both were very small. The Lutheran church was closer to the Presbyterian religion than the Catholic church. I went to the Lutheran church once, and someone told me that I had sat in someone else's place. I moved to another pew only to discover that this pew also belonged to someone else. After the third time, I decided we were probably not welcome, but I stayed for the service anyway. I felt uncomfortable during the entire service, knowing that I probably was still sitting in someone else's place. I did not want to impose on anyone. I went to that church only one other time, and that was when we had Zoltan baptized. But our faith in God remained strong, even though we could not find a church home.

CHAPTER 11
THOU ART WITH ME

In the summer of 1948, the news for which we had been waiting so long finally arrived. The Australian Consulate contacted us about immigrating to Australia. We had finally received some good news, and we were so excited. We had reconciled ourselves to the fact that we could not return to Hungary. Our hopes and prayers had been that we could immigrate to a country where we might begin a new life for our family. Australia was one of the places we were hoping would accept us. Some refugees went to South America, and we would have accepted that option, but it was not as good as Australia. Like so many other refugees, our first choice was actually America, but Australia was our second choice. Both were English-speaking countries, and we had decided we much preferred to learn English rather than Spanish or some other language.

We immediately contacted the Australian authorities and learned that we qualified for Australia because we had only four children, the maximum number allowed to immigrate into the country with the parents. We could hardly contain our excitement! The authorities provided us with the necessary application and made it clear that they needed workers to relocate to Australia. We immediately began the application process. As we prepared the necessary paperwork, I was so overjoyed just thinking about going to Australia. But just before we were scheduled to return the application to the Australian consulate, I received the most devastating news: I was pregnant with another child. This time I knew the doctor had not made a mistake.

This would be our fifth child, and we were certain that this addition would disqualify us right away. We immediately stopped the application process. I was back where I had been before, stuck in the tiny one-room house to look forward to another harsh Austrian winter.

I became very bitter about this pregnancy. I did not want another child at this time. The pregnancy with Zoltan could be blamed on the doctor for misdiagnosing a pregnancy, because it was only after the misdiagnosis that I became pregnant. But this time, I had no one to blame except myself. We finally had received a chance to escape this miserable refugee situation and start a new life. We desperately wanted to establish a permanent home for our family. The birth of this child ruined everything for us because we would have too many children even to be considered. I could not stop blaming myself. I went over and over my situation and could not figure out how I had allowed this pregnancy to happen. I thought we were taking all the necessary precautions to avoid my becoming pregnant. Already we were far too crowded in our house. Now that I was pregnant, we not only had missed out on going to Australia, but, in addition, we were bringing another person into the already cramped, small quarters.

Over the years, we had learned to swallow so much of our pride in order just to exist. We had learned to deal with one disappointment and hardship after another. Now we would not qualify for meeting the Australian immigration requirements. This was the most severe, depressing disappointment yet. We were trapped in a miserable, hopeless situation, doomed to live a life of meager existence in a country where we really were not wanted. We were struggling to provide for four small children, and now an unplanned, unwanted child was on the way. All the faith I'd had in a God who had been protecting and providing for us was beginning to diminish. Why would He allow us to struggle for so very long only to allow us to come close to rescue and then have the opportunity slip away?

During the entire winter, I was miserable. I was so upset with myself and with the pregnancy that I could hardly function. I could not overcome the disappointment of missing the opportunity to leave Obertraun and being able to have place to call home. Each day seemed more difficult than the one before. I was depressed. I was despondent. Hope had vanished, and I was living in a fog, attempting to complete day-to-day chores necessary for our existence.

Just when I thought things could not be any worse for us, Helen, who was now four years old, suddenly became ill on March 8, 1949 (Zoltan's namesday). This came as a total surprise to us. Helen had experienced no problems since she had fully recovered from the malnutrition in 1945. Even though she was thin and somewhat frail from her earlier sickness, she seemed to be a healthy little girl. We noticed that she was not feeling well when she would not eat a piece of the small namesday cake I had baked for Zoltan. She would not even come to the table. She had become feverish during the day, and she was acting very unusual. That evening she had blood in her urine.

Upon this discovery, we immediately went to Mr. Schilcher's house and called Dr. Ballick, whose office was in Hallstatt.

Mr. Schilcher was the only person in the area who had a telephone, but he did not mind letting the neighbors use his phone in case of emergency.

Dr. Ballick made house calls to the villagers in the area on his motor scooter. He was constantly going between Obertraun and Hallstatt. People rarely went to his office, located in his home. When people became ill or ran a fever, they would call the doctor, and he would come as soon as he could.

Because he had an unusually large number of patients to see, the doctor said that he could not come until late in the evening. He finally arrived about eleven and began examining Helen. He could not specifically determine what was wrong with Helen, but he thought it might be a very serious kidney infection. He said that we needed to get her to a hospital as soon as possible. Dr. Ballick went back to Hallstatt and called for an ambulance from Bad Ischl to pick up Helen and take her to the hospital there.

The ambulance arrived at our house about an hour later, and Julius rode in the ambulance with Helen. Dr. Ballick had planned for her to be taken to the Children's Hospital in Bad Ischl. As they were approaching the Bad Ischl General Hospital, the ambulance attendant suggested they stop at the General Hospital instead. The attendant felt that the General Hospital was a larger, better-equipped hospital than the Children's Hospital. They stopped at the General Hospital; fortunately, the hospital allowed Helen to be admitted and began treating her.

The General Hospital was a community hospital owned by the city of Bad Ischl. Many Catholic nuns served as nurses there. They provided excellent care and were very dedicated to helping in any way they could.

The doctors immediately began to run a series of tests to determine exactly what was wrong with Helen. They said it might take a few days to obtain final results. They assured Julius that Helen would be cared for, and that it was not necessary for him to stay at the hospital. Since he needed to work the following day, Julius took the next available train back to Obertraun.

The next evening as we were preparing for bed around ten in the evening, Dr. Ballick's wife came to the door. She had walked from Hallstatt to Obertraun to tell us that the hospital called her and told her that a family member needed to go to the hospital immediately because Helen was very ill. We were shocked and frightened, thinking that Helen had died or was going to die very soon. We could not take the train to Bad Ischl that late at night because the last train had already run, and the next train was not until the following morning. That might be too late. The only other alternative was to ask our neighbor, Mr. Schilcher, to drive us to the hospital.

Mr. Schilcher was the deliveryman for the area, and we knew him fairly well. He was a very nice man, always willing to help in any way he could. We were careful never to take advantage of the fact that he had the only truck and the only telephone in the area. Julius did not like asking Mr. Schilcher for help, even though he needed it and even though he knew Mr. Schilcher would be willing. Nonetheless, Julius went to Mr. Schilcher's house late that evening to ask if he could take him to Bad Ischl. Mr. Schilcher was already in bed, but after Julius told him the situation, he said he would be glad to take Julius to the hospital.

Mr. Schilcher and Julius began their trip to Bad Ischl. It was still wintertime, and this was a particularly cold night. Mr. Schilcher's truck was old. He was having problems with the oil flow lines, which repeatedly kept freezing because of the cold weather. Mr. Schilcher and Julius had quite a difficult time getting to Bad Ischl. They had to stop two or three times to take out the oil filter and thaw out the line. Julius finally arrived at the hospital early in the morning. He was certain the hospital would tell him that Helen had died.

Julius quickly ran into the hospital and identified himself to the nurse. The nurse told him she was very glad he was there. She said that Helen was, indeed, alive, but that she was a very sick little girl. The nurse feared for Helen's life, and therefore she had called to have him come because she thought it would be terribly sad for a child to die without somebody from the family being there with her. This was not what Julius wanted to hear. He told Mr. Schilcher to return to Obertraun and tell me that Helen was very sick but that she was still alive. Julius remained at the hospital.

The doctors could not determine what was making Helen so sick. The worst symptom was that her red blood cell count was very low. It should have been four and one half million per cubic millimeter, but it dropped below a million to eight hundred thousand per cubic millimeter. Once it went below a million, it stayed there. The doctors could not understand how Helen could still be alive with her red blood cell count so very low. They had run numerous tests, but none revealed conclusive results as to indicate what was attacking the red blood cells.

Our situation became even worse. To complicate matters, Elizabeth, young Julius and Zoltan all became ill with whooping cough. As a result, I could not spend much time at the hospital. I went as often as I could. Being torn between four ill children, three at home and one in the hospital, was almost unbearable. When I was at one place, I felt that I should be at the other. Emotionally and physically, I was exhausted by my responsibilities as a mother, by my depression, and by my guilt for becoming pregnant and causing us to miss our chance to have a better life in Australia.

During one of my visits with Helen, I witnessed a violent argument between two of the doctors treating her. They clearly could not agree on a diagnosis or on a treatment. The doctors then began to question me. They asked what seemed like a thousand questions about Helen's prior medical condition. They asked if Helen had ever had scarlet fever. I said no. One of the doctors disagreed and said she must have had scarlet fever. I told the doctors that the only illness of which we were aware was malnutrition. I told them briefly of the circumstances around the illness. The doctors all seemed to feel that Helen had been ill before and just had not been diagnosed. In their frustration, they were seeking any plausible answer to rationalize their thoughts.

A young doctor strongly argued that the only thing that would help Helen was a blood transfusion. The older doctor was not convinced. At best, he felt a blood transfusion would be experimental. Furthermore, Helen was so sick that in order for the blood transfusion to be successful, the blood would have to be an exact blood type match to Helen's. The doctors had tested Julius's blood, but his blood was not an exact match. He had type "O" blood, which could be given to her, but because it was not a match, the doctors felt it was far too risky. The doctors knew that my blood type was "A+," exactly the same as Helen's, but I was eight months pregnant. The young doctor felt I was perfect for the transfusion and insisted they try a transfusion of my blood to Helen. The older doctor refused. He said medical science had learned many years earlier that it was not safe to take blood from a woman in her last months of pregnancy. The older doctor simply ended the discussion with his vehement and firm refusal to try the transfusion. I had to return home and take care of our sick children there. The doctors' arguments had not helped my mental condition in the least. Adding to my already despondent disposition and guilt for our being unable to go to Australia was the additional guilt for being pregnant and unable to supply blood for Helen, whose very life seemed to depend on a transfusion. Literally, I was only existing, not living, as I went back and forth between the hospital and our home, never knowing as I made the journey each way what would await me when I arrived.

The doctors were clearly struggling to find the proper diagnosis and treatment for Helen. Each day her condition continued to be critical and changed very little. She was not eating, and she slept almost all the time.

Julius stayed at the hospital for a week at Helen's side. Helen did not speak German, so Julius served as interpreter. Because the hospital did not have the equipment to continually check Helen's pulse and did not have enough nurses either, Julius monitored Helen's pulse constantly. When her pulse slowed, he would tell the nurses. The doctors ordered caffeine shots to stimulate Helen's heart when her pulse became very low. This happened fairly regularly to the extent that the nurses said that

Helen would not be alive if it were not for her father at her side, continuously keeping watch over her. As Julius continued his vigil, the nurses became concerned about his health because of his lack of sleep. All the nurses were very kind and so very compassionate. They did all they could, not only for Helen to keep her comfortable, but also for Julius in order for him to be as comfortable as possible. Although the caffeine shots increased Helen's heartbeat and provided some temporary improvement, they did not improve the red blood cell count. The low red blood cell count continued to be the symptom that most disturbed the doctors.

I wanted so badly to go more often and stay longer with Helen in the hospital, and I felt guilty each time I left Helen because I never knew if I would ever see her alive again. On the other hand, I had three very sick children at home, and I knew they needed me, and I had a responsibility toward them. I could not leave my children at home for long periods of time. When I was in the hospital, I always worried about the children at home. When I was at home, I always worried about Helen and her struggle for life in the hospital. The nights were especially difficult for me. Each night I went to bed with a chorus of coughs serenading me; finally, I would fall asleep. My thoughts and emotions ran rampant. As irrational as it seems, I thought perhaps my pregnancy somehow contributed to everyone's illness. I simply could not understand why everything was happening the way it was. I prayed often during this time, but I was receiving no answers to my prayers. Perhaps my prayers were not leaving the stone house. Perhaps my anger, my depression and my guilt all prevented my being worthy of God hearing my prayers. I struggled more with my faith during this period than at any other time in my life. The one thing for which I was always thankful was that Julius had decided to take off from his work to stay with Helen at the hospital. Although I still felt guilty that I, her mother, was not at her side, I was relieved that at least her father was with her.

Helen had been in the hospital almost a week when I made one of my visits to see her. This particular day she was fairly alert. When I walked in the door, she smiled and said she was glad to see me. We had a very nice but short visit because, as usual, I had to hurry home to her brothers and sister. As I left the hospital, I was somewhat optimistic because Helen did seem a bit better, and we had enjoyed a brief conversation. Hurriedly, I walked toward the Bad Ischl train station, which was about a ten-minute walk from the hospital. As I was waiting to cross a very busy street, a little girl about nine or ten years old reached up and grabbed my hand for help in getting across the street. I did not say anything to the girl, and the girl did not say anything to me. The cars, trucks, motorcycles and bicycles on the road would not yield to the pedestrians. Finally, a small opening occurred in the traffic, allowing me to safely cross the street with the little girl holding my hand. Once safely across the street, the little girl simply let go of my hand and walked on her way. I thought how trusting this little girl was to know that I would guide her safely across the street. She never hesitated to reach for my hand. Words were not necessary; she depended on me to take care of her in a dangerous situation.

The next evening as I was at home with the children, I heard a knock at the door. It was Mr. Schilcher. Julius was on the phone, and he needed to talk with me. Quickly, Mr. Schilcher and I walked back to his home. Julius told me that Helen was still not responding to any treatment to increase her red blood cell count. Furthermore, she had lost consciousness during the morning, and her condition had worsened during the day; the doctors and nurses did not feel that she would survive until morning. Julius asked me to gather Helen's best clothes and her favorite doll and bring them to the hospital. He said he wanted Helen buried in her finest clothes with her favorite doll. The last train to Bad Ischl had already run that evening, so he told me to take the first train in the morning. He said he did not want to leave Helen's side if she were still alive in the morning because, if she died, he wanted to be with her. But if she died overnight, he would meet me at the train station. I understood the plan clearly: If Julius was at the train station in the morning, Helen would have died during the night. If I did not see him there, I would know that Helen was still alive, and I should hurry to the hospital as quickly as I could.

That night after returning from Mr. Schilcher's house, I sat in the damp, small, one-room house with the three children who had whooping cough, knowing that Helen would likely be dead in the morning. I was totally exhausted and in the depths of depression. I had three sick children in my care; if one child did not cough, another coughed. There was no quiet time. I had already spent another weary day, and the news that Helen was dying was overwhelming. I cried uncontrollably. I began to think that this was God's answer to my prayers. I thought that this was God's way of punishing me for not wanting to be pregnant. I had been so upset about this pregnancy and had told myself over and over that I did not want this child. Now, I was feeling that God was going to take a child from me because of my selfish feelings about the pregnancy and the fact that the pregnancy had caused us to miss the opportunity to go to Australia. During this emotional turmoil, I realized just how much I really did want this child I was carrying and how I could not bear to lose a child.

SURVIVING THROUGH FAITH

This was the worst day of my life. I had been depressed before and I had been frightened before. I recalled how I had felt when we were fleeing Hungary and when we had run out of food in the Enns Valley. The events of this day were far worse than those I had experienced then. I did not know what to do. I had no place to turn. I had no place to run. I did not have another room where I could go and close the door and experience total silence for a moment. I did not even have the comfort of reaching for Julius's hand to give me strength to go on.

Again, as I did every night, I began praying. Perhaps my prayers would escape the walls of the stone house. But this night, my prayers were a bit different. I asked the Lord to forgive me for my selfish feelings and for not wanting another child. I asked the Lord for forgiveness for all of the terrible thoughts I had entertained during the past months about the pregnancy. Then I remembered again what Edesapa had said to me: "Trust in the Lord. In life you can lose everything, but I emphasize to you, never lose your faith. Remember, never lose your faith! Often it is only through faith that people survive." At that very moment, I remembered Edesapa's words as though he were sitting beside me saying them to me. He always emphasized: "The Lord's will be done."

In no way could I accept that it was God's will that Helen die. I began to question Him: "Lord, why are all of these terrible things happening to my family and me? Why do You want Helen? Why? Why? Why?" I could see no way that I could deal with this tragedy; in no way could I survive this tragedy.

Suddenly, and without warning, I remembered the little girl I'd seen in Bad Ischl the previous day. This little girl had not known whose hand she was holding. She simply had trusted that the hand she was holding would safely guide her across the busy road. My mind began to race! Why can't I be like this little girl who just looked in my eyes and knew without saying anything that I would help her cross the road safely? Why can't I trust the Lord in the same way this little girl trusted me? She did not question me. She did not ask if I could guide her safely across the road; she had faith that I would do so. Why, then, should I question the Lord about my situation? I needed to be like this girl. I had been taught that I should have the faith of a child. The little girl had exhibited this to me in a very real way. All I had to do was reach up and hold onto the Lord's hand. He would guide me through this crisis. No doubt, this was the faith about which Edesapa had spoken so many times—the faith to trust in the Lord always and to pray that His will be done. What a simple answer. What a wonderful promise. The Lord was there. He knew my needs. All I had to do was to trust in His will for my life.

Again I prayed, but this time my prayer was more sincere, more genuine and more valid than any I had ever prayed. I prayed to the Lord: "Helen is in Your hands. Your will be done. Thou art with me." And I promised the Lord that I would accept His will, whatever it might be.

Once I completed this prayer, I suddenly felt a calm come over me like I had never felt before. I knew then that all was in the Lord's hands, and that He was taking care of everything. In the midst of the heavy coughing and the noisy breathing of the children, I was now very relaxed. My submission to the Lord was complete; my faith was whole again. I went to sleep immediately. I awoke the next morning with the comfort of knowing that for the first time in months I was at peace with myself. Somehow, I felt that nothing bad had happened overnight. I grabbed the clothing and the doll that Julius had requested, rushed to the Obertraun train station and boarded the train to Bad Ischl.

As we were approaching Bad Ischl, I was confident that Julius would not be at the station because I felt that Helen was still alive. I was certain that my prayers had been answered in a positive way. As the train pulled into the Bad Ischl station, I saw Julius waiting. My heart sank, and I literally became ill. My heart pounded, and I became nauseous. This was not at all what I expected. I was so sure Helen would be alive that I almost did not bring the clothes and doll for her burial. This was the worst feeling I had ever experienced, the feeling of losing a child. But I had made a promise to God the night before. He understood what it was like to lose a child. After all, He had given His Son for us. He knew what was best for Helen, and this was His will for her. As I had promised in my prayers the night before, I was ready to accept the will of the Lord.

Stoically, I got off the train carrying Helen's burial clothes. Julius came running toward me. As he came close enough for me to hear, he began to shout, "Hurry up! Come on! We must run! We must go quickly to the hospital!" I could not imagine what was wrong with Julius except that he was overcome with grief. Helen was dead, so there was really no need for us to hurry. At eight months pregnant, I had great difficulty walking fast, much less trying to run and keep up with Julius.

Finally, I pleaded with Julius, "Slow down! I can't keep up. Why are we in such a hurry?"

Realizing he had not told me his news, he slowed and told me that Helen was indeed still alive! He explained that late during the night the doctors had met once again to discuss Helen's case; for some reason the older doctor finally agreed to the blood transfusion they had been discussing for days. Even though the older doctor agreed to the transfusion, he still insisted that he did not like the idea of taking blood from someone expecting a baby in about a month. Finally, however, the older doctor agreed to the transfusion as a last desperate attempt to keep Helen alive. Julius said the doctors were preparing for the blood transfusion, and he was so excited that he had decided he would come to the train station to make sure that I came as quickly as possible. He told me that Helen was still unconscious and barely holding onto life. I was thrilled beyond words that Helen was still alive. I thanked God that He had spared her until I could reach the hospital.

When we arrived in Helen's hospital room, the doctors had already placed two beds side by side ready for the transfusion. Helen was in one of the beds and I was told to get into the other. The doctors began looking for a vein in Helen's arm in which to insert the transfusion needle. Her arms were so frail that they had a very difficult time finding a vein. Finally, they succeeded and began the transfusion. They did not have time to take my blood and put it in a container and then give it to Helen. They simply connected us directly to each other and made a straight transfusion from my arm into Helen's.

Very soon after the transfusion was completed, Helen regained consciousness, opened her eyes, looked at me, smiled and said, "Edesanya." I had never heard a more beautiful word! It all happened that quickly. It was like a miracle! Helen was herself again. The nuns were overjoyed that the doctors had found a treatment that at last seemed to work.

The doctors, on the other hand, were only cautiously encouraged. However, they were happy enough with the initial results that they suggested we try another transfusion the next day. Soon after the transfusion, I returned to Obertraun with Helen's clothes and doll to take care of our other children.

Sometime after midnight that night, Helen continued to improve and became much more alert. She told her father that she was hungry and would like to eat an apple. Julius became so excited that she had asked for an apple. He knew this was a positive sign that she was feeling better. She had not asked for anything to eat since she had become ill over a week earlier. He ran all over the hospital in the middle of the night looking for an apple. He even went outside trying to find a store where he could buy one in the middle of the night in March. No place was open. He came back to the hospital and asked every staff member he could find if they knew where he could get an apple, but no one had any ideas. Finally, someone found one. Julius quickly gave Helen a piece of the apple. The fact that she was alert enough to eat the apple was encouraging. Just hours before, the doctors had not expected her to live. Now, she showed remarkable improvement as she ate a few bites of the apple.

I returned to the hospital the next morning so that Helen could receive another blood transfusion. Already the red blood count had begun to rise slowly. On this day, Helen was conscious. When she realized that she was going to get another needle in her arm, she did not want any part of it. When the doctors began looking for a vein in her tiny arm, Helen began screaming. Julius and I both tried to hold her and calm her, but she was fighting too hard for the doctors to find a vein in her frail arm. As a result, the doctors were forced to cut a hole in her right arm, technically called a "cutdown," to find a vein in which to place the needle. They opened her skin and inserted the needle, and we began another arm-to-arm transfusion. Helen was still crying and fighting so much that we lost some of the blood during the transfusion, but nonetheless we were able to complete the transfusion.

Soon after the second transfusion, Helen began to have seizures. The doctors told us that this happens sometimes when blood from a healthy adult person has been mixed with the blood of a sick person, especially when the sick person is a child. Helen became delirious, and she threw herself around and did not respond when we tried to calm her. After a few minutes, she finally calmed down and then completely lost consciousness. Her heart and breathing stopped. The doctors gave her a caffeine shot to get her heart started, as they had done many times before when her pulse had become dangerously low. But this time, the caffeine did not work. The doctors tried to massage her heart, but that did not work either. It appeared that the doctors were about to give up and declare her dead when I said, "Let's give her artificial respiration." The doctors and nurses felt the situation was hopeless and a waste of time. They were ready to declare Helen dead.

Julius disagreed and immediately began giving Helen artificial respiration. Once he began, the nurses and I helped. We worked on Helen for over an hour, and Julius and I refused to stop. If anyone stopped, Julius would just jump in and perform the procedure himself. As the nurses or we were performing the artificial respiration, Julius would lean over Helen and tell her to breathe. He would demonstrate with his own breathing what he wanted her to do. Finally, after about an hour, Helen started to breathe, but only on command when Julius told her. She was not consistently breathing on her own. Every time Julius told her to breathe, showing her how to inhale and exhale, she tried to do it herself. She seemed to want to breathe and was trying to force herself, but she was not able to do it consistently. Her heart would either stop or become very irregular. The doctors and nurses monitored her heart with their stethoscopes to determine if it was working properly. This went on for what seemed like hours. Finally, Helen began to breathe normally, and her heart began beating without being massaged. By this time, it was approaching early evening, already long past the time I needed to get back to the children at home, but I wanted to stay until we felt Helen was out of danger. I knew that if Elizabeth needed anything, she would go to Maria, who was always there and would help in any way she could.

Just before I left, one nurse said to us, "After watching what has just happened, I know this child can be very thankful. Her parents have given her life for the second time."

Because Helen was so close to death, the doctors were still not confident that the second transfusion would ultimately help. They still considered it more of an experiment rather than a normal medical procedure. They did not even take the time to properly sew Helen's skin back on her arm, where the cut had been made for the second transfusion needle. They simply provided a minimal number of stitches to stop the bleeding. They refused to believe that she would recover. (The skin grew together in such a way that it left an ugly scar on Helen's arm.)

Later that evening, Helen's red blood cell count began to increase rapidly. The doctors were completely amazed. They said they had never seen nor heard of a human being living after having gone through what she had. All they could surmise was that a child could survive with such a low blood count, whereas an adult could not. They were overjoyed that the transfusion had somehow worked.

By morning, the red blood cell count had increased and was still going up. The second blood transfusion had brought the count up to one and one quarter million from eight hundred thousand. This was still about a third of what it should be. Helen continued to improve every day, and the tests indicated that her red blood cell count was still rising. No more transfusions were ordered once her condition started improving consistently. The doctors were still not sure she was completely out of danger, but for the first time they were optimistic about her full recovery.

I was elated to hear the doctors' optimism. Helen had come so close to death. I was thankful that the doctors had agreed to the blood transfusion, which appeared to be the only thing that had saved Helen. I was certain that the older doctor had changed his mind about the transfusion as an answer to my prayers the night Helen was so critically ill. It was the will of the Lord that she live. Finally, after a week and a half in the hospital, Helen's health was improving.

Less than a week after the transfusions and after Helen began to feel much better, she came down with whooping cough. The doctors asked Julius if he knew how she might have gotten whooping cough. He told them that all of the children at home had come down with whooping cough right after

Helen went to the hospital. Evidently, Helen was exposed by the other children before she went to the hospital, and the actual infection did not surface until after she was there. Fortunately, Helen was feeling better and had regained some of her strength before she developed the disease.

With the whooping cough, the hospital staff said they could not keep Helen in the children's section of the hospital any longer. They needed to find another place for her and isolate her from the other children to protect them from the disease. The children's section presented too high a risk of transferring the germ by direct contact. Whooping cough can be very dangerous to young children.

Two ladies who were recuperating from surgeries in another section of the hospital were willing to allow Helen into their room with them. These ladies knew that whooping cough was not that dangerous to adults, especially since they had already had it. They were kind, gracious women who said they would not mind the inconvenience of having a child with whooping cough in their room. They were willing to accept the annoying effects of the disease. People with whooping cough were very noisy with a continuous bad cough and noisy breathing. Sometimes, the person coughing would choke and gasp for air. This was a major inconvenience for the ladies, and we were very grateful for their kindness.

After Helen contracted whooping cough, Julius no longer stayed at the hospital every day. He visited only about twice a week. Actually, hospital policy did not permit parents to visit their children while they were in the hospital. The hospital had learned through the years that every time parents came to visit the children, they reacted violently when the parents left. The hospital found out that it was much easier to handle the children in the hospital if their parents were not there. They had made an exception earlier for Julius because they feared that Helen might die at any time, and they wanted a family member beside her in that case. Also, since Helen did not speak German, she would not attempt to talk to anyone except her father. The hospital staff had felt it very important for Julius to be there during that time. But now that she was alert and out of danger, they curtailed the visitation in accordance with their policy.

Helen soon became accustomed to hospital routine. The nurses and doctors were always amused at what she did when they came into room to give her a shot. As soon as they walked into the room, Helen rolled over, uncovered herself, and exposed the surface that the nurse needed exposed, got her shot and then turned back over without saying a single word. She never cried and never said anything.

Helen would not talk at all in the hospital. The only time she would speak was after her meals. Then, she politely said "thank you" in German.

The few times Julius visited, the staff noticed that she spoke. They liked the idea that she perked up and communicated with someone. They encouraged him to come more often because it seemed to make Helen more active, and she seemed happier. But after a while, they noticed that instead of being happy after her father left, she began to cry for long periods of time. They explained to Julius what was happening and asked him to limit his visits to the hospital. He agreed because he certainly did not want Helen to be upset either.

After Helen had been in the hospital about a month, it became time for me to go to the same hospital to deliver my fifth child. Julia was born on April 9, 1949. Helen and I were now patients in the same hospital. I was in one part of the hospital with Julia, and Helen was in another part with whooping cough. At the time, the Austrian doctors did not allow women to get out of bed for eight days after childbirth. Helen knew that I was in the hospital, and I felt bad that we could not see each other. Finally, after eight days, I went to visit Helen. She was very glad to see me and could not understand why I had not come to see her earlier. She knew she had a baby sister, but she did not show much reaction. She clearly wanted to come home and be with me more. I had seen Helen only a few times while she was in the hospital, and obviously she was a bit homesick. She was still very weak. I held her tightly and told her that we would take her home soon. This was my only visit with her while I was in the hospital.

Two days later, the doctors allowed me to go home with Julia. After examining Helen, they said she could go home, too. Julia, Helen and I went home on the same day but in two different trips. Julius took Helen home in the morning in an ambulance after her more than five-week stay at the hospital. Even though Helen was much improved, the doctors felt that because she was still weak, it would be better to take her home in an ambulance rather than on the train. In the afternoon, Julius came back and took Julia and me home on the train.

As we were leaving the hospital, we thanked the doctors and nurses for all they had done to help save Helen. We knew they had struggled to determine what was wrong with her. The doctors said they felt they had done nothing to deserve thanks. It was clear that some of the doctors and nurses felt Helen's recovery was a miracle. They confessed that they had not known what was wrong with Helen and thus did not know how to treat the disease. All they knew for sure was that her red blood cell count was so low that they could not believe she had survived. They had known of no medication to treat her illness. They had tried a variety of treatments but still could not pinpoint if any were actually improving her health. Nothing had seemed to help except the blood transfusions. If it had not been for the young doctor's insistence on a blood transfusion, Helen would not have survived. Somehow or somewhere, either through his studies or intuition, the young doctor had known that the blood transfusion was what she needed. He persistently insisted that it be done until the older doctor finally agreed. I was still convinced that the older doctor only agreed because of God's help through my prayers.

Helen had stayed in the hospital for more than five weeks. The last three weeks were spent with the kind ladies. Fortunately, because of the social system in Austria at the time, the long hospital stay did not cost us any money. Because we were refugees in Austria, the medical treatment was paid for from a fund that existed for this purpose. The community hospitals were there to serve the people, and we were glad they did just that for us.

Before we brought the two children home from the hospital, the family doctor, Dr. Ballick, had told us to separate Helen from Julia to protect Julia from the whooping cough. He cautioned that children less than six months old who contracted whooping cough rarely survived the disease. He said that because babies could not cough up the mucus, they frequently died from choking. He further said there was no way to treat a baby with whooping cough. He also informed us that a third person could not carry and transmit whooping cough between two persons. There had to be direct contact. Consequently, I could handle and care for both children, but I could not allow them to be together. As important and necessary as this arrangement was, we realized that in our little house it was impossible for us to comply. There was no way to isolate Julia from Helen, but we had to do something.

We tried to locate a place in the neighborhood where I could keep Julia until the whooping cough danger was over. A very good friend of the Kieningers lived just a few minutes' walk from our house. They said I could stay with Julia in their workshop, which was a small building beside their home. They straightened and cleaned the workshop, converting it into a baby's room.

For short periods of time, I would leave Julia sleeping in the workshop by herself while I checked on our other children. When I was away, the homeowner stopped by to check on her from time to time. I went over and fed her regularly, changed her often during the day and spent the night with her. I made frequent trips between our house and where Julia was staying. I was still able to cook and do other chores at the house when I was not with the baby. It was comforting to know that I could travel freely between the two places without fear that I might be spreading whooping cough. Julius was extremely helpful during this time. I know he hated to do some of the chores I usually did, but he never complained. Each day after work he would come home eager and willing to help in any way he could.

About the time Julia was five to six weeks old, she developed a very bad diaper rash. Although I was with her frequently, I was not always there when she needed to be changed. As a result, the rash spread and became so bad that Dr. Ballick said she must be watched constantly and changed frequently. Since the other children were near complete recovery, the doctor said we should take Julia home so that she could be watched more closely. He felt that the diaper rash presented more of a danger now than the chance of her getting the whooping cough. Finally, Julia joined the rest of the family.

Now, we were seven in our cramped, one-room home. With a fifth child added, we needed to make adjustments to accommodate her. Julia took over the baby buggy in which Zoltan had been sleeping, and Zoltan began sleeping on the baby bed. Helen slept on a straw mattress on the floor.

During most of the time Helen was sick, Julius did not work because he was at the hospital. At one point, he stayed at the hospital for nine straight days. When I was at the hospital with Julia, he stayed home to take care of the other three children. After he returned to work, Julius was surprised when the forest service paid him for all the time he had not been working. He never expected to be paid for any of the time off. He told the forest ranger who was in charge of his working schedule that he had been overpaid because he had not been working on many of the days for which he had been paid. The forest ranger responded that in the last four years Julius had never been sick and had never taken any sick leave. He said Julius had accumulated the sick pay. The forest service simply felt that even though Julius had not been sick, in this case, they wanted to give the sick pay to him. It was a goodwill gesture of appreciation by the forest service. We were very happy that they understood and, of course, we were happy with the money that we did not expect.

After her time in the hospital, Helen was very weak and could not walk. Because of a combination of the illness and the lack of use of her legs, she had to learn to walk all over again. By summer, Helen had learned to do this but with difficulty. She walked like a little duck.

One day during the summer, we went to the lake nearby. Helen was with the other children who were playing in the water. I was visiting with the lady from Vienna who was staying with the Perstls for her annual summer vacation. A pharmacist from Vienna was with this lady. When he saw Helen walking so funny, he asked what was wrong with her. I told him the whole story. He said that he was not a doctor, but he had seen enough of this in Vienna to recognize that this was a form of polio affecting the bone marrow that caused the blood count problem. He said he had heard of a number of cases in Vienna. Very rarely did anyone recover from what was considered a fatal disease. He said he was confident that the antibodies in my blood had saved Helen. All the time that Helen was hospitalized, the doctors never mentioned anything about the possibility that she might have had polio. The doctors just knew that the blood transfusion saved Helen.

The pharmacist wrote later in the fall that his best friend's son became ill with the same symptoms as Helen. He told them about my story and that the only thing that appeared to help was a blood transfusion from a pregnant donor with a perfect match. The doctors gave the boy a perfect match blood transfusion, but it was not from a pregnant woman because there was not one available with the right blood type. The boy died.

We never knew for sure what disease Helen had. After the conversation with the pharmacist, we always assumed it must have been some form of polio because of the similar symptoms described. The red blood cells must have been attacked by a germ or bacteria, and the fresh blood with the antibodies destroyed them. We were confident, based on what happened and what the pharmacist had told us, that it was my blood that saved Helen's life. Obviously, antibodies in my blood as a result of the pregnancy were the secret to her healing. The pregnancy that kept us from going to Australia was the pregnancy that saved Helen's life. My faith grew even stronger after this experience.

The Perstls heard on the radio and passed on to us some very disturbing news about the refugees from Upper Austria who were notified about immigrating to Australia at the same time we received our notification. We all had made application at the same time, and we were all accepted except that Julius and I had to withdraw because of Julia's impending birth. All of those people who were immigrating to Australia perished on the ship that was transporting them there. We were told the ship caught fire and sank in the waters. There were no survivors. We never learned the name of the ship or where it departed from in Europe or any other information about this tragedy. We believed the story to be true because we knew a family that was to have been on the ship and the family had promised to write after they arrived in Australia, but we never heard from them. This incident made me realize again that the Lord had intervened in my life with the pregnancy. The pregnancy clearly saved us from the tragedy that occurred at sea. When I was initially upset and bitter with the pregnancy, I had simply looked at my situation from my narrow perspective as a human. God clearly had other plans.

CHAPTER 12
HE RESTORETH MY SOUL

By the summer of 1949, we had been in Austria for four years. We were still officially declared displaced persons and were considered temporary residents of the country. Although Julius provided for us by working for the forest service with a reasonably respectable job, we never had been accepted as being a permanent part of the community. This never changed throughout the time we were there. We knew that we had no future in Obertraun or in Austria. We were sure that we would never be given an opportunity to improve our standard of living. Julius felt the only job he had for the future was to continue to cut wood in the forest around the area. He had a good relationship with the forest service, and he knew he could stay and cut wood for as long as he wanted to. But he was an educated man, and he wanted so much to move to a place where he would have an opportunity to improve our situation.

Julius continued to encourage me and attempted to boost my spirits about our future. Each season he would say this might be the time. Let's just try to make it through this next season. He knew how much I wanted to go back to Hungary or find a good home for our family, so he always was very careful not to tell me that we would not be leaving anytime soon. I realized the situation myself. I knew our chances were few, but I always wanted to hope. Julius wanted me to focus on getting by for just a few months at a time. At that time, we would reassess our situation and our options. Julius always left me with some hope.

I had a Bible and I read it often. I read the story of Job over and over because it provided me with so much encouragement. Satan and God agreed to test the faith of Job, who not only was a wealthy man but also a God-loving man. Satan argued that if Job were to lose everything. He would then lose his faith in God. Job was not aware of the pact between Satan and God. Job did lose everything. His belongings were stolen, his servants were murdered, his sheep were killed, his house was destroyed and his children were killed. Despite all these calamities, Job never lost faith in God. Even though he lost all his worldly possessions one by one, which included vast wealth and his family, he continued to praise God. Satan was certain that Job would finally curse God. Despite everything that happened, Job did not curse God. He clung to his belief in a loving, just God even though everything in his experience and all the evidence pointed against such. Job waited patiently for his situation to change. Finally, Satan gave in and told God that he could not do anything to this man to destroy his faith and that he would give up. God had proven to Satan the strength of a man's faith. It was then that God gave Job back twice as much as he had before. He was given a large family, thousands of animals and far more than he had before.

I saw some similarities between our situation and that of Job. I never believed that God had made a pact with Satan in our situation like he did with Job, but I did believe that our faith had been challenged in the same way as Job's. Job's story affirmed to me that God is not deaf to our cries for help, and that God is in control of the world no matter how circumstances might seem otherwise. I knew our prayers had been answered on a number of occasions, and that fact reinforced my faith. But my prayer to settle into a new home where my family could live more comfortably had not yet been answered, and we had been in Austria for over four years. I relied on reading Job's story to sustain me, but I could see my patience waning. How long was God going to wait before he answered our prayer for a new home?

The options for immigration were few, and the future still looked bleak. After all of these years, we had no home and no prospect of a home. Austria was overcrowded. The government did not want us, and we knew they were doing all they could to find us a home but without any results. We cherished our freedom too much to return to communist Hungary. We kept wondering, "Would any country really want a family with five children?"

All of the countries accepting immigrants not only had restrictions concerning the profession of the head of the household, but also concerning the size of the family. We were discovering that all of the countries wanted either single people or families with one or two children. The countries were concerned that large families might not be financially stable with the low-paying jobs that were available to the immigrants. The countries did not want to risk having the government support the immigrants after they entered their country.

Over the past years we had heard that several places in the world had opened up for refugee immigrants, but all of them wanted to take only common laborers who would work cheaply and who had small families. That was the case with Australia, England, Canada, several countries in South America, as well as with the United States. England took some educated people for a while, but what they really wanted were common workers for the least desirable jobs that their citizens did not want to do. The countries opened their borders to allow specific quotas of agriculture workers, forest workers, semiskilled laborers, welders and similarly skilled people. No professional or well-educated people were wanted. No one wanted doctors, lawyers or teachers.

Several of the families who had been a part of our group that had come from Hungary were able to immigrate to other countries. For a while, we kept in touch with some of the refugee families, but eventually we lost contact with all of them. Australia offered the first opportunities for people to leave Austria. Later, various countries in South America also opened their doors to refugees.

We were willing to go to any country that would offer us an opportunity for a home and a new and better life. As was our choice all along, we preferred to go to a country where English was spoken. Regardless of where we went, we had to learn a new language, and if we needed to learn a new language, we thought we wanted to learn English. Going to Australia sounded very good when the opportunity had been presented a year earlier, but going to America sounded by far the best of all. From what I had learned in my history studies in school, the United States sounded like a wonderful place to live. During the long winter months I did a lot of wishful thinking and dreaming about places like America and Australia.

In late 1949, Obertraun was buried in snow. Our future looked as dim as the winter weather. All I could think about during the entire Christmas season was what a wonderful gift it would be if we finally had an opportunity to leave Obertraun and start a new life somewhere else.

We knew that the Protestant organization Church World Services was working very hard to find us a homeland, but they had not been successful for over four years. We continued to pray that someday we would receive a letter from them with good news about an immigration opportunity. One day in early January 1950, our prayers were answered when we received such a letter. The letter stated that the United States had removed the limitation on family size and had begun accepting applications from anyone who met the specific job quotas for skilled or semiskilled workers or laborers. The letter explained that there was a large immigration quota for agricultural laborers. We could hardly believe what we were reading. This meant we might have an opportunity to go to the United States. Just the idea that we actually had a chance to go to the United States and live in America seemed to be an incredible dream. America was like a place in a fairy tale to us. It was so far away and so desirable but always seemed unreachable. The thought that we could possibly go was practically unreal. We had waited so long, and we had hoped so much. Maybe we could finally leave Obertraun.

We already knew that the United States was not looking for educated or professional people. We were appreciative of the opportunity to be able to go to America, but Julius just could not understand why they did not want educated people. He placed such a high value on education. He was so proud of growing up on a farm and being able to go to the Teachers College and then continuing on to earn his doctorate degree. Julius was so pleased that he had achieved the highest overall grade possible at the Teachers College. He was the first student in twenty years to achieve that score. The last person to achieve the highest possible grade at the Teachers College in Budapest was the Chairman of all of the Teachers Colleges in Hungary at the time when

Julius graduated. The man graduated from the Teachers College in 1912, the year that Julius had been born. In the summer of 1932, Julius proudly had shown me his diploma with the signature of his future father-in-law and the signature of the person who had achieved the perfect score twenty years earlier. All of this hard work had been of no value to him in the past five years; it now appeared that it would be of no value to him to as a way to enter America.

The important thing to us was to move our family to a place where we could start life anew, where we could have a home large enough to raise our five children and give them a chance for a better life. Even though Julius had his doctorate and I, too, was educated, we felt our best chance to qualify to go to America was to de-emphasize Julius's education and to emphasize his farming skills.

The letter stated that Julius should go to Linz, the capital of Upper Austria, on January 10 to determine if we qualified to make application. He was to meet with a United States officer at an American facility there. Because he knew they were looking for agricultural workers, Julius went to Linz pretending to be a farm worker. The American officer who was handling his case noticed the Dr. before his name and quickly questioned how he could possibly be a farmer. He asked Julius for written proof that he knew something about farming. Julius told the American officer that he had grown up on a farm and had worked on the farm for his father for years. The American officer asked Julius about his education. Julius told the officer of his qualifications as a teacher and that he had a doctorate degree in zoology, botany and anthropology.

As Julius had feared, his education and professional qualifications worked against him instead of for him. The officer explained that they were not looking for educated people or qualified teachers, only farm workers. He said he would like to put Julius's name down as a farm worker, but the immigration policy required some form of written documentation that he was qualified to be a farm worker. Because Julius had not been working on a farm, he did not have any work papers or any other documentation that supported his claim that he knew farming. The officer suggested that Julius go to a nearby agricultural trade school in Linz and ask the teaching staff to give him an examination to prove that he knew farming. The officer said that if Julius could pass the examination to prove that he knew how to work on a farm, the school would give him a farm worker certification that he was to bring back to the officer.

As instructed, Julius went to the school, but the school was not in session. Everyone was still out for the Christmas vacation. He walked around the school trying to locate someone with whom to talk. Finally, he located the dean of the school, who happened to live on the campus. Julius told him of his problem. The dean agreed to help. He took Julius to a part of the campus used for storing a variety of agricultural tools and equipment such as plows, harrows, tills, etc. The dean asked Julius to identify each tool and piece of equipment and to tell him the use of each. Julius told him everything about the equipment and each of the tools. The dean quickly realized that this was a ridiculous exercise and that they were wasting their time. Julius obviously knew farming and agriculture. He immediately gave Julius a certificate to indicate that he knew agriculture. Julius was delighted because he now had the proof he needed to document himself as a skilled farm worker. He had high hopes that he now had a chance to meet the quota required and thus be able to go to the United States.

Julius returned to the American officer again to complete his application. This time a different American officer was there. Julius explained what he had done and presented the officer with the farm worker certificate he had received. This officer reviewed the whole situation. He also knew of Julius's doctorate degree in natural sciences. This officer seemed to want to give Julius the best possible job in the United States. As he reviewed Julius's papers, he noticed that Julius worked for the forest service in Austria. Julius explained that he had worked as a lumberjack four and a half years in the forest in Austria. The officer told Julius that if he knew the theoretical part of forestry as well as the practical side of working in a forest, he might have a better opportunity applying as a forest ranger than as a farm worker. The officer suggested that Julius try to secure a certificate that confirmed that he knew forestry work. Then, he could register as a forest ranger. The officer thought that a forest ranger's job would be a much better paying job and a better opportunity than a job as a simple farm worker.

The officer sent Julius to a college nearby that had a program specializing in forestry. Julius met with the dean of the school and explained his situation. The dean took Julius outside and asked if Julius knew the names of a few trees around. Julius was able to name every single tree, not only with its common name but also with its Latin name. Sufficiently impressed, the dean immediately issued Julius the certificate. After a short visit, the dean wished Julius the best for his future.

Again, Julius returned to the American officer and gave him the certificate. The officer accepted the certificate to qualify Julius under the quota as a forest ranger. The officer indicated that he liked Julius and thought that he would be a good asset to the United States. He explained to Julius that once he arrived in the United States, he was not obligated to work as a forest ranger, a farm worker, a laborer or anything else. Once in the United States, he told Julius, "You can do whatever work you want to do." He further explained that the United States officials would not deport him if he chose to do something other than the work stated on his immigration papers. The officer explained that quotas were required to enter the United States, but that they really didn't mean anything once an immigrant arrived in the United States. Julius thanked the officer for the very encouraging information and for his personal concern. The officer told Julius to return to Linz with his wife in ten days to finalize the immigration process. A very happy Julius returned to Obertraun.

Those ten days seemed like the longest ten days in my life. I thought that Friday, January 20, would never arrive. I was so excited that morning when we took the train to Linz. Once we arrived, we were required to complete all kinds of forms and answer question after question about what each of us did in Hungary and in Austria. After we completed all of the paperwork and responded to all of the questions, the American officer informed us that we met all of the requirements to immigrate to the United States. What a wonderful thing to hear! It now appeared that our prayers were answered and that we could begin our journey to a new home.

Once we received approval to immigrate, we met again with our Church World Services sponsor later the same day in

Linz. The sponsor informed us that we would be going to a place called New Windsor, Maryland, where our local sponsor would meet us. Once in New Windsor, we would learn where Julius would be assigned to work in the forest. The sponsor told us to go home and that we would receive notification from the Church World Services of the date, location and means of transportation for our departure. When we received this notification, we could begin packing everything for our departure because then we would know for sure that all arrangements for our trip to America had been finalized. Julius and I were overjoyed as we left Linz to return home. This time it really seemed we would be leaving Austria for a better life.

We had never left our children alone for the entire day, not even when Helen was sick and in the hospital, but on this day, January 20, 1950, we had no choice because we both had to go to Linz. Elizabeth, who was very mature and responsible for an eight-year-old, was left in charge. We trusted her with the four smaller children. We left in the dark at about four-thirty in the morning, and we did not return until late in the evening. The only help Elizabeth received was with starting the fire in the stove. I had asked our neighbors (the Perstls) if they would come over at seven in the morning to start a fire for the children. Elizabeth handled all the rest of the chores that day. She managed to feed and care for all of the other children, including changing Julia's diaper.

After we returned from Linz, we learned from neighbors that some Americans had been asking a number of questions about us the previous few days, obviously trying to determine if we might be some kind of risk to the government of the United States. They asked if we participated in any political parties, especially the socialist or communist parties. Of course, their answer had been no. When we lived in Austria, we always had been very careful not to belong to any political party, and we always were careful to avoid making any political comments or statements that might upset anyone. We had no time to become involved with politics.

We easily passed the investigation. Later, we learned more about it. Because we were from Hungary and because Hungary had been under the control of Germany, the Americans considered Hungary an ex-enemy of the United States. We never understood this designation because Hungary was a weak country that was overrun by the Germans. The people of Hungary never accepted German control. The Hungarians simply tried to make the best of a situation they did not want. We learned that the investigation was conducted by the Central Intelligence Agency (CIA) to determine if we were a political risk to the United States. We had not been aware before we went to Linz that the United States was conducting an investigation as part of the approval process for immigration.

Everything seemed to be working out. We were finally getting closer and closer to realizing our goal to immigrate to the United States. We actually were going to be able to leave Obertraun and Austria. As it became more certain that we were going to be leaving soon, I felt I should thank the clerks at the city hall who were the only city workers who were very nice to me. I had gone to city hall frequently to pick up ration cards for the Kieningers, the Perstls, and for us. I had become well acquainted with all of the clerks. I wanted to say goodbye and thank each one of them personally.

I went to each individual clerk to say goodbye and tell each one where we were going. While I was still in the office, one of the clerks said that she had mentioned to the Burgermeister that I was leaving, and the Burgermeister said that he would like to see me before I left. The clerk encouraged me to see him.

The last person I wanted to see was the Burgermeister, and I certainly did not want to talk to him. He had been relentless in his opposition to our being in the community. He had taken advantage of every opportunity to make our lives miserable. He had stolen food from us that the Americans had ordered soon after we arrived in Obertraun. He had been instrumental in our not being able to rent decent housing. He had withheld clothing ration cards from us. These were just a few of the many evil things this man had done. Even though I did not want to talk to him, I went to see him.

The Burgermeister, who was a communist, began questioning me as to why anyone would want to leave this beautiful and wonderful country with its socialism to go to a capitalistic country like the United States. He asked me if I thought I would have a better life there. I did not need to answer, because before I could, he gave me his evaluation explaining how awful life was going to be in the United States. He went on and on and on about what a mistake we were making to leave this place and these people and this government to go to a capitalistic society. Finally he said, "America is going to be a hell for you."

I had had enough of his pathetic ranting about where we were going and I decided to respond: "Frankly, the biggest hell I can think of is not any worse than the hell you created for us here. You have done everything in your power to make our life miserable. You have contributed to our hunger, you denied us adequate housing, you denied us adequate clothing, and you have attempted to turn the entire community against us. Now you tell me how America can be worse than that!" I then stormed out of his office. I knew there was nothing he could do at this time to retaliate, and I knew I would never have to see his mean and evil face again. As I walked home after having rebuffed the Burgermeister, I realized I had absolutely no idea what we were going to encounter in America, but I did know that it had to be better than our situation here.

I then went to tell Dr. Ballick goodbye as well. Dr. Ballick had been one of the best friends we had, and I wanted him to know how much we were going to miss seeing him and his family. I told him about my exchange with the Burgermeister, and he laughed and said he had not thought I had it in me to say something like that to the Burgermeister! While I was visiting with Dr. Ballick, he told me how he had been fighting for years with the community council to allow us to find a better place to live. Because Dr. Ballick was the community doctor, he was the person in charge of the whole community's health. He was not a voting member on the community council, but he served as an ex-officio member on the council. He had been trying to make life easier and better for us, but primarily because of the Burgermeister, he had not been successful. Better, more livable places were available for rent in Obertraun, but nobody would rent to us because the Burgermeister had instructed them not to do so. Dr. Ballick told me on this visit how he had explained to the community council that if we continued to live in that old one-room house, he was afraid that the entire family would come down with tuberculosis or some other disease. Dr. Ballick had come by from time to time to visit us. I had thought it was a social call.

After our discussion, I realized that he had been concerned about our health. He was checking to see if we were really all right. We recognized what a wonderful friend Dr. Ballick had been to us, but not until we were about to leave Obertraun did we know how hard he had been working to try to help us. He was a true friend!

After reflecting on what Dr. Ballick had said, I realized that Julius and I were not sick a single day in the almost five years we lived in Obertraun. Neither one of us developed so much as a cold. The only time the children were ill was when Helen was in the hospital and when they all became ill with the whooping cough. Based on Dr. Ballick's assessment of the potential for disease in this house, I concluded that the watchful hand of the Lord must have been protecting us.

I also told Julius about my visit with the Burgermeister, and he told me that he would not talk to him. He said if he ever talked to him again, it would be as a visitor to the community, and he would have money in his pocket to spend freely in his presence. I realized at that moment how oppressed he felt, and that he held the Burgermeister responsible! We had recently learned that the Burgermeister had told the community that all the refugees were the enemy, and the people of the community were not to harbor them. He had attempted to intimidate the entire community into completely ostracizing us, but because we refused to allow it to happen, he failed. He did succeed, however, in keeping us from achieving an adequate standard of living.

On January 29, 1950, which was just over a week after our application had been accepted in Linz, we finally received the news for which we had waited for years. We received our official notice from the Church World Services to report to Linz in two days to begin our trip to the United States. We were incredibly excited. Our lives were about to change. We would, indeed, begin the long-awaited journey to the United States.

For four and a half years, we had lived in this small, one-room house. Julius was always thankful and so proud that all the time we lived in Austria we never even once lived on welfare. Our children never took any charity while we were there. We never even took advantage of the Marshall Plan that gave food packages or care packages. We never wanted to go to any refugee camp. Most of the refugees went to camps that provided food, shelter and clothing for the refugees, and the refugees had to do nothing in return. We had far too much pride to accept that kind of charity, and we never would have accepted any kind of welfare. After Julius started to work, he earned every penny that we used. He worked for everything and paid for everything. The pay was never very much, but we lived on what he made.

On the day we received the official notice, Julius quit his job with the forest service. He took the tools that had been assigned to him to return them to the forest service. His supervisor told him he could keep the tools because he had been such a good employee for the entire time he had worked for them. He had been with the forest service for four and a half years and had worked long enough to earn a retirement. He received a statement when he separated from the forest service that indicated the amount of retirement he could collect at some future date. Julius had earned the respect of his supervisor and his fellow workers.

We were so excited when we began packing. We had received specified instructions ahead of time as to how we should pack our belongings. We first packed up the large crates that were made from the wood intended for a coffin for Julius's grandmother. We had kept them and the footlocker from our trip out of Hungary. This time we packed them with joy and anticipation rather than with the fear and anxiety we had experienced before. We wanted to take everything that we could but only those things that were necessary. We took the baby buggy that Julius had built for Zoltan. We decided to take the radio and bicycle that we had bought, but we did not take the chairs. We left the chairs and everything else we had to the Perstls, who had been so kind to us. We returned the beds and stove that had been loaned or given to us when we moved into the house. We took the saws and tools that Julius used to cut lumber in the forest. We also gave away the skis and sled that Julius had made for Elizabeth and young Julius. In spite of giving away many things we did not need, we barely had room for everything we wanted to take. Each family was allowed to bring no more than 400 kilograms per person. We also packed knapsacks for Julius, the older children and me. In these knapsacks, we packed items we thought we might need on the trip.

Admittedly, our emotions were mixed. Our excitement was overwhelming. A hint of sorrow crept in too, however. Austria's beauty had certainly been one of the positives of our being there. We never lost touch with the beauty of the countryside around us. The mountains, the river, the lake and the village were all magnificent. In the midst of the tremendous joy we had in leaving Obertraun and going to America, an element of sadness entered. We had spent almost five years here, and, in spite of the hardships, we had some fond memories. We had made wonderful friends, particularly the Kieningers and the Perstls, whom we loved dearly. Saying goodbye to them was not easy. They had done so much for us, and we were very grateful to them. Once again, Mr. Schilcher provided us transportation but certainly for a happier occasion than most of the other times he had come to our rescue. He took us and all of our belongings to the station in Obertraun, where we caught the train to Linz.

We met the Church World Services people in Linz, where we stayed a couple of days. The Church World Services had handled all of the arrangements for getting us from Linz to Salzburg on a special train that took refugees like ourselves on the three-hour trip.

In Salzburg, we, along with the other refugee families, were housed in large army barracks, where soldiers had lived during the war. They packed as many people into the barracks as they could. People were everywhere: on the beds, on straw sacks, on the floor—just about anywhere. The conditions were primitive. We stayed in those barracks in Salzburg for about a week. During this time, the Church World Services provided orientation sessions so that we would know what to expect when we arrived in the United States. They also explained some of the laws and customs in the United States that might be different from those in Europe. This time also allowed the Church World Services to get everything organized for the special train from Salzburg to Bremerhaven.

Almost immediately after we arrived in Salzburg, Zoltan became ill. He constantly had a high fever. He did not show much sign of sickness because he was as active as always, but he had an upset stomach, was vomiting and had a high temperature. The doctors and nurses gave me some medicine to treat Zoltan, but nothing seemed to help.

We began to worry because we knew that the authorities would not allow sick people on the train to Bremerhaven. The train to take the refugees ran only once a week, so Zoltan had to be well before we could leave Salzburg. We talked to the nurse who was treating Zoltan about our concerns. We asked her if she had any idea what was causing him to be so ill. She said she had seen this before with some of the refugee families. She felt the problem was caused by the food. The refugees were given a large quantity of food once a day, and it was all very greasy. The nurse said that since Zoltan was not accustomed to eating greasy foods, his body was having trouble handling all of the grease. The nurse agreed that it was very important to get Zoltan out of this environment. Once he was away from here, she said, everything would be all right. The nurse told us not to say anything to anyone about Zoltan's being ill. The nurse told me that mothers with small children (Julia was less than one year old) traveled in the Red Cross hospital wagon on the train. She would put Zoltan with Julia and me in the hospital wagon. We were very thankful that the nurse helped make sure that we caught the next train to Bremerhaven.

While in Salzburg, someone from the Church World Services noticed that I was wearing a dress that Mr. Kieninger had given to me after his daughter had died. This daughter had been a very large woman. The dress was worn and just hung on me, but it was the only dress I had. My shoes were the uncomfortable pair that the priest had given to me in Bad Ischl.

The woman from the Church World Services told me that they did not want me going to America in those clothes. She gave me some good shoes and a dress. For the first time in a long time, I received a pair of shoes that actually fit. She also gave me a light navy blue dress that was a little faded at the pleats in the skirt. It appeared that the dress had been in a store display window. The sun had faded a portion of the dress. I thought these clothes were new because they appeared not to have been worn. The tag on the dress read Nieman Marcus, which did not mean anything to me. Evidently the clothes had been donated to a charity such as the Salvation Army or some organization that provided clothes for refugees to wear coming to America. The Church World Services wanted the refugees to look as good as possible when they arrived at their new home.

When the time came for us to leave Salzburg, Julia, Zoltan and I went to the hospital wagon as the nurse directed us. Julius was lucky to have a whole compartment on the train for the rest of the family. So Elizabeth, young Julius, and Helen were with their father. Just as the nurse had predicted, when we arrived in Bremerhaven two days later Zoltan was no longer ill. During the forty-eight-hour trip to Bremerhaven, Zoltan had fully recovered and showed no signs of the illness. Once on the train, he never vomited again, and the fever went away almost immediately. From then on, he was healthy again. Obviously, the nurse was right. He simply could not properly digest the greasy food.

Bremerhaven is a port city on the English Channel in the northern part of Germany. We stayed in Bremerhaven about a week until transportation to the United States was organized. Our departure was planned for Saturday afternoon, February 18, 1950, at four o'clock from Bremerhaven aboard the USAT *General A. W. Greely.*

As soon as the departure date was announced, the Jewish passengers immediately protested vehemently. Almost half of the refugees making the trip were of the Jewish faith, and they were sponsored by a very powerful Jewish organization. The Jewish people were upset because the trip was beginning on the Jewish Sabbath. It was their belief that a journey should not begin on the Sabbath. The Jewish passengers said they would not board the ship on the Sabbath, and that was final! After very long discussions, the American authorities lost their patience. They told the Jewish passengers that if they were not going to board the ship, they would stay in Bremerhaven, but the rest of the passengers were going, and the ship was going on schedule.

Finally, the sponsoring Jewish organization came up with a compromise. If the Jewish passengers boarded the ship on Friday, they technically would be starting their journey on Friday instead of on Saturday. The American authorities reluctantly conceded to the request and agreed that the Jewish passengers could board on Friday. They boarded before the other passengers on Friday evening. Unfortunately for the rest of the passengers, they took all of the best accommodations. What was worse was that they hoarded all of the medicine that was onboard, including the seasickness pills that were intended for use by all of the passengers.

The remaining passengers boarded the ship on Saturday, February 18. The vessel was a military transport ship intended for eight hundred troops. The guns had been dismounted, but the bases for the gun mountings were still visible. The passenger-carrying capacity had been increased from eight hundred to twelve hundred, fifty percent more than the original intended capacity. The ship was very crowded with passengers in every possible available space. In order to carry more passengers, the ship carried a minimal crew and utilized the passengers to perform many functions normally handled by crew members. Most of the men were assigned a job to do aboard ship.

We began the journey on schedule at four o'clock in the evening on that Saturday. The ship quickly pulled away from the dock into open water. We were unbelievably thrilled and excited to begin the long boat trip to America. As we looked from the deck to the empty shores, we said a prayer and thanked the Lord for America, a country that opened her doors for us, wanted us and offered us a new life. We had just left the shores of Europe, but we were already in love with America. The ship was bitterly cold as we pulled away, but we did not mind at all. The excitement of the moment warmed us, plus we had on our warm clothing. We felt that we were in a safe place, and we were all together as a family going where we had dreamed of going. We totally enjoyed the moment.

Julius's assignment on the ship was as a policeman, and his job was to keep order among the passengers. His main job was to make sure that the passengers did not go into areas of the ship that were off-limits to passengers, such as the engine room and the crew quarters. He worked in four-hour shifts twenty-four hours a day, worked for four hours and rested for four hours.

Soon after we departed, everyone in the family became seasick except Zoltan. I went to the nurse on the ship. She asked why we had not taken our seasickness pills. It was then that we learned that the passengers who had boarded early had taken all of the medicine aboard the ship. We suffered from seasickness almost the entire trip.

By the time it was dark on the first evening, we were in the English Channel. Shortly after we reached the channel, the ship stopped and a small boat tied up next to us. An English pilot boarded the ship to guide us through the English Channel. Because we were in British waters, an English pilot was required to navigate the ship.

The next morning we were still in the English Channel, and in a very heavy fog. The *General A. W. Greely* was equipped with radar, which was turning and appeared to be working. The ship sounded its foghorn frequently in the heavy fog that Sunday morning. While he was on duty at about noon, Julius looked up to see a ship suddenly emerge from the fog and headed directly toward our ship. The other ship collided with us, and metal pieces from the ship's railing broke and flew all over the place. Passengers on the deck at the time began screaming and running away from the railings. Julius himself was near the railing at the time, and he, too, moved away quickly. Although the ship sustained damage, it did not appear at the time that the damage threatened its ability to stay afloat.

The ship that collided with the *General Greely* was a similar American transport ship. It was going to Bremerhaven to pick up the next group of immigrants. Both ships immediately stopped. After they were safely separated, they anchored in the English Channel. From about noon to about eight o'clock that evening, the ships did not move, and the passengers learned nothing about the condition of the ship. By evening the fog had cleared some, but by then it was dark. At about eight o'clock, we heard the engines working again. The ship pulled anchor, and shortly afterward we were in the port of Dover. After the English pilot got off at Dover, the ship departed. The passengers still did not know exactly what had happened or about the condition of the ship.

The next day the Captain called all of the passengers on board and explained what had happened. He told us that the incident was very serious, and that it could have been a tragedy. He said that fortunately the collision was not head-on, just a side-to-side hit. At the last moment, the English pilots from each ship steered away enough so as to avoid a straight-on hit. The Captain then explained why we had remained anchored in the channel so long during the afternoon. He said the crewmen had thoroughly inspected every part of the ship to assess the damage and to determine its seaworthiness. Although they knew at the time of the accident that we were very close to Dover, the crew needed to evaluate the condition of the vessel to determine if the ship needed to be towed to Dover, if the ship could go under its own power to Dover, or if the ship could cross the Atlantic Ocean without any repairs. From the inspection, they found no leaks or any damage to the integrity of the hull. The Captain did report a few dents in the steel hull, but there was no danger that the hull would create any problems for us on the trip. They decided it was safe to continue the trip to the United States without making any repairs to the ship.

After the excitement at the beginning of the trip, everyone settled into a routine of trying to stay as comfortable as possible on the crowded boat. Many people who had boarded on Saturday were suffering from seasickness and did not want to do anything except lie around. Because the ship was crowded, sick people seemed to be everywhere: lying on the stairs, on the deck, or just about anywhere they could find a place to lie down. Since the children and I were part of this group, we understood why the people with seasickness just wanted to be left alone and did not want to be bothered by anyone for any reason.

Julius stayed in a different part of the ship from the children and I. The practice on the transport ships was that the women and children lived in one part of the ship, and the men lived in another part. We never really understood why we were separated for almost the entire trip.

As we crossed the ocean, we went through one storm after another. We were happy that the ship remained upright through some of the storms. The ship swayed from side to side. One day the ship would lean in one direction, but about the time we became accustomed to that, the next day the ship would lean the other way. If we felt well enough to eat, this made eating a real challenge with plates going everywhere. These storms caused everyone to continue to be sick. Fortunately, no one died from the seasickness. Finally, later in the voyage, most of us began to recover and feel better.

We were allowed to go on deck when the weather let up enough. The weather in February was seldom very good with the prevailing winter conditions. With the cold temperatures and storms, the deck was often icy. We did enjoy those few times we were allowed on deck.

On the ship, the children were introduced to food that was very strange to them. One was ice cream and another was fried chicken. The children had never seen ice cream before. They were very suspicious at first, but the strange, cold substance tasted very good, and soon they could not get their fill of it. Fried chicken was a different story. In Austria people ate chickens only when they were sick and unable to produce eggs. So when the children saw the chicken pieces, their first reaction was "what was wrong with this chicken?" It took me a while to assure them that those pieces came from a perfectly healthy chicken.

We had not had Julia baptized in Obertraun before we left, but we did not want to bring her into the United States not baptized; therefore, we decided to have her baptized on the ship. The captain had the authority to baptize passengers, so he baptized Julia in his cabin on the *General A. W. Greely*, while we were crossing the Atlantic Ocean.

At one point in the journey, Julius saw birds appear around the ship and realized we were close to the Azores Islands. The birds followed the ship, trying to pick up food or anything that the ship might dump into the sea. We were thrilled to see the birds because that was just another sign we were closer to our new homeland.

Despite the difficulties at sea, our spirits remained high. Our anticipation was so great that these inconveniences seemed minor compared to what we had experienced the past five years. At least we now would have an opportunity for a better life. We hoped we would have a house large enough to accommodate our family a bit more comfortably, and we hoped Julius would have a job that he enjoyed and that would allow him to care for his family. God had definitely answered our prayers. America had seemed so far out of reach, but now we were on our way to the land of freedom and plenty. God in his mercy, God in his grace, God in his glory had restored our faith and our souls!

SURVIVING THROUGH FAITH

The following is a condensed version of an article written by a passenger aboard the USAT *General Greely* and published in the ship's newsletter which we recived a day before we arrived in the U.S.

We are a strange people with a mixture of cultures. We are poorly clothed and do not make a very nice picture when we are together. We were once folks who had homes and all that belongs to it, but the war came and when the worst was over there was nothing else left for us but our bare hands, undermined health and a longing to return home. We could go back and give in to the new governing deity. We didn't do that. For the sake of liberty we ran away over the boundaries of our old countries. And because of liberty we are bound for America. We love liberty above all. We didn't ask for anything but a decent job, a good roof above our heads and freedom of thought and speech. We have a firm aim, to become good citizens of the state giving us refuge and a new home. If the need arises we shall defend this new home. We left the bitterness behind us on the shore at Bremerhaven and we are sailing for the new world with the pleasure and enthusiasm of new human beings. The period of poor living is over. In America we shall start to live a new life again!

The following is an article written by the ship's staff to the passengers in the same newsletter.

Now you are on the eve of the arrival in the new land, the promised land, and soon you will be seeing the famous skyline of the largest city of your future country. In a short time you will be ashore and the ups and downs, of the voyage, will be but a memory of the past. After all your vicissitudes you will be at last in freedom and safety; your dreams will have come true. When I look around and see most of you going cheerfully about your daily tasks, I sometimes think of those others, relatives friends, fellow country-men who have not had your good fortune; I mean these who never got out, those who died, those who for one reason or another had to return, and those still waiting anxiously to follow you. Think of them, I am sure you do, and count your blessings. You are all, so to say in the role of ambassadors, representatives of the culture, ways and civilization of your race and country. Your splendid spirit of camaraderie displayed throughout the entire voyage proves beyond doubt that peoples of various nationalities and religions really can live together in peace and harmony. As you conduct yourselves, so will the people with whom you will come in contact with, form their opinion of the lands and cultures from which you have sprung. The future now lies in your hands, make of it what you can, with thankfulness, cheerfulness and loyalty. Before we part I wish to thank all those who have so cheerfully and so unselfishly helped us accomplish all the tasks which have to be fulfilled on such a trip. And to all passengers, I now wish a really happy and successful life in the USA.

CHAPTER 13
MY CUP RUNNETH OVER

Our schedule called for us to arrive in New York Harbor on Friday, March 3. As we approached New York on the last part of the trip, the weather was again awful. Everything was frozen and covered with heavy ice. It was very cold, and rain and some snow still fell. The conditions on deck were treacherous. Except for those who were necessary on deck, the crew required that everyone remain in quarters. The ship entered the Hudson River and passed by the Statue of Liberty at about two o'clock in the morning, while we were asleep. When Julius reported for duty at four o'clock, some of the passengers told him that we had passed the Statue of Liberty two hours earlier. Julius had heard the ship drop its anchor in the river just before he reported for duty. From the deck of the ship, he could see the lights on the enormous buildings everywhere. He was in awe. We had arrived in America!

The ship waited in the Hudson River until about seven in the morning, when two small tugboats arrived to pull the big ship to dock. Julius watched carefully as the ship pulled its anchor, and the tugboats pulled the ship into Dock 61 on Manhattan Island. Just as the ship docked, the clouds broke open and the sun peeked through the New York skyline, indicating the dawn of a new day. We officially arrived in America at seven-thirty in the morning on March 3, 1950.

Because the deck was so icy the passengers were not allowed on deck until the ship was safely docked. Afterward, as we looked out over Manhattan that icy morning, we experienced our first glimpse of America in daylight; the windows in the shimmering skyscrapers glowed like pure gold in the sunshine. I could hardly control my emotions with the thought that this was America. This was our new home! It was far more grand and beautiful than I had imagined.

As soon as the ship was securely tied down, the authorities from New York came aboard to process the passengers through passport control and immigration. This was done in alphabetical order onboard the ship. The first people came off the ship at about eight o'clock that morning; since we were the last in the alphabet, the very tired but very happy Zsohar family came off the ship at about twelve o'clock noon.

As soon as we were processed through immigration and off the ship, we learned through an interpreter from the Church World Services that we could not go to our original destination of New Windsor, Maryland. They had learned the day before our arrival that New Windsor had a measles epidemic, and the health authorities had declared the area quarantined to children. New Windsor was the designated site for immigrant forest rangers to meet their local sponsors and be taken to their final destinations. Because Julius was on the forest ranger quota, we were assigned to New Windsor. However, the interpreter quickly informed us that Church World Services already had found us another location.

At first when Julius received the news that we could not go to Maryland, he was concerned about his designation as a forest ranger on his immigration papers. Then he recalled what the American officer in Linz had told him when he registered him as such. The officer had told him that he did not have to work as a forest ranger; that designation was just to get him to America. As soon as he arrived in America, he was free to work any job he wanted to work, and he was not obligated to anything regarding the quota of entry. He recalled the officer told him he could be anything he wanted to be.

For the past five years we had become accustomed to uncertainty and change, so we were not overly concerned about our destination; we knew the change would not be a problem. In fact, we were somewhat hopeful that perhaps Julius would not be working as a forest ranger after all. Perhaps something far more suitable would be available at our new destination. Neither the quota requirement nor the destination had ever been particularly important to us. The only thing that we wanted was an opportunity to establish a new and permanent home for our family in a free country.

When the Church World Services learned of the quarantine at New Windsor, they frantically began to look through their list of potential sponsors. Their responsibility was to get the families they were sponsoring safely to New York and assigned to a local sponsor. Once the families were in New York, the local sponsor would take over and support each family to their final destination in the United States. At that time, immigrants could not come to the United States without someone who could guarantee that the immigrating family would not be a burden to the taxpayers for at least the first two years. The local sponsor had to provide proof of financial resources to sustain the family for two years or guarantee some other way that the family would not be a burden on the taxpayers. Many individual churches assumed this responsibility. A church could easily qualify under the guarantee criteria because of the number of members in the church and the reputation churches had for sponsoring immigrant families.

The Church World Services in New York searched their records and found that the Central Presbyterian Church in Waxahachie, Texas, had made an inquiry about sponsoring a family beginning in the summer when the cotton-picking season was to begin. In 1950 the cotton-picking machine was too expensive for most farmers. They needed workers in the area to pick cotton. Cotton was big business in Waxahachie, and the farmers in the area were short of workers. They wanted to bring low-paid immigrant workers into the city to help with the cotton harvest. Because the work did not pay enough to support large families, the ideal immigrant family, at the very largest, would be a couple with two children.

Central Presbyterian Church in Waxahachie had agreed to sponsor a small family to help fill the need for cotton workers, but they had not planned for anyone until the summer. It was only March, but the Church World Services urgently needed to place us. They called the Central Presbyterian Church and explained the emergency situation to see if they would agree to take a family earlier. In the Presbyterian church, the minister does not make the final decision on matters such as this. The Session, which is the ruling body of the church, has the responsibility for making the decisions for the church. The minister called a quick meeting of the Session that Thursday evening and he received approval to take a small family immediately.

The next morning in a telephone conversation with Mr. Anderson, the head of the Church World Services organization in New York, the Central Presbyterian minister, Don Swain, said that their Session had voted to sponsor a family with "few" children. Mr. Anderson misunderstood and thought that Rev. Swain had said "five" children. With great excitement, Mr. Anderson told him that this was perfect because they had exactly what the Session wanted. As they were finalizing the details for travel, Don Swain began to realize that there had been a big misunderstanding about the number of children. Unknowingly, he had committed his church to sponsor a family of seven. But because of Mr. Anderson's excitement, Don Swain did not say anything, even though he knew he needed to clarify the situation. He decided to ask the Session to approve the sponsorship of the larger family, and the Session accepted. Everything was not finalized until the Friday morning we arrived in New York. The church in Waxahachie had less than two days to prepare for a family of seven, who were scheduled to arrive early Sunday morning.

The Church World Services had just finalized the local sponsorship minutes before we got off the ship. We would be going to Waxahachie, Texas. The train to Texas would leave from Grand Central Station at eight o'clock that night. Church World Services took the children and me away. Julius remained behind to claim the baggage and go through customs control.

The original plan had been to take us to a hotel so that we could clean up and prepare for our train ride. A mix-up occurred, however, with the hotel room, so instead of taking us to the hotel, our sponsor took us directly to Grand Central Station. The Church World Services representative bought us sandwiches when we arrived. It was the first time we had eaten that day. Because of the early morning arrival time, the ship did not serve breakfast. By midday we were very hungry when they served us the sandwiches. We waited at the train station all afternoon for Julius to arrive with the baggage. Although benches were readily available for us to sit on at the train station, the children were very fidgety, and they did not like sitting still. The constant waiting on the ship and then later at the train station made this a very long day.

While the passengers were going through immigration, the ship's personnel were unloading all of the baggage and luggage. Before we left Bremerhaven, the ship personnel sealed our luggage and boxes. The authorities sealed the wooden boxes that Julius had made in Hungary with steel bands so that they could be safely loaded onto the ship. Earlier that morning as we had waited aboard the ship for our turn through immigration, Julius had watched as the ship's personnel unloaded the belongings from the cargo hull. When we finally got off the ship, all of the baggage was in a huge warehouse sorted out in alphabetical order. They had put the first initial of our last name in large letters pasted on the baggage. There was a big "Z" four inches high on every piece of luggage. Julius just had to go to the end of the alphabet to find our baggage.

Customs inspection was also in alphabetical order except for the Jewish passengers. Julius watched in amazement as the belongings for Jewish passengers were separated from the others and loaded onto baggage carriers and taken through customs without inspection. He learned later that the Jewish sponsoring organization was very powerful in the United States. They were able to make arrangements with the customs agents to allow the belongings of the Jewish passengers to come into the United States without inspection. As a result, the Jewish people did not have to wait in the long line to go through customs like the other passengers.

Since the officials were processing people in alphabetical order, Julius was the last person through customs inspection. He was required to open every bag, box, crate and piece of luggage we had. The customs agents were interested in everything. What surprised Julius the most was how interested they were in the camera he had with him. The customs officials wrote down every number that was on the camera, even the lens number. This was a camera that did not even belong to Julius. It belonged to a friend in Budapest who had loaned the camera to Julius to take to Kisrakos for pictures at Christmastime in 1944. Julius had tried to return it to his friend on several occasions, but his friend insisted that Julius keep the camera because if he had tried to send it back to Hungary, the Russians would have taken it from the mail. Even though Julius loved photography and even had a darkroom in our house in Budapest, he never used the camera while we were in Obertraun because film and developing were very expensive.

It was approximately five o'clock in the evening before our luggage passed the customs inspection. The Church World Services people picked Julius up at about five-thirty and brought him to Grand Central Station to join us and catch the eight o'clock train. Julius had not eaten anything all day. He did not have any food, and he did not have any money to buy food. When he arrived at the train station, the Church World Services representative bought him a sandwich.

Soon after Julius arrived at Grand Central Station, a Hungarian man came up to us, asking where we were going. Julius told the man we were going to some place in Texas with a name we could not pronounce. The man shouted, "Texas!" He went on to say that Texas was the worst place to live in the United States; that Texas was not at all like Hungary; that it was very hot and dusty and had no trees. The man repeated over and over about how hot the weather was in Texas. We did not know anything about where we were going. All we knew was that we were going to a place called Waxahachie, Texas. The man spent several minutes informing us of the undesirable aspects of Texas. Then, he simply turned and walked away.

After the man left, I began thinking about what he had said and about where we were going. The name of the place was Waxahachie. After his comments, the name became much more frightening even if I could not begin to pronounce it. I recalled from my school studies and from movies Julius and I had seen when we were still in Budapest that there were three kinds of people in Texas: millionaires, cowboys and Indians. As new immigrants with no money, I knew we were not going to relate well with the first kind of people, and the other two did not sound too appealing to me either! Suddenly, just the thought of where we were going and what awaited us when we arrived began to frighten me. In a matter of minutes, I went from being extremely excited about our future to being very apprehensive about what America was really like.

The Church World Services made sure our luggage made it onto the train. They gave us train tickets to Dallas and a total of seventeen dollars in cash. The Central Presbyterian Church had paid for the tickets. Until we were given this money, we did not have any at all. While we were in Germany and being instructed about the immigration process, we were told that bringing any foreign money into the United States was against the law. This was emphasized several different times in several different ways. We were assured that once we arrived in the United States, the Church World Services would care for us.

The representative from the Church World Services apologized for not having any more money to give us for food on the train ride. He said that normally they would provide enough money to feed the entire immigrant family on the trip to their final destination. But, he said, on this day they had so many people that needed money that they did not have much to give us for the long trip to Texas. He gave all he had left, the seventeen dollars, to Julius and said that he hoped this would allow him to buy at least something for the children on the train. The representative also said that when we arrived in St. Louis, where we would change trains, someone would meet us and buy us a meal.

When departure time came, we boarded the train with our knapsacks, found a comfortable place, and settled into our seats. In a very few minutes, the conductor came to us and said that we could not sit in this part of the train. He took us to another, nicer part of the train to sit. We were very puzzled about why we had to move. Later, we learned that we had encountered our first experience with segregation. We had sat in the Negro section of the train, and white people did not sit there. We had never experienced anything like this, and we had never heard of such a thing. We did not know there was a difference in seating for Negroes and whites.

I had seen Negroes in Budapest, because almost all of the hotels had porters who were Negroes, but I had never actually talked with one. The Negroes did not seem to receive any different treatment than anyone else in Hungary. They certainly did not have different seating on public transportation.

My first actual encounter with a Negro had occurred on the ship coming to America. He was a worker on the ship, and he stopped to talk to the children and me. He obviously liked the children, and he came by regularly to teach the children some words of English—very simple greetings and courtesies. On occasion he would give the children some candy. The children and I appreciated his kindness so very much. He was the first Negro with whom I had ever conversed, and he was such a kind and gentle person. He was extremely nice to us throughout the voyage, and the whole experience with this Negro man had been very positive and good.

We had a very strange feeling about having to go to a nicer part of the train because of segregation. Being asked to move indicated to us that it was not acceptable for us to associate with Negroes. I felt disappointed about what had happened. We were total newcomers to the United States. We had not been born here, we were not citizens, we could not speak the language, and we did not have any connections in this country. Yet, we, as immigrants in the United States for less than one day, had more rights than the Negro who probably had been born in the United States of a family who had been in America for generations. The only reason for this was simply because of the color of his skin. Because of the way we had been brought up, we found this to be a very strange practice indeed.

We finally settled in the appropriate place in the train. The train went directly from New York to St. Louis. It traveled all night, while we relaxed in our seats. The children placed their heads in our laps and slept, but Julius and I were too excited to sleep. We remained awake most of the night, looking out the window at our new homeland.

During the daylight hours, we traveled through the beautiful countryside of Pennsylvania, Ohio and Indiana. My anxiety about America caused by the Hungarian man at Grand Central Station began to subside quickly. The American countryside looked peaceful and not that much different from Hungary. As we traveled each mile, I became more excited about going to our new home.

Early Saturday afternoon, we arrived in St. Louis. We had a couple of hours before our next train left. As we got off the train, we were thrilled to be greeted by a couple named Gray who were there to meet and feed us. The Grays were a wonderful couple and very kind. The Grays, lay people and members of a Presbyterian Church in St. Louis, had volunteered to meet us after being called by the Church World Services. The Grays took us to a restaurant and fed us very well. We had already run out of money for food, and we were ready for a big meal. The couple took us to a cafeteria-style restaurant so that we could choose our food simply by pointing.

During dinner, through an interpreter, we told the Grays that the Central Presbyterian Church in Waxahachie sponsored us. The Grays said they had a good friend named Bill Baker who was a very active member of that church. Bill Baker and Mr. Gray had been classmates at Trinity University, when it was located in Waxahachie. We all thought this was an amazing coincidence, that we would be going to a place where Mr. Gray had lived and had known someone very well.

We had a wonderful meal and a very nice visit with the Grays. We boarded our new train at five o'clock in the evening to leave St. Louis, heading for Dallas. We arrived in Dallas at about eight o'clock the following morning. Originally, we had understood that we would have to change trains in Dallas and take another train to Waxahachie, but the train official indicated to us that we were to get off the train at this time. When we got off the train, a station official somehow knew that we were refugees (maybe it was because we were the dirtiest and most tired-looking group there). Using sign language, he indicated that we should sit down on the benches nearby and wait for someone to pick us up. One of the train officials gave the children some money so that they could buy some popcorn at the popcorn stand nearby.

We must have made a very interesting picture when we arrived at that Dallas train station. Each of us, including the children, had our knapsacks with the individual items that we had needed during our travels. We were sitting there with our knapsacks, wearing very heavy clothes because we had been in subfreezing weather in Austria and Germany, as we were leaving. It had also been very icy and cold in New York. But in Dallas, it was a beautiful March day, and the temperature was nice and warm. It had been months since we had experienced such warm weather.

We had not had a chance to change our clothes or to take a bath during this entire trip. The last place we had bathed was in Bremerhaven in Germany on February 17, before we boarded the ship. There was no place to take a bath or shower on the ship during the thirteen days crossing the ocean. Since we did not have an opportunity to clean up in New York either, it had been over two weeks since we had bathed or changed clothes. We were a terribly bedraggled-looking group at the train station.

Soon after the train arrived, we saw approaching us the most beautifully and immaculately dressed men and women you could imagine. We knew immediately they were the people there to meet us. When they spoke to us, all we understood was the word "Presbyterian," and then we knew for sure that they were from the Central Presbyterian Church in Waxahachie. I wondered what they thought when they looked at us. We must have been a shock for them. We were dressed so inappropriately, and we were so very dirty. In spite of our nasty appearance, they all opened their arms and greeted us with a warmth we never expected. We knew immediately we were where we belonged. God definitely had a plan for us. Our fellow Hungarian whom we had met in Grand Central Station was entirely wrong about Texas!

The church members introduced themselves. They were Dr. and Mrs. Mayo Tenery, Mr. and Mrs. Charlie Graham, Mr. and Mrs. Bill Baker, whose friends had met us the day before in St. Louis, Mr. and Mrs. Doug Langford and Mr. L. T. Felty.

We could not speak any English, and none of the church members could speak Hungarian or German. As a result, we used much sign language! The seven of us were divided between the five cars that had come to Dallas, and we began the drive to our new home in Waxahachie, about thirty miles south of Dallas. The children had no hesitation about getting in the cars with strangers. We knew we were going to our new home because we recognized another word, "home," which has the same pronunciation in the German language that it has in the English language.

The car ride itself was very exciting. We had never ridden in a private car. In Hungary we had occasionally taken a taxi somewhere, but almost nobody owned a car. We had not ridden in any kind of car since we had left Hungary. A few times we had been in a dilapidated truck, but we had not been in a car in a very long time. I could not believe how nice and smooth the ride was. The crates and baggage were brought to Waxahachie in a separate vehicle later.

As we approached Waxahachie in anticipation of our new home, we were incredibly excited. I marveled at the size of some of the homes as we drove through the town. As we were driving down Marvin Street, I could tell by the church members in the car that we were getting close to the house that would be our home. I saw a large white house near the end of the street, and I thought, what a beautiful house. I was amazed when we pulled in front of the house and the people in the car proudly pointed that this was our new home. It was so huge, especially compared to the one-room house where we had lived in Austria. It was even larger than the wonderful house where we had lived in Hungary. We simply could not believe what we were seeing.

As we got out of the car, the children did not know what to think. At first, they appeared a little frightened and nervous because they, too, were a bit awed by the size of the house compared to the cramped quarters to which we were accustomed.

When we entered the house, we were even more over-whelmed. The house contained nine rooms, and each room was larger than the house we had lived in for the past five years! Each of the nine rooms was furnished. The kitchen was fully furnished with utensils, stove and an electric refrigerator with meat in it. The pantry was full of all kinds of canned food. Chairs, tables, lamps and beds were in various other rooms. In the master bedroom, we had a very nice washbowl with a pitcher. The house was even furnished with a radio and an old wind-up record player. The church had furnished linens, towels—everything we needed to begin living in the house immediately. They even had toys for the children. Everything was exactly in its place and very neat.

The members of the Central Presbyterian Church did an incredible amount of work in less than two days after they agreed to sponsor us to Waxahachie. During this time, they had found and rented the house and scrubbed it from top to bottom to get it clean. We were later told that women who had probably not done any housework in years had cleaned the house. They had housekeepers in their homes! While the women were cleaning the house, their husbands, who were prosperous businessmen, were using pickup trucks to gather furniture from people who had called and said they had furnishings to donate. Others were out buying groceries or collecting donations of clothing, linens or other household items. In less than two days, they completely furnished the house with everything required for our family of seven to move in and start living. They even put fresh-cut spring flowers on the dining room table!

No one knows what it truly means to have a place to call home, until his own home has been taken from him. Five years earlier we had been shocked to suddenly lose our freedom in Hungary and become refugees almost overnight. We had been forced to live out of a wagon for six months. Now, after all these years, in a matter of just two days, we had gone from being a refugee family to being legal residents of the United States of

America, and we would be living in a huge house with everything we could possibly need!

This new home was like a fairyland castle to me. The nine-room house that was waiting for us was more than a dream come true; it was a magnificent answer to prayers. We were amazed, surprised and thankful that the members of the Central Presbyterian Church went to this extent to make a happy and warm home for a family they had never met. Not only had they not met us, they did not even know we were coming until two days before. The Lord truly had blessed us. I was certain that we were part of a miracle that day. I was thankful that God had given me the patience to wait for this incredible day. We were blessed with an abundance of love and possessions that we could not have imagined. On this Lord's Day, Sunday, March 5, 1950, I now knew the Lord's will for my family and for me. He wanted us to be in Waxahachie, Texas, this town whose name we could not pronounce, with these people who had greeted us with warmth and open arms, in a new country that would become our country. Finally, we were home again!

The men's Bible class at the church had initially suggested that the church sponsor an immigrant family to Waxahachie, and the entire church immediately got behind the project. The head of that class, Ed Clark, addressed the congregation at the morning worship service that Sunday and told them of the events of the past few days. He informed them that the Zsohar family had arrived in Waxahachie that morning and were in their new home. He told how all the members worked together for the love of Christ, and in less than two days, they had the house ready for the family. At the conclusion of his comments he said, "Today, we became a church!"

When we had arrived at the house that Sunday morning, a German-to-English dictionary lay on the table. We tried to find the words in the dictionary to be able to communicate with the church members. This did not work too well, so we reverted to using sign language.

That afternoon a German missionary couple visiting in Waxahachie stopped by. We could converse with the couple because German was a common language we could all speak. This couple also allowed us to communicate with others who dropped by from time to time during the afternoon. We were surprised and pleased that a Baptist preacher, who knew we were Presbyterian, was among the visitors who stopped by just to welcome us to the community. The missionary couple did not stay long, but it was nice to talk with someone who spoke a language we knew and who could do some interpreting for us to begin to express our gratitude for everything that everyone was doing for us.

Before they left, the missionary couple interpreted from one of the visitors that we were invited to dinner that evening at the home of one of the church members, Mrs. Curlin. It was her adult son Tom's birthday. Mrs. Curlin's daughter, Luella Autry, and her family and Tom's family were all present for the dinner. Seeing how badly we needed to bathe, Luella took the children one by one and bathed them, while Julius and I bathed and dressed. Finally, after sixteen days, we were clean and had clean clothes to wear.

Words could not adequately express the joy and love we felt that day. We did not want the day to end, but by late in the evening we were very tired. We were glad to get back to the house to get some sleep.

The following morning when I woke, lying in a bed for the first time in weeks, I was afraid to open my eyes. I was afraid that the events of the day before had been just a dream, and that I would waken and still be a hopeless refugee in Austria in that tiny house. What had been happening to us was just too good to be true; it must all be a dream. When I finally gained the courage to open my eyes, I confirmed that I was in my new home, and everything was the way it was the day before, and it was still so wonderful. I continued to find it hard to believe that people who did not know us could be this amazingly kind. We had more than we could imagine. Indeed, our "cup runneth over."

As the days passed, we continued to be stunned by the welcome we received. The people were all so warm and so eager to help. Many people came to visit, and everybody brought something to the house. Some people brought food already cooked; others brought fruit. Some people brought more fresh flowers for display. Mr. Gregg, who managed K. Wolens department store, took the children to his store and gave them all new clothes. The generosity was continuous and overwhelming. In our wildest, most optimistic dreams we never could have imagined that this many kind, generous and giving people existed in one place. Our world had drastically changed in such a short period of time. We never had expected to be in a house like they had for provided us. Only a few days earlier, most of us had been feeling terrible on the ship from seasickness. Because we were so sick, we really had been more concerned about completing our journey than about what was waiting for us in America. We had no idea what a big surprise awaited us in Waxahachie, Texas.

After I learned to speak English and began to know our neighbors, I once mentioned to them about how amazed we were when we arrived at our new home to find it completely ready for our arrival. They were all Baptists, and one of them said they were also amazed at what they saw that Friday and Saturday. They laughed when they said that all of a sudden out of nowhere all of these people converged on this house and looked like a bunch of ants working into the night Friday night and then from early morning into the late hours of the Saturday night. The neighbors had no idea what was going on, and when they learned they were Presbyterians, they said they could not believe it because they had never seen a bunch of Presbyterians work together like that!

The children had no problem settling into their new home. Among the things the church members had included with the furnishings in the house were several toys, which the children loved. They had never had store-bought, manufactured toys like the ones they now had.

When we arrived in Waxahachie, Julius was thirty-seven years old, and I was thirty-one years old. We were now prepared to begin a new life with no money and five children in the country, where we knew opportunities would be endless. We remembered what the American officer had said about being anything we wanted to be. We knew the first step to taking advantage of these opportunities was to learn English. We knew that once we learned the language and American customs, we could create opportunities that we could not have created any other place in the world. We were optimistic, but we knew from experience that we were going to have to work hard and make opportunities come our way. We certainly were not afraid of hard work. For five years, we had worked tirelessly just to survive.

SURVIVING THROUGH FAITH

Our prayers had been answered; our Lord had provided us with more than we had ever hoped for or wanted.

Julius found a job immediately and began working. He briefly worked several extremely low-paying jobs before he was hired by Tyler Fixture Company as a janitor. Because he did not know English, he was not offered jobs that would allow him to use his education. He was offered only the lowest paying labor jobs. He was satisfied with those jobs initially, but soon he looked for jobs that would allow him to use his education. This proved to be harder than he expected, but he never lost his determination to work hard and to get the best possible job he could find. It was not easy for him, but he never expected it to be easy. He was so happy to be in America, and he was determined to make the best of the opportunity. Ironically, he did not work a single day as a farm worker or as a forest ranger.

After I had time to reflect on what incredible hardships we had to overcome to get to this country, I thought about those other people who started with us in the original seventeen-wagon group. Because of the hardships, some had decided to return to Russian-dominated Hungary and communism. I felt bad for those people because I realized that those refugees had not had the benefit of the strong faith in the Lord that Edesapa had instilled in me. I knew from the letters we were receiving from my parents that they were surely suffering under communism in comparison to the wonderful opportunity we had to be happy and prosper. The other refugees were so sure when they left our group that they would be safe and secure back in Hungary. They could not have been more wrong. If only they had had the faith in the Lord that He would guide them to safety and security. If they had only believed that God would direct them in their lives; if they had only believed and had faith in the Lord. I never stopped believing, even during the most difficult times. Edesapa had cautioned me that I might lose everything. But he also cautioned me that I should never lose my faith. Thank God I did not, because it was that faith that got me to this country and to this community. Never in my most optimistic dreams did I imagine that we would end our journey in such a wonderful place with such wonderful people. It was clearly our faith that made this long journey possible.

I had no doubt that God wanted us to be in this place. I thought back over all of the choices we made with the guidance of prayer and faith, and I was amazed at the events that allowed us to survive and arrive at this place. Julius made it out of Budapest just in time; he avoided the emergency draft; he received a wagon and oxen when he needed it; we received food when we needed it the most; we arrived in Obertraun and I met Maria Perstl; we did not qualify to immigrate to Australia; we did qualify to immigrate to America; and most significant of all: we could not go to Maryland, but, instead, the Lord directed us to this congregation in Waxahachie.

Soon after we arrived in the United States, I wrote a letter in German to Dr. Ballick. I wrote about the trip and how wonderful everyone had treated us along the way. I told him in detail about the unbelievable reception that we had experienced when we arrived in Waxahachie, and how we were provided the house, the furnishings and all of the food. I wrote how the people in the United States were helping Julius to get established. I also told him that we did not have to deal with ration cards for food or clothing.

I received a response from Dr. Ballick in only a few short weeks. I was delighted to hear from him, but I was even more delighted with the news he gave me. Before we left Austria, I had told him about my discussion with the Burgermeister. After he received my letter, he decided to take it to the next community council meeting in Obertraun. He read it aloud before the council meeting. After reading the letter, he told the council there was no more he could add. He told me the Burgermeister did not say anything, but that his face was very red. He did not know if he was angry or embarrassed. He wrote that reading this letter to the council was one of the most satisfying things he had done in a long time!

I also wrote a letter to Edesapa soon after we settled into the house. I told Edesapa in the letter how much I appreciated the discussions he and I had when I was a child. I told him that as a child I had no idea how important his advice was, but that what he had taught me had helped me to survive as an adult. I told him how often during the five years that we had struggled as refugees that I had gathered strength from his words concerning faith, about which he had spoken to me so frequently. I told of the many times when I had to rely on my faith to overcome desperate obstacles. I told him of the strength it gave me to know that throughout the difficult times during the past five years, I knew that whatever was happening was the Lord's will. I thanked him for those precious times we shared together, and I told him how I would cherish those times forever. I then told him that I looked forward to the day when I could express these feelings to him in person. Edesapa's lessons in faith had given me strength. Without question, my family and I had survived through faith, and we would continue to live through the faith and knowledge that the Lord's will be done.

AFTERWORD

From the time we arrived in the United States, Julius worked in a variety of nonprofessional jobs; however, throughout the years he pursued his love for art and painting. Soon after we arrived in Waxahachie, he began teaching private art lessons on a part-time basis. After a few years, he began teaching art in various recreation centers for the City of Dallas. He developed a reputation as an outstanding artist and art teacher.

In 1967, Julius quit his job as produce manager for a Tom Thumb grocery store and opened an art school and studio in Dallas. He became a full-time artist and teacher. For several years, he also taught art at Hill County Junior College. Over the twenty-eight years that he maintained the art studio, he taught art to hundreds of students. A longtime member, past president and inductee of the Hall of Fame of the Association of Creative Artists, he was a charter member of the Southwestern Watercolor Society and a member of the Compini Society of Fine Arts in San Antonio. Although Julius won numerous awards for his paintings, one of his most cherished honors was being named a Keeper of the Flame of the Baylor Foundation. Upon his death, his paintings, which numbered over a thousand, were donated to the Baylor Foundation, which would display them in various hospitals in the Dallas area.

Until Julius opened the art studio, I stayed home and raised our seven children. After coming to the United States, we had two more children, Isabel and Leslie. As I had done during our years in Obertraun, I found various part-time jobs I could do at home to help supplement our meager income. This time Julius knew I was working at home! About the time that our last child went to college, Julius opened the art studio. I then joined him at the art studio to help him with his business.

I still live in the same house that the Central Presbyterian Church rented for us in 1950. My son Julius now owns the house. I remain an active member of the church and have been an elder for forty years.

Raising seven children, Julius and I never were able to accumulate the funds required to send them to college. However, we made it clear that we expected the children to obtain at least an undergraduate degree. Just as their father before them, our children relied on scholarships, part-time work and loans to attend college. All seven children graduated from Waxahachie High School and received university undergraduate degrees. Five children earned graduate degrees, including one doctorate.

The following provides a summary of their accomplishments and where they are today. Needless to say, Julius and I have been very proud of their successes.

Elizabeth was born May 19, 1941, in Budapest. She prefers to be called Liz. She received her bachelor of arts degree in elementary education in 1964 from Trinity University in San Antonio and began teaching school in San Antonio immediately upon graduation. While teaching school during the day and attending classes at night, she earned a master of education degree from Trinity University in 1966. Beginning in 1966, she spent four years teaching school for the Department of Defense Overseas Schools in Kaiserslautern, Germany. She returned to the United States in 1970, when she accepted a teaching position at Northwood Hills Elementary School in the Richardson Independent School District (RISD). She taught in RISD for the next twenty-eight years until her retirement in 1998. During that twenty-eight-year career, on two occasions, Liz was an exchange teacher: one year in Nelson, New Zealand, and another year in Adelaide, South Australia. On two other occasions she participated in Fulbright summer study/travel programs: one to India in 1991 and one to Mexico in 1995. After both of these programs, she wrote curriculum for classroom study about each of the countries.

Active in various professional educational organizations for her entire career, Liz has served in numerous leadership roles. She not only has served on numerous committees, but she also has served as president, making major contributions to these associations over the years. She is a member of Delta Kappa Gamma. An active member of the First Presbyterian Church in Dallas, Liz is an elder, Shepherd and a Stephens Minister. She is very active in mission work, participates locally in the Stew Pot and Habitat for Humanities missions, and has participated in foreign missions in Mexico (seven summers) and South Africa. She also volunteers for the Susan G. Komen Race for the Cure and is a member of the Dallas County Affiliate of the Susan G. Komen Foundation Board. In addition, Liz finds time to drive for Meals on Wheels.

One would never guess that her true passion is travel! Liz began her overseas travel while still in college, when she attended a summer work program in Finland. Rarely a summer passes that she does not make a long trip. Through the years, she has visited all seven continents.

Julius, Jr., born on September 13, 1942, in Budapest, received a bachelor of science degree in civil engineering in 1966 and a master of science degree in civil engineering in 1971, both from Southern Methodist University in Dallas. He served three years in the U.S. Army as a combat engineering officer. During this time, he served one year in Vietnam, where he was awarded the Bronze Star medal. He worked for twenty years as a general contractor in Dallas and was part owner and president of Goodberry Construction Company. For the last eleven years, Julius has been the construction manager for the University of North Texas. In this position, he administers major construction projects for the university. He is a Registered Professional Engineer in the State of Texas.

He has volunteered as an adult leader of the Boy Scouts of America for the past twenty years and has served as a Scoutmaster for thirteen of those years. He also has served as a Republican Precinct Chairman and Election Judge for twenty years. An active member of the First Presbyterian Church in Dallas, he has been an elder for twenty-seven years and a Sunday school teacher for twenty-three years. He enjoys woodworking, jogging and bicycling.

Julius has been married to the former Janet Odell for over thirty-one years. Janet teaches at Northwood Hills Elementary School in the Richardson Independent School District. They have two sons.

Julius, III, 29, is married and is a first-year medical student attending the University of Texas at San Antonio Medical School. Jeffrey, 27, is a fourth-year medical student attending the University of Texas at Houston Medical School.

Helen was born August 16, 1944, in Budapest. Probably because of her experience in the hospital in Bad Ischl, she always knew the career field she would follow. From early childhood, she wanted to be a nurse. In 1965, she graduated from the School of Nursing at Methodist Hospital of Dallas. She received a bachelor's degree in nursing from the University of Texas Medical Branch in Galveston in 1967. Four years later, she received a master's degree in nursing with areas of emphasis in medical-surgical nursing and nursing education from the University of Texas at Austin. Helen began her teaching career in nursing at the newly created University of Texas Health Sciences Center School of Nursing in San Antonio in 1970. She taught there until 1974, when she decided to attend Arizona State University (ASU) in Tempe, Arizona, to pursue a doctorate in educational technology. While she was earning her doctorate degree, she taught several courses in the undergraduate program at the ASU College of Nursing. She received her doctorate in 1982 and remained to teach at ASU. Helen coauthored a textbook on basic nursing that was published in 1984. The following year she moved to Salt Lake City, Utah, to become a faculty member at the College of Nursing at the University of Utah. Currently an associate professor, she is also the Coordinator for Student Affairs at the College of Nursing. She has received several awards for teaching, including being named recipient of the University of Utah Distinguished Teaching Award in 2000.

Helen is active on the Utah State Board of Nursing, which is a member of the National Council of State Boards of

Nursing. Making major contributions over the years, she has served on numerous committees and as president. Helen also works with the Commission on Graduates of Foreign Nursing Schools (CGFNS) on their research and evaluation committee.

Zoltan was born May 29, 1947, in Bad Ischl, Austria. He usually goes by his first initial, Z. He received a bachelor of science degree in mechanical engineering from the University of Texas at Arlington in 1970. Immediately upon graduation, he began working as an engineer for Mobil Oil Corporation in Dallas. A number of engineering assignments with Mobil relocated him and his family to places such as Wichita, Kansas; Kalamazoo, Michigan; North Plainfield, New Jersey; Jeddah, Saudi Arabia; and London, England. Upon his return from London in 1980, he moved to California as the engineering manager for all of Mobil's pipeline facilities in the western United States. The following year he was transferred to Dallas where he left the engineering field and managed the budgeting and financial analysis function for all of Mobil's pipeline facilities. He later managed the department that was responsible for all of the accounting functions for the same facilities. In 1995, Z. was assigned to Mobil's technology company. Here, he used his broad technical and business background to support several of Mobil's largest capital projects throughout the world. With the advent of the Exxon and Mobil merger, he elected to retire from Mobil on May 1, 2000, after over thirty years of service. He is a Registered Professional Engineer in the State of Texas.

Z. has served in numerous leadership positions, including president of various homeowner's associations in areas where he has lived. He has also served on the Board of the Downtown Dallas YMCA. Presently, he serves his community as a member of the Lake Highlands Exchange Club, and he drives for Meals on Wheels. Z. is a member of the Preston Hollow Presbyterian Church of Dallas, where he is an elder. In the past, he has taught Sunday school.

Z. and the former Shirley Banks have been married for thirty years. Shirley teaches at Lake Highlands High School in the Richardson Independent School District. They have three daughters. Lara, 28, graduated from Texas A & M University in 1996 with a bachelor of science degree in civil engineering; she presently works for Alcatel USA in Plano, Texas. Amy, 26, graduated from Stephen F. Austin State University in 2000 with a bachelor of arts degree in speech communications and history; she presently teaches high school in Plano, Texas. Lisa, 21, is a junior at Texas A & M University, where she is majoring in electrical engineering.

Z.'s hobbies are travel, sports and fitness. He has run several marathons, including the Boston Marathon three times, and he has completed several 100-mile bike rides. His early retirement from Mobil allowed him the opportunity to document the journey and experiences that led the Zsohar family to immigrate to America and settle in Waxahachie.

Julia, born April 9, 1949, in Bad Ischl, Austria, received her bachelor of arts degree with high honors in elementary education in 1971 from Trinity University in San Antonio. She returned to Waxahachie and taught for two years in the Waxahachie Independent School District. In 1973, she moved to St. Charles, Missouri, where she taught school in the Pattonville School District in St. Louis, Missouri. While teaching school during the day and attending night classes, she earned a master of education degree in 1977 from the University of Missouri in St. Louis. In 1981, she and her family moved to Orlando, Florida, where they lived for two years before moving to Lewisville, Texas, in 1983. Julia has been teaching elementary school since 1983 in the Lewisville Independent School District. In the last few years, she has been teaching the gifted and talented students.

Julia has been married to Harold Cave for twenty-eight years. Harold is a contract engineer working for IBM. They have three children. Allen, 24, graduated from Stephen F. Austin State University in 1999; he is presently attending law school at University of Texas in Austin. Colleen, 20, is a junior at Texas Tech University in Lubbock, Texas, majoring in music education. Michael, 18, is a freshman at Lon Morris College in Jacksonville, Texas, majoring in English or history with the intent of eventually attending law school.

Julia is a member of the Trietsch Memorial United Methodist Church where she has taught Sunday school and has participated in numerous mission projects. Very gifted in creating various arts and crafts, she has made Christian jewelry for sale in support of mission projects.

Isabel, born January 18, 1951, was the first of the children to be born in the United States. She received a bachelor of arts degree in math from Trinity University in San Antonio in 1973. Upon graduation she began teaching school in San Antonio. She has taught there for the past twenty-eight years. She has taken full advantage of her summers off from teaching to pursue her love for traveling. She especially enjoys "adventure traveling." She has kayaked in Prince William Sound in Alaska, climbed mountains in Wyoming, toured by bicycle through most of the states, provinces, and territories of North America, and backpacked in almost as many states as she has toured on bicycle. She has spent three summers working for the National Wildlife Federation in their summer Teen Adventure program in North Carolina. Recently, she has become very interested in windsurfing.

When she is not involved in traveling, windsurfing or teaching, Isabel is building a cabin by hand, one stone at a time, in the Texas Hill Country. Ironically, the cabin is almost the same size as the stone house the family lived in for five years in Obertraun.

Isabel has a favorite story she likes to tell about the day in 1983 when she was riding her bike through Canada to Alaska. As the group of seven cyclists was riding through the Yukon, a Royal Canadian Mounted Policeman came up to her and asked if her name was Isabel Zsohar. She acknowledged that she was. He said he had an emergency message for her. It seemed that the Alamo Heights School District had a job opening! Their efforts to contact her on the road had failed, so they resorted to calling the Royal Canadian Mounted Police in the nearest town, according to the itinerary she had left with the school district. She has been teaching at Alamo Heights High School ever since!

Leslie was born on December 3, 1954. He received a bachelor of science degree in electrical engineering from the University of Texas at Arlington in 1977. He received a master of science degree in electrical engineering from Southern Methodist University in 1981. Leslie has spent his career in computer hardware design. Since the late 1980s he has been more specifically focused on telecommunications design. Leslie has a passion for participating in the start up of computer chip-related companies. He participated in a number of start-up companies in the Dallas area before moving to Round Rock, Texas, in 1999. He was one of the early participants in a new company, Agere, Inc., in Austin. Recently, he has become associated with an Internet security chip start-up called Layer N Networks.

Leslie and the former Sheri Erickson have been married for eleven years. They have two daughters. Sarah is eight years old and in the third grade; Louisa is five years old and in kindergarten.

Leslie is very involved with the YMCA Indian Princess program and presently is chief of all the tribes in the Brushy Creek Nation in Williamson County. He also is the chief of the individual tribe that includes his daughters. Leslie enjoys music and participates in gospel music programs, ensembles, solo and instrumental work.

After the war, the remaining family members in Hungary struggled under communism. After his arrest and trial, my father was banished from all references to education in Hungary. He also was stripped of his government pension until my brother, Marci, was finally able to secure at least a partial payment of his pension after many years of legal proceedings. My mother died in 1970, and my father died in 1973. Finally, in 1985, my father's place in the history of education in Hungary was reinstated, and he was honored with a permanent exhibit at the Teachers College. Julius and I loved my father very much, and Julius always was appreciative of the fact that he was able to attend the Teachers College on scholarship. In the year my father was reinstated as an outstanding educator in Hungary, we established a permanent scholarship fund at the Teachers College in Budapest in his name.

After he recovered from his wounds from the war, Marci returned to the University of Budapest and received a doctorate in veterinary medicine. Because of the severe injury that disabled his arm, he was unable to lift animals, so he pursued a career in veterinary research medicine. He struggled to support his family and my parents for many years after the war under the communist rule that he so opposed. Through his veterinary research, Marci became internationally known for his participation in the discovery of a vaccine for farm animals. In recent years, he has been very active in securing government funds to support disabled World War II veterans in Hungary. Through his efforts, hundreds of veterans and their families are receiving financial help from the government. In recognition for his work in support of the veterans, Marci recently received the highest honor ever given to a civilian by the military in Hungary.

Mama (Julius's grandmother) died soon after we fled Hungary. The family farm was sold, and the proceeds were divided among Julius's brothers in Hungary. Julius signed his rights to the property over to his brothers soon after we arrived in the United States. Mihaly still lives in Hungary. Laci and Ilona have died. Geza, who left Hungary the same day we did, moved to England and then to Canada in 1952. Somehow we lost touch with him in 1952 as he was moving to Canada, and we did not know where he was and did not hear from him for years. One day in 1994 when Julius went to the mailbox, he found a letter from Geza Zsohar. Geza's son, Mike, had traveled to Hungary to trace his roots. He met Mihaly who gave him our address in the

United States. After forty-two years, Julius and his brother Geza were reunited! Geza still lives in Canada.

With the help of Liz and the other children, Julius and I returned to Hungary in 1969 for the first time since we had fled in 1945. At the time, Liz was teaching in Germany. As a result, we could acquire affordable tickets to Europe. My parents were still alive, but their health was deteriorating. It was such a thrill to see them again and be able to walk with my father, Edesapa, in the neighborhood as I had done as a child. This time I enjoyed the walks, and I could personally tell him how much his talks had meant to me over my lifetime. We had so much to share and so little time to share it. As a side note, the communist squatter who had occupied the basement during the war was still living in the basement. All efforts to have her evicted had failed.

On this same trip to Europe, we returned for a visit to Obertraun. Because Liz was working for the military in Europe, she could buy an American car. No one can imagine how proud Julius was to drive into Obertraun in an American car less than twenty years after we had left in 1950! The Burgermeister was still in charge, but surprisingly, he was extremely friendly, as were all of the other people in the community. I am sure they thought we were very wealthy. We did not do or say anything to indicate otherwise! We had wonderful visits with our very good friends, the Perstls and the Ballicks. Mr. Kieninger had died.

The proudest and happiest day of our lives was on March 3, 1956, exactly six years to the date after the ship docked in New York. On this day, we became citizens of the United States. The Central Presbyterian Church that sponsored us to Waxahachie held a wonderful reception for us. Words could never express the gratitude we felt toward the church members for their love and support of our family. In recognition of the tenth anniversary of their sponsorship of us to our new home, we made a gift to the church of a new American flag, which had just been issued with the fifty stars in recognition of Hawaii being added to the Union. We also made a gift of a matching Christian flag.

From the time we met when Julius was a student at the Teachers College, he and I always shared a passion for learning and for education. We always felt strongly that the education of children is of utmost importance. Although he did not have money, Julius had not let the fact keep him from receiving an education. He secured scholarship money and worked part-time to earn both his teacher's certificate and his doctorate. Subsequently, we did not have funds to send our children to college, so they, too, had to secure scholarship money, work part-time jobs and secure other financial aid, such as government loans to receive their college education. We always were grateful for the financial support provided by those people who generously gave their money so that our children could earn their college degrees.

To commemorate the fiftieth anniversary of our coming to Waxahachie, Julius, the children and I wanted to express our appreciation to the church for everything that they had done to help us through the years. All of the children had careers and were financially stable. On Thanksgiving Day 1999, two weeks before Julius passed away, the family met and agreed that we would establish a scholarship to celebrate our fiftieth anniversary in Central Presbyterian Church. We felt an appropriate way to express this appreciation was to establish a scholarship fund so that other generations might receive some financial support for an education in the same way as our children. We decided to make the gift to the church in memory of Dr. Mayo Tenery and in honor of Mrs. Barbara Tenery. The Tenerys were youth sponsors at the church for nineteen years, which covered the years our children attended youth fellowship at the church. They unselfishly gave their time, energy and talents to instill Christian education, spirituality and morals to our children and hundreds of others who attended the youth fellowship over those years. On March 5, 2000, exactly fifty years to the day we were met at the train station in Dallas, Barbara Tenery was present with our family when we presented the church with a scholarship in her and her husband's honor. We were all very saddened that Julius could not be there for this special time. He would have been gleaming with pride as the pastor acknowledged us before the congregation. At least he had been a part of the decision; he knew we were doing exactly what he wanted. We were so happy to be able to establish this scholarship as a token of appreciation for the enormous positive impact the church had had on our family over the prior fifty years.

Many people in the Central Presbyterian Church and the Waxahachie community made wonderful contributions to bring us into this community and to nurture us so that we could easily assimilate into American culture. We thank all of them from the bottom of our hearts!

My parents' wedding picture. Edesanya and Edesapa are standing, and Mamsika is sitting. (1918)

Edesanya and Edesapa are standing. My twin brothers, Marci and Emre, are between Mamsika and me. (1928)

Marci, Emre and I are ice skating. Photo taken in January 1932, about the time I met Julius.

This is my first long dress that I received for my thirteenth birthday. I wore the dress to the Scouts Ball on February 1, 1932, the night Julius and I made our lifetime commitment to each other.

My confirmation picture taken Pentecost Sunday, 1933.

From left to right: Marci, Edesanya, Edesapa, Mamsika and Emre. I am standing in the back. (1936)

Picture taken for the presentation of Julius's doctorate in 1940. For such an occasion, he is wearing Hungarian formal attire.

My graduation picture taken prior to receiving my teacher's diploma in June 1940.

Our wedding picture taken in the
Calvin Plaza Presbyterian Church in Budapest on July 22, 1940.

Julius and I are exiting the church after our wedding.

Our official wedding picture taken July 22, 1940.

Elizabeth helping Mamsika, Edesanya and me
with our needlework. (fall 1941)

University botanical excursion in 1941 led by
Julius (sitting holding a cane) into the eastern part of Hungary.
Others in the photo are his students and colleagues.

Julius with his professor (man with hat) in the
university botanical gardens in 1941. Julius created
illustrations for the professor's books.

Family gathering on March 25, 1943. From left to right: Julius, Emre, me, young Julius, Edesapa, Elizabeth, Edesanya, Marci and Mamsika.

Julius, the children and I are enjoying a walk in our backyard
only days before the bombings began in May 1943.

Our visit to the Zsohar family farm in Kisrakos during the summer of 1943. Julius was born in this farmhouse. Papa is holding Julius, and I am holding Elizabeth. Laci and Mama are in the background. The cows pulling the wagon are much smaller than the oxen we had for our trip through Austria.

We are enjoying the animals at the farm during the 1943 visit.
From left to right: Julius, Laci, me, Mama, Elizabeth and Papa.

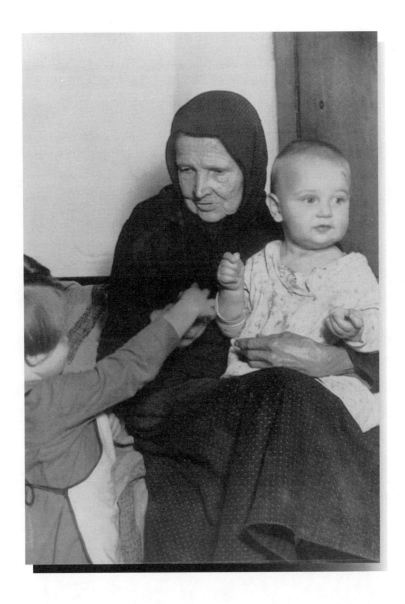

Mama with her great-grandchildren: Elizabeth and young Julius.

The smaller of the two wooden boxes made from Mama's intended coffin wood. This box was filled with food when we left Kisrakos.

One of the few pictures taken while we were in Obertraun.
From left to right: me, Helen, Elizabeth and Julius.

Baby buggy built by Julius in Obertraun. The buggy has handmade wheels, springs for a comfortable ride and an adjustable sunshade.

Photo made of the children and sent back to the
family in Budapest during the fall of 1947.
From left to right: Elizabeth, Zoltan, Julius and Helen.

In 1952, the family proudly poses in front of the
first car we purchased, a used Henry J.
From left to right: Julia, Zoltan, Helen, young Julius,
Elizabeth, me holding Isabel (who was born
in the United States) and Julius.

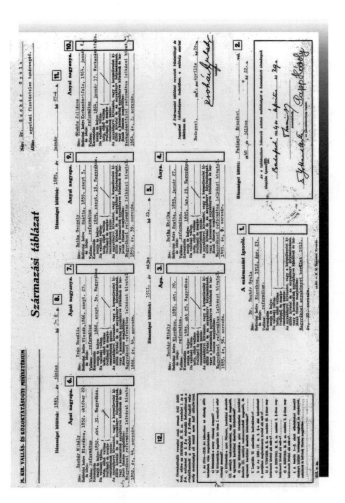

Everyone was required to submit documentation that proved their religion, their parents' religion and their grandparents' religion. This document was issued to Julius after he provided the authorities with the necessary proof of religion. The Hungarian government under the direction of the Germans was trying to locate all of the Jewish people.

People were required to register with the local village if they traveled and stayed overnight away from home. This document states that we have registered to be residents of Kisrakos on April 24, 1944, the day we began our eleven-month stay on the Zsohar family farm.

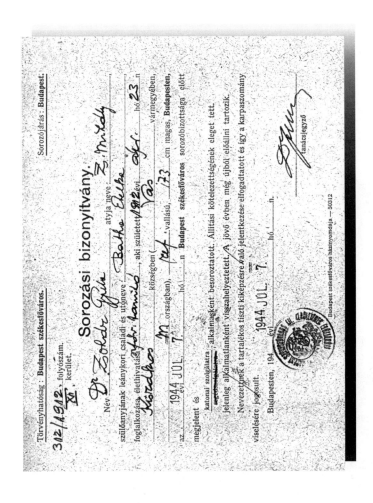

On July 7, 1944, this document was issued by the draft board and states that Julius has been examined and is fit for military service. He did not have to enter the military because the law in Hungary at the time exempted fathers with small children.

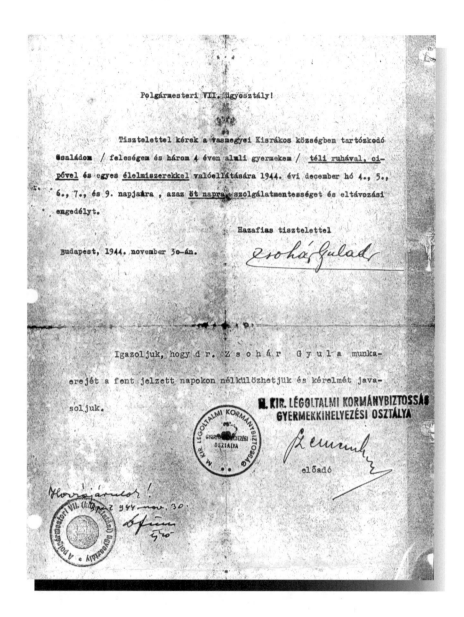

The top half of this document is Julius's request for approval to take five days off in early December 1944 to bring us the winter clothes we needed. The bottom part shows the approval. Later, the dates were changed to allow him to make the trip at Christmas.

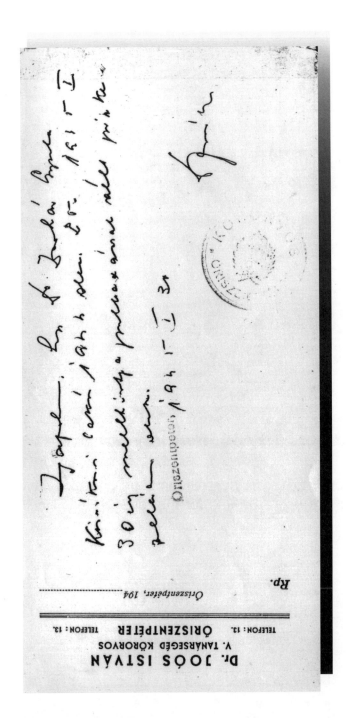

The official doctor's notice that was presented to the military draft board stating that Julius came down with pleurisy on December 25, 1944, and would not be available for military service until January 30, 1945.

Document registering to be a resident of Obertraun. The document indicates that he has been working for the forest service since June 17, 1945.

Temporary residence permit issued on September 3, 1945, which allowed us to stay in Obertraun until January 19, 1946, at which time we would have to apply for another permit. The permit was signed by the Burgermeister.

M - 28/c

Gmunden, 8. Feb. 1946

Receipt of application.
Empfangsbestätigung!

Zsohar	Julius	Obertraun Winkl 7	Ungar
Familienname.	Vorname	Wohnort	Nationalität
Name	surname	Address	Nationality
	mit Familie		

has applied for temporary exemption from repatriation and requests
to remain in Austria. This application is pending action by reviewing
authority.

hat nachgesucht, von der Rückführung ausgenommen zu werden und in
Österreich zu bleiben. Der Antrag läuft bei der Behörde, wo.er
aufgenommen wurde.

Dienstsiegel

Bezirkehauptmannschaft

Application for exemption from repatriation written in both English and German.

U 28/c

MILITARY GOVERNMENT
Detachment E1A
6824 Hp & Hp Co, CAA
APO 777 U.S. Army

15.2.46.
date

TO WHOM IT MAY CONCERN:

1. The bearer ___Zsohar Julius___ , recorded as a Hungarian citizen now living at ___Obertraun, Winkl 7___ , Bezirk ___Gmunden___ employed at ___Forstverwaltung___ in ___Goisern___ will be permitted to continue residence temporarily in Austria at the above address.

2. This stay of repatriation and temporary residence permit is null and void after (date) **1.5.46.** , if there are not issued contrary regulations about repatriation of Hungarian citizens.

3. The bearer is granted this permit for the following reason:

___forestry worker___

4. On presentation of this permit, Austrian food and supply authorities will issue regular civilian ration cards for those persons living outside organized settlements.

By order of Colonel HANNA:

FRANK DI GIACOMO
Major, Infantry
Displaced Persons Officer

Official stamp.

═══

Oberösterreichische Landeshauptmannschaft
Amt für Umsiedlung 15.2.46.
Datum

1. Der Inhaber ___Zsohar Julius___ , gemeldet als ungarischer Staatsangehöriger, z.Zt.wohnhaft in ___Obertraun, Winkl 7___ , Bezirk ___Gmunden___ beschäftigt bei ___Forstverwaltung___ in ___Goisern___ hat die Erlaubnis, seinen Aufenthalt in Österreich unter obiger Anschrift vorübergehend fortzusetzen.

2. Diese Aufenthaltsgenehmigung verliert ihre Gültigkeit am **1.5.46.** (Datum), wenn nicht vorher gegenteilige Bestimmungen über die Rückführung ungarischer Staatsangehöriger erlassen werden.

3. Diese Aufenthaltsgenehmigung wird aus folgendem Grund erteilt: ___Waldarbeiter___

4. Der Inhaber ist zum Bezug von Lebensmittelkarten (bzw.in Siedlungen zum Empfang von Gemeinschaftsverpflegung nach den für Österreicher gültigen Sätzen berechtigt.

Dienstsiegel

Für den Landeshauptmann:

mit Familie

The stay of repatriation and temporary permit issued on February 2, 1946, by the United States military allowed us to be issued ration cards. These permits were temporary and had to be reissued every few months.

THE WAXAHACHIE DAILY LIGHT • March 6, 1950
Displaced Family Arrives Here To Find Home Waiting

Waxahachie's new residents arrived here Sunday and were immediately stunned by Texas hospitality.

Waiting for them in their home at 1400 East Marvin was a house completely furnished, all furnishings had been acquired in one day by donations from members of the Central Presbyterian Church. Included among the gifts which will start them on their new life was as electric refrigerator, all necessary linen, and a supply of food which should make them forget the hunger they knew in Europe.

Julius Zsohar, thirty-seven, is the father of the family. He is a man with a pleasing personality, a ready smile, and a superb education. He doesn't quite understand our brand of English yet, but anybody wishing to communicate with him may write what they have to say and he can understand it. His wife, Elizabeth, thirty-one, and their five children range in age from eight years to ten months. Elizabeth is the oldest, and Julia is youngest at ten months. The other three are Helen, five; Zoltan, two and a half years; and Julius, seven. Julius and Helen plan to enter school as soon as they can understand enough of their future language.

Members of Ed Clark's Men's Bible Class and other members of the Central Presbyterian Church who sponsored the family's entrance into this country, said that the father has indicated he desired work at anything in order to support his family. Several prospective job offers have already been tendered, it was stated.

The family arrived at Dallas yesterday at 7:30 a. m. and were driven here by members of the Men's Bible Class.

UNITED STATES OF AMERICA

DECLARATION OF INTENTION

No. 4 2 0 8

(Invalid for all purposes seven years after the date hereof)

United States of America

Northern District of Texas

In the United States District Court

of Nor.Dist. of Texas at Dallas, Texas

(1) My full, true, and correct name is Gyula Zsohar
(2) My present place of residence is 1400 East Marvin, Waxahachie, Ellis Co. Texas
(3) My occupation is Teacher (4) I am 38 years old. (5) I was born on April 23, 1912
in Kisrakos, Hungary (6) My personal description is as follows: Sex male
color white complexion fair color of eyes blue color of hair brown height 5 feet 9 inches, weight 197 pounds,
visible distinctive marks none race white present nationality Hungary
(7) I am married; the name of my wife or husband is Erzsebet Ilona Zsohar born Padanyi 7-22-40
at Budapest, Hungary ; or she was born at Leva Czecho-Slovakia
on January 16, 1919 ; and entered the United States at New York
on March 3, 1950 ; and now resides at Waxahachie Ellis Co. Texas
(8) I have 5 children; and the name, sex, date and place of birth, and present place of residence of each of said children who is living, are as follows:
Erzsebet, Zsohar F. 05.13.43 Budapest, Hungary, 1400 Marvin, Waxahachie, Texas
Gyula, Zsohar M. 08.18.44 Budapest, Hungary, 1400 E. Marvin, Waxahachie, Tex
Ilona, Zsohar F. 08.18.44 Budapest, Hungary, 1400 E. Marvin, Waxahachie, Tex
Zoltan, Zsohar M. 05.29.47 Bad-Ischl, Austria, 1400 E. Marvin, Waxahachie, Tex
Julia, Zsohar F. 04.09.49 Bad-Ischl, Austria, 1400 E. Marvin, Waxahachie, Tex
(9) My last place of foreign residence was Obertraun, Upper-Austria, Austria (10) I emigrated to the United States from
Bremerhaven, Germany (11) My lawful entry for permanent residence in the United States was
at New York, N.Y. under the name of Gyula Zsohar
on March 3, 1950 on the SS Gen. Greeley
(12) Since my lawful entry for permanent residence I have not been absent from the United States, for a period or periods of 6 months or longer, as follows:

DEPARTED FROM THE UNITED STATES			RETURNED TO THE UNITED STATES		
PORT	DATE (Month, day, year)	VESSEL OR OTHER MEANS OF CONVEYANCE	PORT	DATE (Month, day, year)	VESSEL OR OTHER MEANS OF CONVEYANCE

(13) I have not heretofore made declaration of intention: No. on in the

(14) It is my intention in good faith to become a citizen of the United States and to reside permanently therein. (15) I will, before being admitted to citizenship, renounce absolutely and forever all allegiance and fidelity to any foreign prince, potentate, state, or sovereignty of whom or which at the time of admission to citizenship I may be a subject or citizen. (16) I am not an anarchist; nor a believer in the unlawful damage, injury, or destruction of property, or sabotage; nor a disbeliever in or opposed to organized government; nor a member of or affiliated with any organization or body of persons teaching disbelief in or opposition to organized government. (17) I certify that the photograph affixed to the duplicate and triplicate hereof is a likeness of me and was signed by me.
I do swear (affirm) that the statements I have made and the intentions I have expressed in this declaration of intention subscribed by me are true to the best of my knowledge and belief: SO HELP ME GOD.

Dr. Gyula Zsohar

(Original and true signature of declarant without abbreviation, also other name if used)

Subscribed and sworn to (affirmed) before me in the form of oath shown above in the office of the Clerk of said Court, at Dallas, Texas
this 9th day of August, anno Domini 19 50. I hereby certify that Certification No. A-7431791 from the Commissioner of Immigration and Naturalization, showing the lawful entry for permanent residence of the declarant above named on the date stated in this declaration of intention, has been received by me, and that the photograph affixed to the duplicate and triplicate hereof is a likeness of the declarant.

[SEAL]

George W. Parker
U.S. District Court
Clerk of the Court.
By *Jeffie B Moody* Deputy Clerk.

Form N-315
U. S. DEPARTMENT OF JUSTICE
IMMIGRATION AND NATURALIZATION SERVICE
(Edition of 11-1-41)

16—39119-1 U. S. GOVERNMENT PRINTING OFFICE

On August 6, 1950, Julius signed the Declaration of Intention to become a United States citizen.

GLOSSARY OF PRONUNCIATIONS

Edesanya:	AIDESH-ahn-yah
Edesapa:	AIDESH-ah-pah
Erzsebet (Elizabeth):	ERR-shi-bet
Erzsike (Elizabeth):	ERR-shi-kay
Feher:	FAY-hair
Geza:	GAYH-zah
Gyula (Julius):	DUE-la
Gyuszi (Young Julius):	DUE-sea
Ilona (Helen):	E-lonh-nah
Ilonka (Helen):	E-lonh-kah
Kerekes:	KAYH-ray-kesh
Kieninger:	KIN-in-ger
Kisrakos:	KISH-rah-kosh
Kormend:	CORE-mahnd
Laci:	LA-tsee
Mamsika:	MOM-shi-kah
Mihaly:	ME-high
Pankasz:	PANH-kahs
Perstl:	PER-shtel
Schilcher:	SHIL-her
Schladming:	SHLAD-ming
Schlattham:	SHLAT-hymn
Szatai:	SAY-tay
Szekesfehervar:	SEY-kesh-FEH-hair-vahr
Szentgotthard:	SAINT-goat-tard
Szombathely:	SUM-buht-hey
Zoltan:	ZOL-tahn
Zsohar:	SHO-har